THE OTHER
EUROPE

By the same author

History of the Communist Party of Czechoslovakia

As co-editor

Totalitarianism
America in Our Minds

THE OTHER
EUROPE

Jacques Rupnik

PANTHEON BOOKS • NEW YORK

To the memory of Jan Patočka

Grateful acknowledgment is made to Cambridge University Press for permission to reprint an excerpt from *Eastern Europe Between the Wars, 1918–1941* by Hugh Seton Watson, Cambridge University Press, 1945.

Library of Congress Cataloging-in-Publication Data

Rupnik, Jacques.
The other Europe / Jacques Rupnik.
p. cm.
Bibliography: p.
Includes index.
ISBN 0-8052-4077-2
1. Central Europe—Politics and government. 2. Central Europe—
Intellectual life—20th century. 3. Central Europe—Relations—
Europe, Eastern. 4. Europe, Eastern—Relations—Central Europe.
I. Title.
D1058.R87   1989
303.48'243047 —dc20   89-42658

Manufactured in the United States of America

Revised Edition

Contents

Preface

Although written to coincide with a television documentary (broadcast at the end of 1988) this book is not a reportage. It tries to provide a background to, not a detailed chronicle of, the spectacular changes under way. Since the introduction and the last chapter were written in May 1989, a Solidarity government has taken office in Poland; the Hungarian Communist Party has changed its name and is run by a man who claims to be a social democrat; tens of thousands of East Germans voted with their feet and fled for the West via Austria and Hungary (or Austria-Hungary?), which became a transit zone between East and West—a metaphor for a new Central Europe in the offing.

The updating had to stop, but the task remains: to treat the present as a problem of history.

This book was written after extensive travel to the countries of the 'Other Europe' with a film crew (known as the 'merry gulag'). My thanks go to Michael Jones and Nicholas Fraser from Panoptic Productions for their generous act of faith in taking me on board; to Tom Roberts, the director, for never taking no for an answer from a Soviet bloc official; and above all to the many Central Europeans who offered their insights and their help. I hope that they recognize themselves in this book. My thinking about the 'Other Europe' owes a great deal to two friends and colleagues in Paris, Pierre Kende and Pierre Hassner. Special thanks are due to Cara Morris, who agreed to be the first reader of the manuscript, for her helpful hints and suggestions.

JR

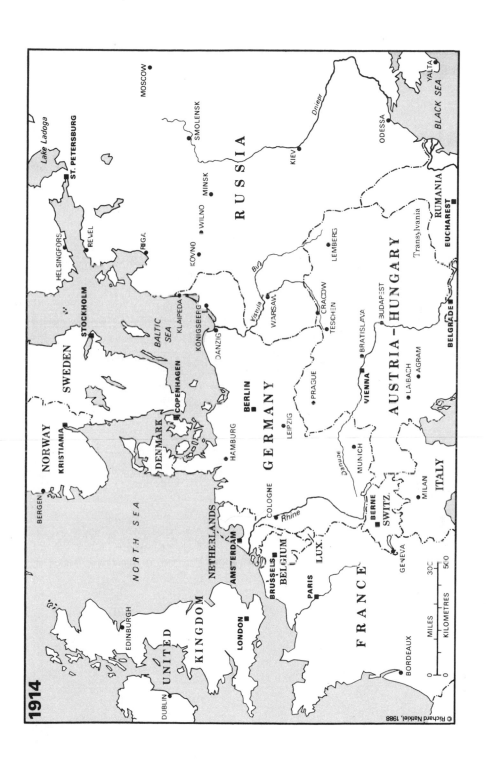

1914

NORWAY
KRISTIANIA
BERGEN

SWEDEN
STOCKHOLM
HELSINGFORS

Lake Ladoga
ST. PETERSBURG
REVEL
RIGA

MOSCOW
SMOLENSK

RUSSIA

Dniepr
KIEV

ODESSA

YALTA
BLACK SEA

BALTIC
SEA

KLAIPEDA
KONIGSBERG
DANZIG

KOVNO
WILNO
MINSK

NORTH SEA

DENMARK
COPENHAGEN

HAMBURG

BERLIN

GERMANY

LEIPZIG

PRAGUE

WARSAW
Vistula
Bug
CRACOW
TESCHEN
LEMBERG

RUMANIA
EUCHAREST

Transylvania

EDINBURGH
DUBLIN

UNITED
KINGDOM

LONDON

NETHERLANDS
AMSTERDAM

BRUSSELS
BELGIUM
LUX.

COLOGNE
Rhine

MUNICH

Danube

BERNE
SWITZ.
GENEVA

BRATISLAVA
VIENNA

BUDAPEST

AUSTRIA – HUNGARY

LABACH
AGRAM

BELGRADE

PARIS

FRANCE

BORDEAUX

MILAN
ITALY

0   30C
MILES
0   5CO
KILOMETRES

© Richard Natkiel, 1988

1920s

© Richard Natkiel, 1988

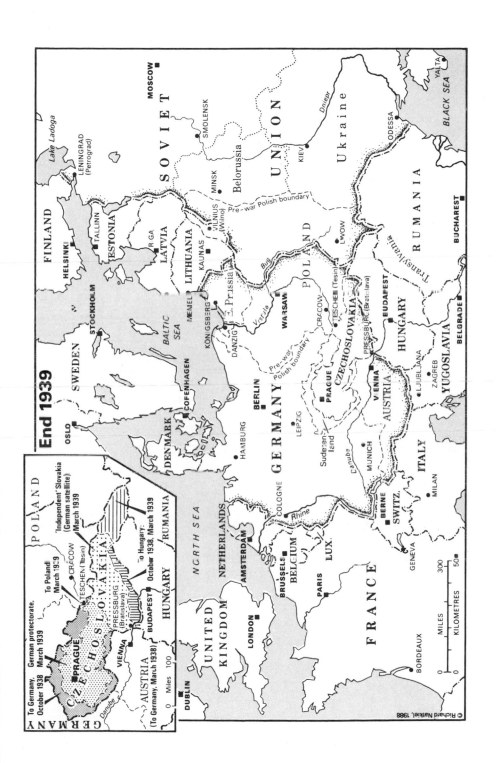

End 1939

MOSCOW

S O V I E T   U N I O N

LENINGRAD (Petrograd)

SMOLENSK

Lake Ladoga

Dnieipr

FINLAND

HELSINKI

Ukraine

BLACK SEA

YALTA

ODESSA

KIEV

MINSK

Belorussia

Pre-war Polish boundary

TALLINN

ESTONIA

RIGA

LATVIA

VILNIUS (Wilno)

LITHUANIA

KAUNAS

BUCHAREST

RUMANIA

LWOW

P O L A N D

SWEDEN

STOCKHOLM

MEMEL

E. Prussia

Bug

Transylvania

KÖNIGSBERG

DANZIG

WARSAW

Vistula

CRACOW

TESCHEN (Tesin)

PRESSBURG (Bratislava)

BUDAPEST

HUNGARY

BELGRADE

YUGOSLAVIA

BALTIC SEA

COPENHAGEN

DENMARK

BERLIN

LEIPZIG

PRAGUE

CZECHOSLOVAKIA

VIENNA

AUSTRIA

ZAGREB

LJUBLJANA

OSLO

HAMBURG

G E R M A N Y

Sudeten-land

MUNICH

Danube

ITALY

MILAN

NORTH SEA

NETHERLANDS

AMSTERDAM

COLOGNE

Rhine

BRUSSELS

BELGIUM

LUX.

BERNE

SWITZ.

GENEVA

UNITED KINGDOM

DUBLIN

LONDON

PARIS

F R A N C E

BORDEAUX

0   MILES   300

0   KILOMETRES   50

© Richard Natkiel, 1988

Inset map:

GERMANY

POLAND

'Independent' Slovakia (German satellite) March 1939

To Germany, October 1938, German protectorate, March 1939

PRAGUE

C Z E C H O S L O V A K I A

To Poland March 1939

CRACOW

TESCHEN (Tesin)

PRESSBURG (Bratislava)

To Hungary: October 1938, March 1939

BUDAPEST

HUNGARY

RUMANIA

VIENNA

AUSTRIA (To Germany, March 1938)

Danube

0   Miles   100

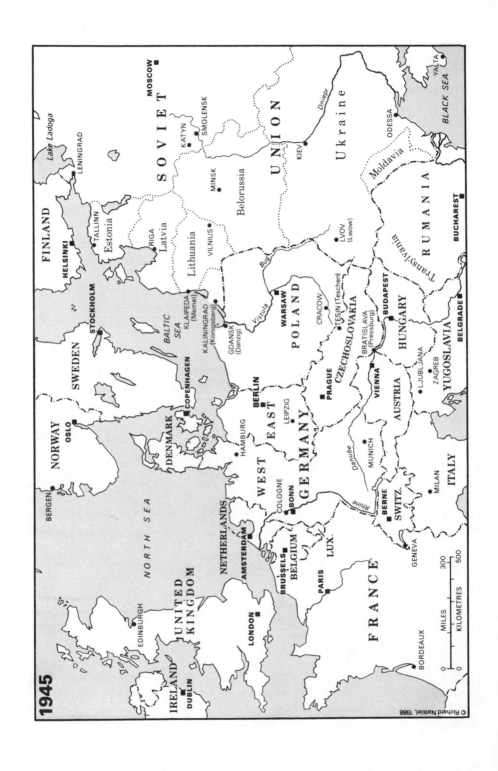

1945

NORWAY · FINLAND · SWEDEN · SOVIET UNION · Ukraine · RUMANIA · BLACK SEA

Introduction

Travelling from Vienna to Prague, you cross the Iron Curtain into what is known as Eastern Europe. In fact you are travelling west; Prague is to the west of Vienna. Politically and militarily, of course, the lands between Germany and Soviet Russia belong to the eastern bloc. Historically and culturally, they are the 'heart of Europe'.

The Other Europe is the last colonial empire still in existence, though it is no longer the monolithic bloc it used to be: national differences are as striking as they ever were. Despite forty years of Sovietization, it could be argued that in terms of culture, of values and of lifestyles, the real Iron Curtain runs further east, on the Russian border with the Baltic countries. Not only, at the end of the Second World War, was Communism imposed from outside, but the Russian centre of the empire was perceived by the nations on its western periphery as economically and culturally inferior.

Nowhere is the identification with Europe as a whole stronger than where it is most threatened, where the defence of a culture is part of a search for alternatives to the partition of the continent. For more than forty years these nations have told us they cannot survive without Europe. By the same token, they have challenged the comfortable yet depressingly empty concept of a Europe confined merely to the Common Market – that is, a concern with taxation and butter mountains rather than ideas and values. Economically the East needs the West, but culturally today the West needs the East, precisely because it is there that the soul of Europe, the idea of Europe as a culture that transcends political divides, has been preserved.

Today the return of the Other Europe is made possible by the terminal crisis of the Communist system and a tentative return of democracy in Poland, Hungary and Yugoslavia which could be a match for that of Spain, Portugal and Greece in the 1970s. There is a formidable acceleration of history in East-Central Europe, in which the risks are proportional to the hopes of overcoming the artificial division of Europe which we call in shorthand 'Yalta'. The pace of change in some countries contrasts with a conservative resistance in others, making predictions extremely hazardous. Who could have predicted only a year ago that Solidarity would be legalized in Poland by the very people who tried to crush it, or that a multi-party system would emerge in Hungary? But similarly: who could have imagined twenty years ago that Czechoslovakia would hibernate so long in the ice age of 'normalization' or that Romania would be run by an extravagant disciple of Alfred Jarry and of the Khmer Rouge!

The current changes in the Other Europe owe more to the decay of the Communist system than to Gorbachev's initiative, though he no doubt represents an unprecedented tolerance of change in what used to be known as the bloc. But that should not be confused with *perestroika*. In the Soviet Union change has been introduced from above and is meant as a rejuvenation of Communism, while in East-Central Europe it comes from below and amounts to the dismantling of Communism. While Moscow might hope that *perestroika* will bring about a new reformist consensus in its relationship with its allies, the latter are looking resolutely Westward. Viewed from Budapest or Warsaw, the chances of Gorbachev's reforms and the reshaping of the system from within ultimately depend on the plausibility of the transformation of a Russian/Soviet political culture which historically has not been conducive to democratic change. Viewed from Moscow, they depend on the possibility of dissociating the reform of the system and the reform of the empire. From Armenia to the Baltic the message is clear: *glasnost* brings to the surface long-suppressed democratic aspirations but also nationalism. The last thing Gorbachev needs is for demands for national autonomy to spread from the inner to the outer periphery of his empire. An explosion there could mean the end of *perestroika* in Moscow.

East-Central Europe is where the Cold War started. The fate of change in that area will also be the test which declares that it has ended. In making up their minds about Gorbachev's offer of a 'Common European home', West Europeans will have the countries of the Other Europe on their minds: after all, they have been part of a 'common house' with Moscow for more than forty years. And their message is: only when each nation has its own house can an all-European house have any meaning.

Today a crisis is brewing at the periphery of Gorbachev's empire. *Perestroika* and *glasnost* were meant as an answer to the crisis of the system, but they also threaten to destabilize it. The most difficult time for decaying empires comes when they try to reform themselves.

Part 1
THE OTHER
EUROPE

1 In Search of Central Europe

> From the standpoint of history, Europe can be divided
> into three blocks: the historicity of the West, the absurd
> history of Central Europe, and the ahistoricity of the East.
>
> (Josef K., Prague, 1980)

'You have to confront yourself with the role of your country in a part of the world that doesn't want your presence in tanks but as tourists.' This is how Hungarian writer György Konrad touched off a debate between Central European and Soviet writers at a Wheatland Foundation conference in Lisbon in May 1988. For the first time, with unprecedented frankness, Hungarian, Polish and other writers from Central Europe confronted their Soviet colleagues with two basic facts that apparently had never crossed their minds: that Central European culture exists as something distinct from the Soviet Union and that in Central Europe Soviet Russia is perceived as an oppressive colonial power. Both came as a shock to Soviet writers. Lev Anninski declared that 'Russian tanks came to liberate. So let's look at causes before we talk about effects.' Tatyana Tolstoya, a writer and descendant of Leo Tolstoy, said that she was amazed at Konrad's question, 'When am I going to take *my* tanks out of Eastern Europe?' and added that this was the first she had ever heard of Central Europeans speaking of their culture as something separate from that of the Soviet Union.

It shows the depth of the divide that the Konrad debate united the Russians, whether from Moscow or in exile. Thus Joseph Brodsky, the Soviet Nobel laureate living in New York, sided with his colleagues from Moscow, criticizing the notion of Central Europe and describing it as 'terribly myopic' for Central Europeans to accuse Russians of imperialism and colonialism. Czeslaw Milosz, the Polish émigré poet and Nobel Prize winner, argued that although the idea of a separate Central European culture was taboo in Russian literature and was abhorred by the Soviet state, Soviet writers today could no longer afford to ignore it. The exchange revealed deep cultural and political undercurrents at work in the Soviet bloc at the end of the 1980s.

The spectre of Central Europe haunts the lands of 'real socialism'.

From Prague to Budapest, from Warsaw to Zagreb (and evoking powerful echoes in Vienna and Berlin), the rediscovery of Central Europe reflects the major intellectual and political trends of the post-Solidarity era. It represents, first of all, an assertion of a cultural and historical identity distinct from the one imposed, for more than four decades, on the nations of the other half of Europe by the Soviet overlord. It is also part of the continuing search for an alternative to the partition of Europe.

The east of the West or the west of the East? Central Europe always had an in-between feel about it: between Germany and Russia before the war; between the United States and the Soviet Union today. Its geographical borders are difficult to establish with precision. But because the quest for a 'third' (middle) Europe, whether as a cultural identity or as a political project, is above all about breaking down certain real and mental boundaries, one should not expect it at the same time to draw new ones. Central Europe is today more a state of mind than a scientific concept.

After successive attempts at emancipation by Poles, Hungarians and Czechs, defeated because of their isolation, there is a growing sense of the interdependence of these nations. Czeslaw Milosz had this to say in the January 1988 issue of the *samizdat* journal *Tygodnik Mazowsze*:

> The idea of a federation of countries from the Baltic to the
> Adriatic existed before the Second World War.... This idea is
> still alive and has been revived in the notions of Central Europe.
> I do not know if it is enough that this idea exists at the spiritual
> level. On the other hand, the enormous intellectual potential that
> is flourishing within Poland and perhaps in the whole of Central
> Europe must be transformed one day into a political force.

To be sure, this 'Europe of the mind' tends to be the domain of intellectuals. The man in the street is probably more interested in a 'Europe of the consumer'. He might be prepared to share some of the superficial nostalgia for the Austro-Hungarian monarchy, especially as nobody actually remembers it. Even without idealizing the past, it is clear to everyone that the Austro-Hungarian Empire, once described as a 'prison of nations', was, compared to Soviet rule, in fact quite benign: 'Better Franz Josef than Josef' is the motto of the day.

The protagonists of the debate about Central Europe range from Milan Kundera, the exiled Czech novelist, to Pope Karol Wojtyla; from dissidents on the eastern side of the divide to pacifists on its western flank. It reveals a growing tendency of the societies in the Soviet bloc (following the post-Solidarity depression and now the cautious hopes under Gorbachev) to think of themselves as subjects, not merely objects of history. Of course, the debate sometimes cannot avoid the trap that it has become an intellectual fashion in the West as well as in the East: Central Europe as a cultural export item? But if that is the price to pay to alter the Central Europeans self-image as well as Western perceptions of the periphery of the Soviet Empire, so be it.

The reactions of the Communist authorities have varied from benign neglect to the old-fashioned authoritarian twitch. A Hungarian literary journal, *Tiszataj*, was banned for its overly outspoken advocacy of the Central European idea. And the official interpretation of paragraph 98 of the Czechoslovak Penal Code states: 'Among the subversive activities threatening the independence of the state it is possible to include, for instance, the advocacy of a Central European federation.' The idea might well be a fashionable one, but it can attract prison sentences ranging from three to six years.

Who actually are the Central Europeans? The answer changes from country to country, affording interesting insights into the motives involved and the perception of one's neighbours. Eugène Ionesco, the Romanian-born playwright, imagines a 'vast confederation' including Austria, Hungary, Romania, Croatia and Czechoslovakia. Poland is conspicuously absent, but then Ionesco is the undisputed master of the absurd.

Czech historian Karel Bartosek humorously poses the difficult dilemma of whom to include in an imaginary Central European federation: 'Besides the Czechs, who should actually belong? The Slovaks? Only just. The Poles? Yes, difficult to do otherwise. The Austrians? Of course. The Yugoslavs? Yes, but not all of them. The Germans? Yes, but how? They are too big for comfort. So we ended up drinking to the launching of the federation with the Hungarians.'

The Hungarians, like the Czechs, tend to consider the territory of the old Austro-Hungarian Empire to be the historical core of Central Europe, which they often prefer to call the 'Danubian domain'. For the Poles the Other Europe covers the whole area between Germany and Russia. In other words, it excludes Germany, but takes in the Baltic states and reaches into the Ukraine, the easternmost outpost of Polish influence where towns such as Wilno or Lwow are still considered vital historical components of Polish culture. There, the Poles would say, is the real frontier between East and West.

On the cover of the first issue of *Nowa Koalicja* (*New Coalition*), a Polish *samizdat* journal, appeared a map of Central Europe without borders, symbolizing a new approach in the dissident movement. As the Soviet bloc states move toward greater isolationism and parochialism, independent-minded intellectuals are challenging some of the old borders between nations, real and imaginary. A group calling for Central European integration was launched in Paris in the spring of 1988 by prominent Polish exiles Miroslaw Chojecki and Bogdan Ciwinski. Their call for regional cooperation mentions both the need to overcome isolation and the inspiration provided by the existence of the European Community in the West. Could Central Europe become, one day, *vis-à-vis* the Soviet Union, what the EEC represents *vis-à-vis* the United States?

The common denominator here is the belief that the small nations of the Other Europe are condemned to remain helpless before the great powers as long as they conceive of emancipation only in national terms. The rejection of an artificially imposed ideological identity through membership in the Warsaw Pact combines here with a critical reassessment of the limitations of nationalism. Sometimes interest in Central European cooperation reflects a deeper disillusionment with the post-First World War minority-ridden would-be nation-states, which proved highly vulnerable to totalitarianism from the right and later from the left.

Each nation has its particular motivation, its own axe to grind. For the Czechs and Slovaks the Central European idea often reveals discontent with their flawed partnership. For the Slovenes and the Croats (who were also members of the Austro-Hungarian Empire) it is a way of distancing themselves from Communism and from Belgrade. Their involvement in the Alp-Adria regional cooperation project that cuts across the East–West divide is a case in point; as well as the two Catholic Yugoslav republics it includes Austria, the Italian provinces of Venezia and Friuli, and Bavaria. Hungary has become an associate member. The Central European idea gives the intellectual and economic elites in Ljubljana and Zagreb a reason to look westward rather than to the south-eastern, backward, orthodox part of their crisis-ridden country; it represents yet another symptom of the disintegration of Yugoslavia.

Central Europe is an attractive balm for the wounds inflicted on the Hungarian national ego by two traumatizing post-war settlements. All things considered, the dual Austro-Hungarian monarchy is now presented by Budapest historians as the most glorious period in Hungary's modern history. No less importantly, the Central European idea affords another, somewhat oblique, means of talking about Transylvania, of detaching it from Romania, which rules the region and its minority of almost two million Hungarians.

What is more, for a Hungarian, Vienna represents the West at his doorstep. As Hungarian art historian Sandor Radnoty put it: 'Budapest could never be Paris or New York. But with a bit of historical luck, we could have enjoyed the same quality of life as the Viennese. It is also quite clear', he adds, 'that the example of Austria's lucky break in 1955 [when the Soviets voluntarily ended their occupation of the country] encouraged the Hungarians in their ill-fated revolution of 1956.'

Poles have always primarily identified themselves with Europe as a whole. To them the term *Mitteleuropa* smacked of German hegemony. Only in formerly Austrian Galicia does one find some receptiveness to the Central Europe discussion. In the editorial offices of the Catholic weekly *Tygodnik Powszechny* in Cracow you can see an interesting combination of visual references: a portrait of the Pope, who was the city's former Archbishop, Emperor Franz Josef and a Solidarity poster. Yet after the crushing of Solidarity Poland experienced a revival of interest in the idea of Central Europe, an idea which is consistent with the traditional Polish sense of mission to defend the values of Christian Europe against the East. Poznan historian Rafal Grupinski gives several reasons for this, including a feeling of powerlessness, of hostility to Russia and of anti-Western resentment: Central European cooperation may be seen by some Poles as compensation for the neglect they suffered during their isolated struggle for Solidarity and an identification with Western values which seem to be abandoned or betrayed by the West itself.

There is an element of megalomania in the Central European complaint, mixing arrogance towards Russia with moral superiority over the West. But there is also an important, if sometimes overstated, point: the partition of Europe is sustained not just by brute force but by a 'Yalta of the spirit'. The bitterness is understandable. 'Europe has not noticed the disappearance of its [Central European] cultural home,' says Milan Kundera, 'because it no longer perceives its unity as a cultural unity.'

The sublimation of politics within the realm of culture is no doubt a major distinguishing feature of Central Europe. This might be

dismissed as a sign of the powerless making a virtue out of necessity.
But it reflects the capacity to see the real stakes behind political
conflicts. Thus in the collective memory of the nations concerned,
the revolts of Budapest in 1956, of Prague in 1968, of Warsaw and
Gdansk in 1980–1 remain not just national tragedies but a tragedy
for Europe as a whole.

What does this identification with Europe mean? Historically,
there is the thousand-year-old identification with Western Christendom. As the result of the great divide between East and West
that goes back to the eleventh century, the Poles, Czechs, Slovaks,
Hungarians, Slovenes and Croats belong to the Roman Church while
the Russians, Ukrainians, Serbs, Bulgarians and Romanians are
Orthodox. How significant are such cultural divides for understanding relations between state and society? Consider the following
statement, an excerpt from the response of Pope Nicholas I to the
106 questions put to him by Boris, Tsar of the Bulgars, in 864:

> You state that it is a custom in your country to guard constantly
> the border between your fatherland and that of others and that
> if a serf or a free man [*servus aut liber*] tries to escape through
> this surveillance, the guards [*custodes*] kill him immediately
> [from answer 25].
>
> What should one do with a free man who escaped from his
> country and who is caught? One should do what is specified by
> law. Still, the history of the saints teaches us that a number of
> saints left their country and found elsewhere greater respect than
> at home. I am not mistaken in thinking that if there is no other
> reason than the departure, he [the free man] cannot be considered
> guilty. Consider in particular what the divine voice had told our
> father Abraham: 'Go and leave your land and your folk' [Moses
> 1,12:1] and that several of our Church fathers had lived for years
> as exiles away from their home. Besides, he who cannot leave
> his country is not a free man; and if he is free and no duty holds
> him, by leaving his country he is not fleeing, the same way that
> the verb addressed to Abraham was not 'Flee' but 'Go and leave
> your homeland'; and in obeying he did not commit a crime that
> ought to be judged [from answer 20].

Although the East–West divide initially represented, in terms of
civilization, merely two variants of European Christianity, it acquired
a different meaning following the Tatar defeat of Russia in the
thirteenth century and the Ottoman conquest of the Balkans about
the same time. From then on, Christendom became co-extensive
with Catholic Europe. As Hugh Seton-Watson pointed out:

The frontier between Christendom and the infidel coincided roughly with the Western borders of Orthodoxy. In Western Europe less and less account was taken of the Christians lost under infidel rule in the East. A large part of the Eastern boundary of Christendom was the frontier of the Polish–Lithuanian Commonwealth, the last bulwark against the Tatars. When a new state, based on the principality of Moscow, emerged from the Tatar yoke led by an Orthodox ruler, the Polish attitude towards its eastern neighbour did not change. From the Polish point of view, Muscovy was the barbarian East. From Moscow's point of view, Poland was the spearhead of the Roman–Germanic world of schismatics who had betrayed the true faith.

Historical vulnerability helps explain the somewhat messianic overtones attached to the word 'Europe' in Poland or Hungary. While Western Europe, preoccupied with trade and colonial exploration, was steadily losing interest in the eastern frontier of its civilization, the nations of Central and south-eastern Europe fought for survival against the Muslim threat as late as 1683 when the Polish army, led by Sobieski, defeated the Turkish siege of Vienna, thereby saving Western Christendom. In contrast to the rise of religious fanaticism in the West, relative tolerance was shown towards the Protestant Reformation in both Poland and Hungary. The principle of religious freedom was proclaimed simultaneously in Warsaw and in Torda (Transylvania) in 1571–2.

While Moscow declared itself the 'Third Rome', Europe became identified (in the aftermath of the Counter-Reformation and especially from the eighteenth century onwards) with an increasingly secularized humanistic culture. This double heritage (Christian and humanist) is still felt today. It explains why both the Church and intellectuals, religion and culture, are in Central Europe still the prime foci of identification with Europe, especially in times of adversity.

This historical divide is important in defining Central Europe's relationship with Russia, a controversial topic because it also implicitly raises the issue of the relationship of the Russian tradition with Communism.

The Central European argument put forward by Hungarian, Czech and Polish intellectuals runs something like this. In contrast to the Western pattern (which includes Central Europe) of separation between spiritual and temporal power, the very origin of pluralism, the Russian tradition is characterized by Caesaro-Papism, the forcible merger of the spiritual with the temporal, of ideology with politics. Hence the long tradition of the subservience of the Church to the state. The concepts of an ideological state and of Russian messianism may have crystallized under the Bolsheviks, but they are traceable to the exalted claims of Tsarist Russia as the Third Rome.

The second major feature distinguishing Central Europe from Russia is the separation of state and society. The Hungarian historian Jeno Szücz has argued persuasively that in Western society, going back to the feudalism of the Middle Ages, the key to an under-standing of social and by extension political relations was the notion of contract, of mutual obligations and individual dignity. In feudal society there was a contract between the lord and his vassal and a similar one between the great barons (who made up the embryo of a political society) and the king, as well as a contract between the central power and the emerging cities. This is closely related to the idea of the rule of law, of an independent system of justice. In the itinerary from the feudal contract to the social contract lie the origins of what we know as the Western freedoms, of responsibility, of the autonomy of civil society. The defining value of European civiliz-ation, says the Hungarian philosopher Mihaly Vajda, is the freedom of the 'individual limited only by that of others'.

> Behind this notion of freedom lies, of course, an interpretation of the human being as a rational being, who is fully capable of deciding on his or her own affairs as well as on those of the community.... A civilization of free individuals has led necessarily to the separation of state and civil society – an increasingly characteristic feature of this civilization as a whole.

The Russian model is quite the opposite: it is not society that shapes the state but the state that permanently reshapes society. From the Mongol invasions of the thirteenth century to Ivan the Terrible, who destroyed the nobility and replaced it with a class of state-appointed officials, from Peter the Great to Stalin, Russian history has been marked by the irresistible rise of the state and its all-powerful bureaucracy on the one hand, and by the fusion of state and society on the other.

Where does Central Europe fit into this dichotomy between Eastern and Western patterns of development? In his brilliant analy-sis *The Three Regions of Europe*, Jeno Szücz suggests that Central Europe oscillated in terms of its social and institutional structures between the other two Europes. From the tenth to the fifteenth century the Polish kingdom of the Piasts and later of the Jagiel-lonians, the Czech kingdom of the Premyslids, and the Hungarian Arpad dynasty belonged to *Europa Occidens*. The model was

Western, even if often fragile and distorted. However, whereas the West was able to resolve its crises through colonial expansion and the consequent development of the cities as the focus of economic activity, Central Europe did not have that option. The landowning class sought to resolve its crisis by shifting the burden on to the peasantry. This became known as the sixteenth-century 'second serfdom', which, as Hungarian Marxist historian Ivan T. Berend explains, pushed Central Europe into Eastern Europe. It is a neat argument: from the point of view of socioeconomic history Central Europe is the failed West; the 'second serfdom' divided Europe (even Germany) into East and West; its borders happen to coincide with those of the present-day Warsaw Pact.

From feudalism to socialism? – the 'roads to serfdom' are varied indeed. The thesis smacks too much of economic determinism to be convincing. Yet it touches on a very real problem, that of East-Central European backwardness. The issue has tormented the political and intellectual elites of the area since the Enlightenment of the late eighteenth century. There is still today, says Hungarian sociologist Elemer Hankiss, a 'neurosis of backwardness', a complex, a chip on Central European shoulders. Is catching up with the West simply a question of a time-lag (for the railroads it was about fifty years, for universal suffrage thirty or forty years)? Or should one speak of a different (East European, Prussian rather than Russian) road to industrial modernity? Central to the question was the non-emergence of a Western-style entrepreneurial class. Unlike in the West, the landowning gentry retained its dominant position (suffice it to mention the Esterhazys in Hungary, the Radziwills in Poland or the Lobkowitz and Schwarzenberg families in Bohemia). Except in the Czech lands, the bourgeoisie remained not only numerically small but also politically powerless. The entrepreneurial and trading class in Hungary and in Poland was often of German or Jewish origin (in the Balkans, the Greek minority played a similar role), and thus did not acquire the power and privileges that accompanied the rise of that class in the West. While the West developed bourgeois political elites, Poland, Hungary and Romania remained gentry nations.

This explains why the state in Central Europe became a powerful – often the dominant – instrument of modernization. In an area hotly contested by military–bureaucratic empires (Russia, the declining Ottoman Empire, Austria and Prussia), from the eighteenth but especially in the nineteenth century the 'enlightened' despotic state became actively involved in economic development, both by building up an infrastructure (roads, canals, railways) and by military expenditure. The state did more than regulate economic activity; it played the role of a leading entrepreneur. As modernization curtailed the power of the nobility and gradually emancipated the peasantry in the nineteenth century, the state itself filled the vacuum faster than the bourgeoisie were able to claim it. As a result, the expanding bureaucracy flourished while civil society remained weak and fragmented, posing little challenge to the growing authority of the state.

The dilemma of the Central European intelligentsia (which, after the weakening of Turkish domination in the nineteenth century, applied also to the Balkans, particularly to the Romanian and Serbian elites) rested on the discrepancy between its identification with Western civilization and culture and their problematic introduction into a backward social and economic structure. The nineteenth-century intelligentsia was the 'inventor' of modern nationalism and at the same time the promoter of Western social and political ideals. Hence the origins of the intelligentsia's love affair with the state, which was thought to be the only possible guarantor of the nation's survival and the sole force capable of bringing the nation into European modernity. The intelligentsia idealized the peasantry as the soul of the nation, the incarnation of the authentic national culture, but it put all its hopes for progress in the state.

Not surprisingly *étatisme*, the faith in the beneficial qualities of the state authority, in contrast to the 'reactionary' features of society, permeated all the main political ideologies in Central Europe from the nineteenth century. The Enlightenment may have been a French invention, but it was really in Central Europe that the lasting partnership between the intellectual and the state was formed. Hegel's *Philosophy of Right* later provided further philosophical ammunition to intellectuals eager to rope in the state to overcome their country's feudal legacy. Both nationalism and socialism, from 1848 the two dominant ideologies in Central Europe, had a strong étatist content. Nationalism moved from culture to politics, from the mere defence of a language and tradition to the assertion of historical and political rights which became identified with a claim to statehood.

Central European socialists, strongly influenced by the German tradition of Lassalle and Marx, saw the conquest of the state as the key to the transformation of the social and economic system. For the socialists as for the nationalists, the key issue in politics was the deep connection between Central European backwardness, the *étatisme* of the main political ideologies and the steady rise of the authoritarian state as the instrument of social and economic change. In this perspective, Central Europe's development is seen as a failed version of the Western pattern, and merely a variation on the

Eastern – thus the irresistible advance of the modernizing state in Central Europe brings, as its final stage, post-Second World War Communism.

It would be misleading, however, to imply that Communism in East-Central Europe could be established and consolidated thanks to the above-mentioned socioeconomic antecedents. Even for Barrington Moore, the author of *Social Origins of Democracy and Dictatorship*, 'the decisive causes of their politics lie outside their boundaries'. Moore's assumption is that only large countries have social systems of sufficient autonomy to affect their political organization in the era of industrial revolution. At any rate, such socioeconomic determinism leads to oversimplification, for instance the attribution of Czechoslovak capacity to maintain a Western-style democracy in the inter-war period (while its neighbours drifted toward authoritarianism) solely to the existence of a strong urban, commercial class which was lacking elsewhere in East-Central Europe.

If the Toynbee approach, which regards religion as the main criterion for defining boundaries between civilizations, has its limitations, socioeconomic determinism applied to Central European politics is simply too reductionist to be true. To bisect the continent into the industrial, urban societies in the West and the backward societies of the East is not very satisfactory. As a result of inter-war economic development, later accelerated by rapid socialist industrialization, the societies of the Other Europe have become both industrialized and urbanized. Moreover, there has always been a backward, rural, authoritarian Europe in the West as well: take Spain, Portugal or southern Italy, for instance.

The original paradox of Central European politics is the incongruity between its endorsement of Western civilization, political ideas and institutions, and the reality of the area's social and economic development, as well as the complexities of its ethnic puzzle. From the first impact of the ideas of the French Revolution this tension has always been present. The celebrated Polish Constitution of 3 May 1791, which was the first coherent statement in Central Europe of the principles of constitutional democracy, says: 'In society, everything is derived from the will of the nation.' But in this case the political nation comprises only the *szlachta*, the Polish gentry. The *szlachta* made up some 10 per cent of the nation (the nobility in France at the time of the Revolution was only 1 per cent, and in Hungary it was about 5 per cent of the population); the point is that in the absence of a 'third estate' individual rights and political freedoms rested in the hands of the aristocracy, at a time when serfdom of the peasantry was maintained.

The revolution of 1848 – the Spring of Nations, as it was called in Central Europe – illustrated the contradiction yet again. The Hungarian revolutionaries endorsed French ideals of 'freedom, equality and fraternity' as a challenge to the Habsburg establishment but refrained from undermining the privileged status of the nobility, and they simply ignored the national aspirations of their own dependent nationalities, such as the Croats or the Slovaks.

The nationality problem was indeed the second main cause of the distortion which Western-style liberal–democratic principles underwent when they were introduced into Central Europe. In contrast to Western Europe, ethnic and political boundaries did not coincide in Central Europe and the Balkans. The 1849 Declaration of Independence of the Hungarian Nation claims 'the inalienable natural right of Hungary, with all its appurtenances and dependencies, to occupy the position of an independent European state'. The Declaration overlooks the 'natural right' of the 'dependencies' – which made up a majority of the population in Hungary – to claim, like the Hungarians *vis-à-vis* Vienna, the same right to independence *vis-à-vis* Budapest.

When democratic ideals among unfree nations are asserted, primacy is often given to the collective rights of the nation over the individual rights of the citizen. Like the Hungarian Declaration of Independence, the Manifesto of the Pan-Slavic Congress held in Prague in 1848 exalts nationhood:

> We Slavs reject and abhor every domination by mere force. . . .
> We demand, without exception, equality before the law and
> equal rights and responsibility for everyone. Wherever one
> person among millions is born into oppression, there true
> freedom is still unknown. . . .
>
> It is not only on behalf of the individual within the state that
> we raise our voices and make known our demands. The nation,
> with all its intellectual merit, is as sacred to us as are the rights
> of an individual under natural law. Even if history allows men to
> develop more fully in some nations than in others, it always shows
> that the capability of development of those other nations is in
> no way limited. Nature, which knows neither noble nor ignoble
> nations, has not called upon any one of them to dominate
> another. . . .

Despite these social and national constraints, the general trend of development, especially since the last quarter of the nineteenth century, was marked by a democratization or pluralization of politics in both Central Europe and the Balkans. The Austro-Hungarian Empire was not a parliamentary democracy of the French or British type, but nor was it a Russian-style autocracy. The state curtailed the power of the nobility but it permitted civil society a limited autonomy. The tradition of local self-government (the Hungarian *comitas*, for instance) was to be of lasting importance. The spiritual independence of the churches was maintained. Above all Austria-Hungary was a *Rechstaat*, a constitutional state, where there was respect for the rule of law. It could be argued that these are among the main features that, a century ago, distinguished the political institutions in Central Europe from those of Russia, and to some extent they still do so today.

The victory of the Western democratic powers in 1918 and the collapse of the bureaucratic empires that had long dominated Central Europe and the Balkans created a historic opportunity for the founding of independent nation-states. Independence, the Wilsonian principle of national self-determination, and parliamentary democracy all came from the West. In a climate marked by Wilsonian optimism about the inevitable triumph of liberal democracy, most of the new states in Central Europe indeed tried to base their political legitimacy on institutions derived from the Western model. Most of them (including the Baltic states) adopted democratic constitutions modelled on that of the French Third Republic. This turned out not to be such a brilliant inspiration, for these constitutions privileged the legislative over the executive branch and at least partly contributed to the political instability of the 1920s, which paved the way for the authoritarian temptation of the following decade.

Despite the various misfortunes and perversions of the democratic process, notably in the 1930s, this was, in the political history of the nations concerned, a period of democratization and political pluralism. Sometimes excessively so: in Poland in the mid-1920s there were ninety-two registered political parties, of which thirty-two were represented in Parliament; in Czechoslovakia in 1929 the figures were, respectively, nineteen and sixteen. Freedom of association (for interest groups, trade unions) and freedom of expression (especially freedom of the press), freedom to trade and undertake economic activity, freedom to travel – all were guaranteed by law. Whatever limitations were gradually imposed on these guarantees by the rise of authoritarianism in the 1930s, they made all the difference between failed democracy and the totalitarian dictatorships that were to come.

Czechoslovakia was the most successful among the 'successor states' that emerged in the aftermath of the First World War, not only in adopting Western-style democratic institutions but also in making them work. The power of Parliament was matched by the almost American-style presidency of Tomas Masaryk. Political fragmentation found its stabilizing counterweight in the *petka* system of coalition between the five leading political parties. Of all the states of the area it was clearly the richest: Czech lands were already the most industrially developed part of the Austrian Empire. Czechoslovakia was, between the wars, the most unabashedly middle-class society, looking westward in terms both of trade and of culture. But it practised capitalism with a social conscience, developing something close to the first modern welfare state. Independence could have exposed the provincialism of the local cultural life. Instead, Czechoslovakia's inter-war period was unquestionably marked by a sense of self-realization and of genuine interaction with the West: from writer Karel Capek, the Anglophile who represents best the liberal spirit of the First Republic, to Vitezslav Nezval and the surrealists (and also the painter Alfons Mucha and the composer Bohuslav Martinu), who considered Paris their second home.

One explanation for the success and the discreet charm of the Czechoslovak experiment was the democratic structure of Czech society. The indigenous Czech nobility had been decimated or forced into exile in the aftermath of the Battle of the White Mountain (1620) and the Counter-Reformation. The rebirth of Czech politics was therefore the making of intellectual and later bourgeois elites. In contrast to the 'gentry nations', namely Poland and Hungary, whose political style was characterized by defiance and a romantic or libertarian commitment to independence, the Czech political style was bourgeois, democratic, fairly egalitarian, rational and pragmatic. The man who embodied the liberal virtues of the inter-war Czechoslovak democracy was its founder and philosopher–president, Tomáš Masaryk.

To be sure, by the 1930s pressures were mounting on the Czechoslovak political system. Despite the left-wing radicalism of the Communist Party in the early 1930s and the right-wing nationalism prevalent among the Sudeten Germans, on the whole the political institutions displayed remarkable stability and continuity until the ultimate stab in the back in Munich in 1938. Masaryk had believed that Czechoslovak democracy needed some fifty years of peace to establish itself and to win the hearts and minds of its minorities. Twenty years was all it was allowed.

Experiments in Western-style democracy were even more short-lived in the rest of Central Europe and in the Balkans. The democratic constitutional façade started to crumble in the 1920s, giving way in the 1930s to increasingly authoritarian and corrupt regimes. In Hungary the democratic interlude under Karolyi lasted merely a few months. Then the 1919 Communist revolution led by Béla Kun was followed by a White counter-revolution. The reactionary Horthy regime very early on set the pattern for the whole area: an inordinate fear of Bolshevism justifying a drift to the extreme right. In Bulgaria the democratic regime collapsed in 1923 when the veteran peasant leader Alexander Stamboliiski was overthrown by a military coup and murdered immediately after winning the elections. In Poland, Marshal Josef Pilsudski, the hero of Polish independence who had repelled the Red Army at the gates of Warsaw, staged his *coup d'état* in 1926 to 'put the house in order' after a period of instability and parliamentary chaos caused by political fragmentation and inexperience. As an astute observer put it: 'everyone wants to be in opposition, on no account will anyone accept responsibility'. That same year a coup was staged in Lithuania. The 1930s confirmed this shift from parliamentary to authoritarian regimes in Romania and Yugoslavia and also, after February 1934, in Austria and in the Baltic countries. Czechoslovakia was by then the only exception to the rule.

There were a number of reasons why the democratic experiment proved unsuccessful. Prominent among them the above-mentioned problem of introducing a political system based on values and institutions derived from the French Revolution in archaic, predominantly peasant countries. In the absence of genuine land reform, what could words such as 'freedom, equality and fraternity' mean to the Hungarian or Romanian peasant? The old stable patriarchal system was breaking down without sufficient provisions for integration of large sections of society into the new democratic system. They – the peasantry, but also many members of the intelligentsia – became vulnerable to the appeal of right-wing radical demagogues.

The persistence of a strong bureaucratic tradition did not endear modern democracy to the mass of the population any more than imported abstract ideals did. Here, too, there were differences from country to country depending on the legacy of the *ancien régime*. Hugh Seton-Watson, after visiting the area in the 1930s, described the problem as follows:

> In the new states of 1918, regions of Eastern (Russian, Turkish) and Western (Austrian) standards were combined together. In Yugoslavia, Romania and Poland, it may be said with little exaggeration that Eastern methods prevailed over the Western. In Bulgaria, the Eastern system has never been challenged. In

Czechoslovakia, the Austrian tradition of honest and fairly efficient administration was continued, and in Hungary, conditions were, as before World War I, somewhere between Western and Eastern.

The old Russian bureaucracy was the offspring of Mongol and Byzantine traditions, while that of the Balkans owes its origin to a combination between Byzantine and Turkish conceptions. Both were essentially arbitrary and dictatorial, but their severity was always mitigated by inefficiency and corruption. The Balkan official regards himself as immensely superior to the peasants among whom he lives and from whose ranks he has sprung. To be an official is the fondest dream of every able young son of a peasant. The Balkan official does not like to work. He considers himself so fine a fellow that the state and the public should be proud to support him and should not ask him to make efforts that will tax his intellect or character. A visitor to a Balkan ministry or police headquarters in the middle of the morning will find the rooms filled with good-natured fellows comfortably enjoying a cup of Turkish coffee and a chat with their friends. The papers lie on their desks. Outside stand, sit and squat patient queues of peasants awaiting their various permits and receipts. Foreigners and citizens with *protekcia* obtain swift and polite attention, but the people can afford to wait. They have waited many hundreds of years for justice and a few more hours will not make much difference. Time counts little in the Balkans.

The second major cause of the rise of right-wing authoritarianism was the unresolved national problem. Hungary and Bulgaria militantly opposed the borders established by the Versailles treaty. Czechoslovakia, Poland and Romania, not to mention Yugoslavia, were ethnically just as diverse as their imperial predecessors – with one difference, however: they lacked a supranational ideology that would help the national minorities (who made up around a third of their population) to feel included, or at least less alienated, in the new state. To be sure, Masaryk displayed great faith in the power of the democratic process: it was meant to bring together the various ethnic components into one political nation of citizens. In practice, the lack of self-government alienated not just the Germans and the Hungarians living in Czechoslovakia but later even the Slovak 'partners'. In Poland, Pilsudski resisted the xenophobic and anti-Semitic tendencies of the nationalist right but failed to give the minorities a stake in the Polish state. During the whole inter-war period Central Europe and the Balkans were racked by a permanent 'private civil war' between states over borders and national minorities. Hungary had territorial claims against all her neighbours. Poland quarrelled with Czechoslovakia over Teschen (Těšín) and with Lithuania over Wilno. Bulgaria claimed the territory of Southern Dobrudzha from Romania, and contested Macedonia with Yugoslavia and Greece. By undermining democratic institutions, nationalism combined with insecurity helped pave the road for authoritarian solutions and rapprochement with the main champion of ethnic nationalism, Nazi Germany. The Great Depression of the 1930s further discredited capitalism and liberal democracy in Central Europe while simultaneously fostering the appeal of the left and that of right-wing radicalism. The local imitations of the fascist and Nazi movements were often caricatures of the original but their growing influence, especially in the case of the Iron Guard in Romania and of the Arrow Cross in Hungary, was part of the prevailing atmosphere of rebellion against Western values on the eve of the war. Corneliu Codreanu's 'A Few Remarks on Democracy' was representative of this trend:

> Democracy destroys the unity of the Romanian people, dividing it into parties, making Romanians hate one another and thus exposing a divided people to the united congregation of Jewish power at a difficult time in the nation's history. This argument alone is so persuasive as to warrant the discarding of democracy in favour of anything that would ensure our unity. . . . Democracy makes Romanian citizens out of millions of Jews by making them the Romanians' equals. . . . Democracy is incapable of perseverance. . . . Democracy cannot wield authority, because it cannot enforce its decisions. . . . Democracy serves big business.

The decline of Western liberalism and the rise of conservative authoritarianism, even fascism, in Central Europe and the Balkans were directly connected with the abdication by the Western powers of their role in continental affairs: America withdrew into isolationism; Britain seemed more worried about French pre-eminence on the continent than about the Nazi threat; France was giving all sorts of vague promises to everyone in East-Central Europe but, when push came to shove, failed to turn word into deed, whether in trade policy or in military strategy. The Maginot Line strategy was not likely to give much credibility to France's commitments to the Little Entente countries of East-Central Europe in the face of rising German influence in the area. Since democracy and independent statehood had been bestowed on the nations of Central and Eastern Europe by the Western powers, Western decline and indifference eventually weakened the shallow roots of democracy in the area. This policy of benign neglect created favourable conditions for Nazi Germany and Soviet Russia, the main powers wanting to revise the Versailles Treaty of 1919, to assert their competing claims to an ideological and political sphere of influence. Munich was not just about the survival (or betrayal) of democracy in Central Europe.

The behaviour of the Western powers does not diminish the importance of domestic ingredients in the growth of authoritarianism and later totalitarianism in the Other Europe. Onslaughts on liberal democracy, such as Codreanu's, are of interest precisely because we can trace the native roots of totalitarian ideologies and practices. With some toning down of the anti-Semitism, the diatribe could have been published in the Bucharest of Stalin's day or under Ceausescu. The idea that individualism and political pluralism associated with 'bourgeois democracy' should be replaced by a 'new order' in which the nation is identified with the state points to threads of continuity between the right-wing totalitarians of the 1930s and their Communist successors in the 1940s.

The political culture of the Other Europe reveals authoritarian predispositions, but also elements that proved resistant to totalitarianism. The chief characteristic of Central European political culture was the duality between authoritarianism and liberal democracy, between East and West, and the discontinuity of its political development, which was always dependent on the political orientation of the dominant great powers in the region. The introduction of modern democracy in the 1920s might not have been an unqualified success, but the 'little dictators' of the 1930s, as Antony Polonski called them, although they produced fairly unpleasant and conservative regimes, never embarked on a permanent totalitarian reshaping and ideological mobilization of society of the kind practised by Hitler's Germany or Stalinist Russia. Though the state became semi-authoritarian, society remained ethnically, culturally and politically pluralist.

Thus, in searching for a Central European identity, in trying to assess the area's relationship with the West and with Russia, one comes up with different conclusions depending on which criterion is chosen. If, like E. M. Cioran or Milan Kundera, we define Europe through its culture and values or, put differently, if we follow the Toynbee approach and consider religion as setting boundaries between civilizations, then we can indeed speak of Central Europe as a 'kidnapped West', to which Russian Communism is fundamentally alien.

How relevant in this respect is the divide between Catholic Central Europe and the Orthodox Balkans? In an essay entitled 'Russia and the Virus of Freedom', the Romanian writer E. M. Cioran gives a very personal view of cultural boundaries. For him, it is in Central Europe, 'beyond Vienna', that the vitality of European values is strongest.

And what about the Balkans? I don't mean to defend them, nor ignore their merits. Their taste for devastation, for internal chaos, a world like a bordello in flames; their sardonic perspective on cataclysms past or imminent; theirs is the idleness of insomniacs or assassins . . .

Europe's only 'primitives' will perhaps give it a new push which it will see as the ultimate humiliation. Nevertheless, if South-Eastern Europe was merely horror, why then, when one leaves it for this part of the world, does one have the sense of a fall – splendid as it may be – into emptiness.

On the other hand, an examination of the lineages of the absolutist states through the prism of social and economic history might make a case for including the lands between Germany and Russia in a backward, statist East European model distinct from the Western one with its emphasis on the autonomy of civil society.

Finally, in terms of political tradition, Central Europe's 'failed liberalism' or semi-authoritarianism occupies an intermediate position between Russia and the West, between despotism and democracy.

Thus the debate about Central Europe hinges on the relative weight of indigenous factors and external forces in the formation there of the post-war Communist system. It is therefore also a debate about Europe and Russia, about the relationship between the Soviet present and the Russian past. For conservative Russians, like Solzhenitsyn, the Communism that brought about the ruin of Russia was a Western import, a virus Lenin brought back from Zurich. Of course, for Central Europeans (Kundera the Czech, Cioran the Romanian from Transylvania, Kolakowski and Brandys the Poles, or the Hungarians György Konrad and Mihaly Vajda), it is the other way round: Communism, as a Russian import, has represented a threat to their Western, European identity and their freedom. In Central Europe, Russia was always seen as 'another world' (Milosz), the symbol of despotism, old and new. The aversion, inherited from history, has been reinforced by the post-war experience of Soviet domination. Kazimierz Brandys explains:

I sometimes hear that the Poles say 'Russia' instead of 'the Soviet

Union' and that this reveals Polish nationalism. But isn't that to ignore that the Poles have experienced at close range not just the Tsarist empire but also the Soviet empire? Two centuries of invasions and violence, of territorial annexations, deportations, imprisonments.... When one speaks of Russia, however, one must also think of Herzen and Sakharov. But, whether we like it or not, it is the worst experiences that are the most easily transmitted.

When Milan Kundera wrote that 'on the Eastern border of the West, Russia is seen not just as one more European power but as a singular civilization, another civilization' he meant to expose the fallacy of the 'community of Slavic nations' thesis which has been used since Stalin's day to justify Soviet expansion westward when other ideological arguments were lacking. His essay on Central Europe as the 'kidnapped West' provoked a most revealing controversy. As soon as you start drawing cultural boundaries you run the risk of being accused either of cultural determinism or of 'excluding' whole nations from Europe. Everyone is always someone else's 'Eastern barbarian'. After all, the Russians too feel that they have been the rampart of the Christian world against the Asian hordes, while in the Balkans, Orthodox Serbs see themselves (even now, in the conflict with the Albanians in the Kosovo) as defenders of Christian Europe against the onslaught of Islam. The discussion on Central Europe should not be interpreted as an attempt to 'exclude' anybody from Europe. Rather, it reveals that there are historically different ways of belonging to Europe and that although the centre of Europe might be difficult to identify, it has several peripheries.

The identification of Russia with despotism is not a Central European invention. It has long been in the mainstream of European thinking about Russia from the nineteenth century until the Second World War (in France it runs from the Marquis de Custine on the conservative side to Victor Hugo on the democratic left). As for the continuity thesis linking Tsarist and Communist Russia, it was most eloquently formulated, back in the 1930s, by Nikolai Berdiaev, a Russian philosopher, in his seminal study, *The Sources and the Meaning of Russian Communism*. Kazimierz Brandys has returned to the subject in the latest volume of his *Notebooks* (1988): 'I am not confusing Russia and Communism. I simply believe that Russia has had a decisive influence on the formation of contemporary totalitarian ideological states; and that there existed in Russia for a very long time their horrible prototype. A prototype, not a model.'

Continuity or radical break? Regardless of its actual merits this eternal controversy is more important for what it reveals about the way the Central European nations perceive their place in Europe and their relationship with their Eastern neighbour, than for what it says about Russia.

2 Perceptions of Russia

If you insist on your dreams of nationhood, of an
independent Poland, and all your illusions, you will bring
on yourself great misfortune.

(Tsar Nicholas I)

It isn't pleasant to surrender to the hegemony of a nation
which is still wild and primitive.

(Czeslaw Milosz)

It has become a standard cliché in examining the relationship between Soviet bloc countries and Moscow to distinguish between the
nations, like Poland or Hungary, whose historical experience
accounts for the strength of anti-Russian feeling, and countries like
Czechoslovakia or Bulgaria, considered traditionally pro-Russian,
which had welcomed the arrival of the Red Army as the confirmation
of Slavic unity against Germany. The stereotype, as always, contains
an element of truth, but can also be misleading. A double contrast –
between Hungary and Bulgaria on the one hand, and between Poland
and Czechoslovakia on the other – may serve to illustrate the point.

For the Hungarians, Russia is generally associated with primitive
culture, arbitrary 'Asian' methods of government and military brutality. This negative image gained wide currency with the emergence
of Hungarian nationalism in the nineteenth century, which increasingly saw Russian-sponsored Pan-Slavism as a threat (until then the
Germans had been regarded as the main enemy): a threat to Hungary
and to all of Europe, according to Miklos Wesselenyi's book on
Russia in the 1840s; a threat to democratic ideals, according to
Kossuth, the leader of the 1848 revolution in Budapest. Their fears
were confirmed by events. The two Russian military interventions
against Hungarian democratic revolutions, in 1849 and in 1956, have

seared the memories of the Hungarians, who also fought opposite the Russians in two World Wars.

The whole inter-war period was haunted by the spectre of the Communist revolution of Béla Kun in 1919. The arrival of Soviet troops in 1945 after a lengthy and bloody siege of Budapest is experienced as a national tragedy, all the more painful in that the official version presents the Red Army occupation as a liberation. Inevitably, there was a strongly anti-Russian component to the Hungarian revolution of 1956. 'Ruski go home' (an echo of the official anti-American slogan 'Ami go home') was among the cries heard in Budapest as Russian troops moved in to 'restore order'. The Kadar regime rightly earned the reputation of being among the most flexible in the bloc when it came to enforcing ideological constraints on the work of writers and historians. But one taboo has not been shaken by the permissiveness of the 1980s, and that is the question of Soviet Russia and Hungarian–Soviet relations.

In contrast, the Bulgarians traditionally acknowledge a debt to Russia for having fought the Turks in 1877–8 to secure Bulgaria's liberation from almost 500 years of Ottoman domination. Ever since Ivan the Terrible first raised the hopes of Orthodox Christian Slavs in the Balkans, Bulgarians have regarded Russia as their patron. Since the eighteenth century the Bulgarians have recognized a cultural debt to the Russians as well, though they dislike any suggestion that their culture is merely an offshoot of Russia's. They prefer to present Bulgaria as the true cradle of a Slavonic Christian culture associated in the ninth century with the missionaries Cyril and Methodius. The cliché about traditional Bulgarian Russophilia is probably an exaggeration. Nevertheless, it is striking that, in contrast to all the other Soviet bloc countries, Bulgaria is the only one not to have experienced any kind of overt conflict with Moscow (whether at the Party level or in the form of popular dissent).

A comparison of Polish and Czech attitudes to Russia also reflects two nations' different historical experiences of dealing with their eastern neighbour. From eighteenth-century partitions to nineteenth-century revolts and twentieth-century Sovietization, the modern history of Polish–Russian relations is dominated by conflict. In contrast, Czech–Russian relations until the middle of this century have been marked less by an absence of conflict than, perhaps, simply by an absence of contact.

'Yes, we are the Scythians, the barbarians from Asia' ... The Poles, on the whole, tend to agree with the Russians' own idea of themselves as being the modern 'Scythians' described in a famous

1918 poem by Alexander Blok, a Russian poet, born in Warsaw.

Poles and Russians are historical neighbours but not actually geographical ones. They are separated by the Lithuanians, the Byelorussians and the Ukrainians, and Polish–Russian conflicts have often concerned the fate of the region and nations that lie between them. Poland viewed Russia first of all as a rival. The Polish–Lithuanian Commonwealth in the fourteenth and fifteenth centuries included most of the territories that today form part of Soviet Ukraine and Byelorussia. But it was only when Russia's eighteenth-century imperial expansion moved westward to the Baltic and to the Black Sea that Poland became her prime target. The West thinks of Peter the Great and Catherine II primarily as Westernizers trying to modernize and 'Europeanize' Russia. But the Poles associate the idea of a Europeanizing Russia with the threat of conquest. Russia's imperial expansion into Europe led to the loss of Polish independence. Partitioned three times (1772–92), Poland succumbed to her two historical enemies, Orthodox Russia and Protestant Prussia.

Russian domination means for the Poles more than the loss of their national sovereignty: it also means the triumph of Eastern despotism over democracy. Despite growing Russian pressure in the eighteenth century, Poland maintained its democratic constitution based upon the predominance of the Diet (Sejm). Historians have often observed that the excessively libertarian spirit of the Poles, as symbolized by the famous *liberum veto* (whereby legislation could be blocked by the objection of even one Sejm member) eventually led to the paralysis of the political system, and weakened the nation's capacity to resist outside influence. Indeed the Russians arrived claiming to 'restore order' in the wake of political anarchy – a justification which would become a leitmotif of Russian–Polish relations. But the lasting legacy for the Poles' collective memory is the crushing of their pluralist and libertarian spirit by the encroaching Russian despotism.

Neutralized as a rival for Muscovy, Poland was now transformed into an internal weakness, the Achilles heel of the Russian Empire. The Polish revolts of 1830 and 1863 are, from this point of view, the antecedents of more recent challenges to the imperial status quo. Then as now the Poles see their struggle against Russian autocracy in broader European terms.

Jacek Wozniakowski, director of a Catholic publishing house in Cracow, says: 'Poles have a tendency to idealize Europe as a whole, the more so since they are convinced it is often betrayed by Europeans themselves. For our Romantic writers the epitome of a tyrant was the Tsar, and they despaired about Europe's abjectness and its blindness to the inevitable, as they saw it, wave of tyranny which would eventually sweep the continent.' Zygmunt Krasinski's warnings to the West about the danger posed by Russian despotism are good illustrations of Polish concerns: the Russian Tsar, he prophesied in 1842, would become an atheist and embark on worldwide domination.

In a famous statement written in Paris in 1832 by two leading representatives of Poles in exile, the historian Joachim Lelewel and the poet Adam Mickiewicz declared that 'Every good Pole will carry to his grave the consolation that if Heaven has not allowed him to save his own fatherland, he has, nevertheless, by this struggle defended for a while the freedoms of a threatened Europe.' This statement was addressed to the Russian 'Decembrists' on the seventh anniversary of their aborted attempt to shake off autocracy, but was met with indifference. Even a Russian liberal like Pushkin resented 'foreigners' who dared criticize the violent suppression of the Polish revolt of 1831.

Russian and Polish interests have rarely been compatible. Similar 'misunderstandings' occurred in 1863: the key question for the Russians was the abolition of serfdom. Alexander II was praised (even by London-based exiles like Herzen) as a liberator, as Russia's saviour. For the Poles, at that time, the burning issue was national independence. Even Russian liberals such as Turgenev, the former Decembrist, considered the 1863 Polish uprising a 'grave mistake'. Poland should remain associated with Russia along the same lines as the association of Ireland and England; there was no need for total Russification, but the Poles should find themselves a place in a universal Orthodox Church. For Katkov, an Anglophile Westerner turned Slavophile, the Poles were a challenge to the very existence of Russia. It was an either/or situation: 'Our struggle against Poland is a struggle between two nations and to give in to the demands of Polish patriotism is to sign a death sentence for the Russian people.' The domination of Poland was perceived as a *sine qua non* for Russia's claim to be a great power. As Katkov warned: 'If Poland were restored, if Russia loses its status of a European great power, she will revert to being a semi-European, semi-Asian state.' Even Russian and Polish democrats were unable to find a common goal: freedom for the peasants or freedom for the nation? The outcome, as Kazimierz Brandys says, was paradoxical too: 'In Poland, the peasant received land but all hope of national autonomy immediately evaporated. In the country of the Tsars, serfdom was abolished, but the prisons were filled.'

The Russian–Polish dilemma between social revolution and

national independence was repeated in different form in the immediate aftermath of the First World War. In August 1920 Red Army troops led by Budyonny and Tukhachevsky marched on Warsaw in what must be considered the first major attempt to export the Bolshevik revolution, but they were defeated in what the Poles still call the 'miracle on the Vistula', by Josef Pilsudski, a socialist who had devoted all his life to the struggle against Tsarist Russia. Afterwards Lenin wrote to his fellow revolutionary Klara Zetkin: 'The Poles failed to see in the Red Army their brothers and liberators, they only saw their enemies. . . . The Poles do not think and do not act in a social and revolutionary manner but only as nationalists and imperialists.'

Pilsudski drew a different lesson from the Red Army invasion: Bolshevism was merely Russian imperialism by other (in fact rather similar) means.

> When I see Mr Tukhachevsky marching in the footsteps of Paskiewich the 'prince of Warsaw' [the pacifier of the 1831 uprising] and knocking on the doors of Warsaw while repeating formulas borrowed from Marx, I cannot help replying to him by quoting the title of a brochure, well known in Poland, from another great socialist theoretician, Liebknecht: 'Soll Europa Kosakisch werden?' [Should Europe become Cossack?]

The experience also confirmed Pilsudski's break with socialism. He told his former socialist colleagues, 'Gentlemen, I am no longer your comrade. In the beginning we followed the same direction and took the same red-painted streetcar. As for me, I got off at "Independence" station.'

Reflecting on the legacy more than fifty-five years later, Adam Michnik wrote:

> We owe to the 1920 victory over the Bolsheviks twenty years of independent Polish thought which inspired and still inspires generations. Yes, contemporary resistance to Sovietization is to a large extent possible thanks to the cultural reserves created by the inter-war Republic. If the Red Army had won the Battle of Warsaw, if a Provisional Revolutionary Committee had started governing Poland, then perhaps I would be living today in Kolyma or in Birobidzhan; who knows whether I'd speak Polish, whether generations of Polish intelligentsia would not have been turned into fodder for polar bears, if Polish culture could have avoided the disaster that befell Russian culture under Stalin's rule.

The Stalin–Hitler Pact of 1939 and the ensuing new partition of Poland between Nazi Germany and Soviet Russia only confirmed to Polish eyes that the Soviet Union was merely the extension of Tsarist Russia. The massacre of some fifteen thousand Polish officers at Katyn and elsewhere on Soviet territory in 1940, and the 1944 Warsaw Uprising, which was put down by the Germans as the Russians watched from across the Vistula – all this accounts for the widespread feeling in Poland at the end of the war that one occupation had ended only to be replaced by another.

Not surprisingly all the major post-war crises had a strong anti-Soviet element. In 1956 it was difficult to talk of de-Stalinization without questioning the Soviet imposition of its terrorist model on Poland. The events of March 1968 started with students protesting against the banning of Mickiewicz's play about students being arrested for conspiring, *Forefather's Eve*, set in Tsarist Russia. In 1980–1 Solidarity refrained from anti-Russian rhetoric, but as the workers' movement turned into a national, albeit self-limiting revolution, old, officially taboo subjects resurfaced: the stab in the back in 1939, Katyn, the Warsaw Uprising. The regime's belief that silence or the imposition of a lie would in due course have the desired effect, at least on younger generations who had not experienced the war, proved to be misguided. As Kazimierz Brandys put it:

> Imagine a Warsaw student who discovers that in 1863 the great Russian writer Leo Tolstoy, an already famous head of a family, wanted to enrol in the Russian Army to fight the Polish insurgents. And the same student finds out another day that in 1940, the Soviet writer Alexei Tolstoy arrived in the Polish town of Lwow, occupied by Soviet troops, and used the opportunity to enlarge his collection of silverware. Think about that student. Wouldn't it be too much to ask of him not to see there evidence of continuity?

In contrast to their northern neighbours, the Czechs and Slovaks have had little or no historical contact with Russia. In the nineteenth century the great Slavic brother was perceived as a useful cultural and political counterweight to German domination. Interestingly, the suppression of the Polish uprisings in 1831 and in 1863 tarnished the Czechs' opinion of Russia. It was only after the 1867 Ausgleich, the transformation of the Empire into a dual Austro-Hungarian monarchy which left the Czechs out in the cold, that political Slavophilia became attractive.

In the two World Wars, the alliance of Russia and the West helped the Czechs recover their independence. Czechoslovakia, unlike

Poland, began to look upon Russia as an ally in the 1930s. While the Polish government-in-exile broke off relations with the Soviet Union over Katyn during the war, President Beneš of Czechoslovakia went to Moscow in 1943 to sign a friendship treaty with Stalin. In Poland the Home Army (known as the AK) continued its underground struggle against Sovietization even after the war. In Prague the Red Army was met with an outburst of pro-Russian euphoria. 'My vas ozidali!' ('We were waiting for you!') was the headline in *Mlada Fronta*. In 1956, unlike the Poles, the Czechs and the Slovaks showed little sympathy for the Hungarians in the face of a Russian invasion. At heart, they were convinced that the Budapest solution would not be repeated, precisely because they had historically a different, conflict-free relationship with the Russians. Surely the Russians would understand that the Prague Spring was not directed against them and would, in the long run, enhance the cause of mutual understanding and socialism ...

The year 1968 was a turning point for both Poles and Czechs. In Poland, the revolutionary Romantic tradition, which had always been the main political outlet for anti-Russian feeling, was receding. The regime's own exploitation of nationalist and anti-Semitic rhetoric for purposes of Sovietization forced society itself to be more discriminating in its use of nationalist themes. In Czechoslovakia, the tanks of August destroyed in one night whatever pro-Russian feeling might still have lingered after 1948.

The alleged pro-Russian feelings of the Czechs (to a lesser extent this also applies to the Slovaks) have in any case been vastly exaggerated, much like the proverbial Russophobia of the Poles. A closer analysis shows that the reality was in both cases much more complex.

In fact, the Poles, like the Czechs, were divided in their attitudes towards Russia. Since the nineteenth century, the main divide in Poland's political tradition has been between the Romantic, idealistic, revolutionary tradition of the left (of which Josef Pilsudski was the leading representative) and the realist, 'positivist' current led by Roman Dmowski on the right. They represented two concepts of the nation and correspondingly two attitudes towards Russia. Pilsudski, who came from Wilno, an ethnically mixed area, favoured the concept of the political nation: he envisioned a large, multinational Polish state and, naturally, considered Russia the main threat. Dmowski and the National Democrats wanted a 'small' but ethnically homogeneous Poland. Their concept of the nation was therefore xenophobic and anti-Semitic. In their eyes Germany was the main threat to Poland, a position that led them to seek accommodation with Russia. Conciliatory gradualism, so-called 'organic work', an emphasis on educating a modern Polish nation rather than insurrection, had been their policy under the Tsars, and the concern over the western border with Germany remained paramount in the inter-war period.

At the end of the war the resistance of the AK, which refused to accept a Soviet-imposed regime, the new borders and the loss of the eastern territories, shows the indefatigability of the Romantic anti-Russian struggle. Yet, following the defeat of the Hungarian revolution of 1956 and in view of Western passivity in the face of the Soviet invasion, the Romantic tradition receded and positivism resurfaced with the Catholic Znak group led by Stanislaw Stomma. As in the nineteenth century, the idea was to improve Poland's lot within the framework of Soviet domination. Without sharing Dmowski's political views, Stomma explicitly referred to Dmowski's famous 1908 essay 'Germany, Russia and the Polish Question'. But, paradoxically, it is the Polish Communists themselves who implicitly claim to be the best proponents of the programme of National Democracy: they have, after all, achieved an ethnically homogeneous Poland while still trying (leaving aside the ideological desirability of the socialist community) to persuade the Poles that living under Soviet dominion is a geopolitical requirement necessary to safeguard the western borders against alleged (West) German 'revanchism'.

The myth of Czech Russophilia is perhaps even more inaccurate than that of Polish Russophobia. Early nineteenth-century cultural Pan-Slavism was widely shared by Czech intellectuals, but the political Pan-Slavism that developed at the end of the century was definitely a minority phenomenon: some right-wing conservatives, frustrated by the Austrian Emperor's reluctance to be crowned king of Bohemia, dreamed of a Romanov on the Czech throne. But the mainstream of Czech politics since 1848 was resolutely anti-Russian.

In 1848, Frantisek Palacky, the Czech historian and political father of the nation, wrote his famous reply to the Frankfurt Parliament, which was planning the unification of Germany. He rejected the prospect of the Czechs being absorbed in it and made the following case for their place in Austria: 'If Austria did not exist,' he said, paraphrasing Voltaire, 'it would have to be created.' The Habsburg Empire was for him a rampart not only against Germanization but, no less importantly, against Russia, 'this power which, having already reached an enormous size today, is now increasing its force beyond the reach of any Western power'. He warned against Russia's imperial ambition to become a 'universal monarchy', which would be an 'immense and indescribable disaster'.

But it was Karel Havlicek (1821–56), considered by Masaryk to be the most original and inspiring writer in Czech politics, who contributed the main blow in the demolition of the myth of Slavic unity centred around Russia. A leading Czech political figure during the 1848 revolution, Havlicek was also one of the Czechs who knew most about Russia. A fine connoisseur of Russian literature and a translator of Gogol, Havlicek spent a year and a half in Moscow in 1843–4. His Russian journey, much like that of the Marquis de Custine (whom he had not read) was full of disheartening experiences. Custine left for Russia hoping to find there arguments against democracy. His brief visit made him promptly change his mind. Havlicek left for Russia a Romantic Slavophile and returned to Prague a hard-nosed liberal determined to dispel any Czech illusions about Russia. Custine's book concludes with advice to a friend: 'If ever your son is dissatisfied with France, follow my recipe: tell him to go to Russia. Anyone who has examined the country thoroughly will be content to live anywhere else.' Havlicek's recommendation is similar: 'Anyone who wants to do the Czechs a real service can do no better than to send them all expenses paid to Moscow.'

In his writings on Russia Havlicek argued first that Slavism was a fraud, a mere tool of Russian imperialism. He also insisted that Russia was despotism incarnate. The Russians, he wrote in 1844, 'are not, as we tend to call them, our brothers; they are instead much greater enemies of our cause and more dangerous to our nation than the Hungarians and the Germans. Let us make use of their language and literature as we see fit, but avoid throwing ourselves into their arms. Otherwise things will end badly.' During the 1848 Spring of Nations, he wrote: 'Russia is a land of despotism, and we, other Slavs, must unfortunately be on guard against our brother as if he were our worst enemy.' Fear of Russia was also the basis for his and Palacky's view that in Central Europe, squeezed between Germany and Russia, only a democratized, federalized Austria could be the 'guarantor' of Czech national identity.

For Havlicek, Tsarist autocracy had its roots in Russian history and a culture that was divergent from the European tradition. In 1855, during the Crimean War, he wrote the following: 'If Russia wins, then Pan-Slavism becomes a reality and is bound to level all Slavic particularism; then God help us! If Russia does not win, without being pushed back into its Mongolian cradle, then Germans will dominate long enough to make the Czechs even more powerless and defenceless against a Russian invasion which is bound to come.' On the prospect of a Russian garrison in Prague, he added: 'Having seen what they were capable of in their own country, I cannot imagine what they would do here.' The problem with prophets of doom is that they tend to be proved right, even a century later. No wonder that Havlicek is among the most avidly read 'classics' in present-day Czechoslovakia.

Tomáš Masaryk considered himself a disciple of Palacky and Havlicek and shared some of their assumptions concerning Russia. Like Havlicek, he developed at first a fascination for Russia and a great expertise in Russian culture and history. Dostoevsky was Masaryk's introduction to Russian culture. The title of his magnum opus *Russia and Europe*, published in 1913, suggests the main line of his enquiry: Russia as the hinge between Europe and Asia. Could Russia, with a culture marked by religious mysticism, its legacy of Byzantine despotism ('theocratic Caesaro-Papism', as he called it), evolve towards a European future?

The Bolshevik revolution of 1917, in his view, gave a negative answer to the old question about the Europeanization of Russia. Having spent the autumn of 1917 and the spring of 1918 in Russia, Masaryk emphasized, upon his return to Prague, the limits of a Russian socialist revolution. Because of its cultural and political backwardness, the Bolshevik revolution was bound to reproduce all the features of autocratic Russia:

> The law of anthropomorphism applies not only to religions but also to politics. The Russians cannot rise above their condition, and their Communism and socialism cannot be really Marxist and scientific. The Bolshevik state and regime has inherited all the flaws of the Russian state, of Russian schools, of the Russian Church, since they are all rooted in the same people and the same level of instruction.

Today, this interpretation might not appear very original, but in 1918 this was by no means the most widespread view of the Bolshevik revolution. Rejecting revolutionary violence, Masaryk argued that the Bolsheviks failed to understand that 'the development of European nations and their ethics reject violence and therefore also aggressive revolutions. . . . In Europe we are able to introduce necessary social transformations peacefully.'

In *World Revolution*, published in 1925, Masaryk summed up his argument as follows:

> Only the primitive conditions of Russia made it possible for a vigorous usurper to bring about the Bolshevist revolution and to establish the rule of a small but organized minority. Uncritical, wholly unscientific infallibility is the basis of the Bolshevist

dictatorship; and a regime that quails before criticism and fears to recognize thinking men stands self-condemned. They managed to get rid of the Tsar but not of Tsarism.

If we add to this the *New York Times*'s reference to the Czechoslovak Legions in Russia in July 1918, when it called Masaryk 'the master of Siberia and of half of Russia', we can, without much regret, discard the traditional stereotype about Czech Russophilia. Indeed, it could be argued that, much like Pilsudski in Poland, Masaryk provided inter-war Czechoslovakia with a consistent, if moderate (both in tone and in practice) anti-Soviet consensus derived from a reading of Russian history.

It took Munich, the betrayal by the West and the onslaught of Nazi Germany, to reverse this trend, especially in the immediate post-war period. The fact that the Communists turned out to be the prime beneficiaries of this policy shift towards Russia should not obscure the fact that it was Edvard Beneš, Masaryk's disciple and successor, who was its main instigator. During the war he reached the conclusion that the Soviet Union was abandoning its Communist ideology and reverting to a less threatening, more traditional, imperial Russian posture. Meanwhile the West was supposedly evolving towards more 'socialism', i.e. more state intervention in the economy. Hence the idea that fitted the spirit of Yalta perfectly, of a Central Europe and particularly of a new Czechoslovakia as a bridge between East and West, between capitalism and socialism.

Post-1968 independent Czech historiography has often questioned that theory of the 'bridge' as an illustration of the flawed thinking of Czech democrats after the war. A bridge can hardly be a political programme for a nation; it is 'at best something to walk on or to sleep under', as one author put it. Masaryk's idea of the continuity between Bolshevik and Tsarist Russia was turned upside down: it became the justification for treating Soviet Russia as a 'respectable' European power. It became a commonplace not just for Beneš but also for Churchill and de Gaulle, who never referred to the Soviet Union other than as Russia. But the theory of the bridge not only minimized the specifically Communist features of the Soviet regime; it was also a distortion of Masaryk's thinking. As early as 1895 Masaryk wrote:

> It is often said that Czechs have as our mission to serve as a mediator between the West and the East. This idea is meaningless. The Czechs are not next to the East (they are surrounded by Germans and Poles, that is, the West), but also there is no need whatsoever for a mediator. The Russians always

had much closer and more direct contacts with the Germans and the French than with us, and everything the Western nations have learned about the Russians they have learned directly, without mediators.

So much for bridge-building in Central Europe.

Despite the very real differences in their historical experience, the Czech and Polish attitudes towards Russia have converged since 1968. In Poland, the traditional dichotomy between Romantic anti-Russian idealists and the neo-positivist 'realists' has receded. The alternative was neither the overthrow of a Soviet-sponsored regime nor capitulation in the name of realism. The question instead was how to foster a gradual emancipation of society without provoking a Soviet intervention. Asked at the height of the Solidarity period whether he feared a Soviet invasion, Lech Walesa replied: 'But they've been here since 1945!'

As for the Czechs, they have rediscovered the hard way, after the Soviet invasion of 1968, what they already knew from Palacky, Havlicek and Masaryk. Only a few months after the invasion, just as Gustav Husák started to give real meaning to the policy of 'normalization', the historian Milan Švankmajer published in the journal *Dejiny a Soucasnost* (*History and the Present*) an article entitled 'The Gendarme of Europe', about Russian attitudes towards democratic revolutions in Europe. Quoting Nicholas I, who upon hearing of the revolution in France in 1848 is reputed to have said: 'Gentlemen, saddle your horses, there is a revolution in Paris,' Švankmajer recalled, for the benefit of his Czech readers, traditional Russian attitudes in times of 'troubles':

> reorganization of the secret police and the attempt to 'cure souls'. . . . Every subsequent government began virtually stereotypically by ostentatiously abolishing the dreaded 'Secret Office' only to restore it again (under a different name and without publicity). . . . All the more important government and public institutions were provided with permanent agents, who were planted even in the major military units. . . . The Russian Empire is in reality constantly exposed to the danger of disintegration, which can be prevented only by a strong central government. . . . Civil rights threaten not just the individual and peripheral interests of multinational empires but their very existence.

Apropos of Russia's violent suppression of the democratic revolution in Budapest in the spring of 1848 Švankmajer concluded:

It was a stroke cunningly and coolly calculated by a sense of self-preservation, a blow against a European revolution, whose civil rights and efforts to assert the rights of national self-determination threatened the very foundations of Russian autocracy.... The Russian Empire was brought to its role as 'gendarme of Europe' not because of differences of civilization, culture, or values but because the evolution of Europe since the end of the eighteenth century had persistently threatened the very foundations of its existence. The reverse, of course, is also true.

From Budapest in 1848 to the Prague Spring of 1968, from 'the gendarme of Europe' to the 'gendarme of the socialist camp', Russia, in Central European eyes, has lost none of its power to assert itself as the symbol of unfreedom.

For the peoples of Central Europe, the past, to use Faulkner's phrase, 'is never dead. It's not even past.' Their historical experience with Soviet Russia has left them with a triple legacy. The first part is that the Soviet-type system has been imposed on them from without; it is a system derived from particularly Russian conditions and traditions that have been forcefully grafted on to societies with a radically different culture and political tradition.

The second is that, perhaps for the first time in modern history, the centre of the Empire is viewed by its periphery not only as an oppressor, but also as culturally alien and inferior. (This, incidentally, is a feeling shared not just by the populace or the intellectuals, but even by a significant section of the Communist establishments in Central Europe.) The official ideology since the war hails the advent of the Soviet model of socialism as progress. It has been perceived by the peoples concerned as a regression.

Finally, there is, after decades of lies and humiliation under the façade of Communist brotherhood, a widespread thirst for truth – truth about the present as well as about the past. The change has to start with language. The humiliation of a nation starts when a Czech or a Hungarian is asked to call the military invasion of his country 'brotherly help' or when the inscription on the grave of Polish officers massacred at Katyn says they were the victims of Hitler when everyone knows they were the victims of Stalin.

Now can Gorbachev make a difference? Can his policies of *glasnost* help to alter, not just relations with the ruling parties, but also the popular perceptions of Soviet Russia? Though it is early days to assess tangible evidence of the impact of his policies in the bloc, the image of the Moscow leader has changed dramatically. Paradoxical as it may seem in a city divided because of the Soviets, young rock fans demonstrated in East Berlin shouting 'Down with the wall!' but also 'Gorbachev! Gorbachev!' Similarly, after nearly twenty years of Soviet-imposed 'normalization', Gorbachev received an enthusiastic popular welcome in Prague in April 1987, while dissidents circulate in *samizdat* the latest translations from Soviet periodicals. Even in Poland, the most sceptical of Soviet bloc countries, Andrzej Rosiewicz, a popular songwriter, now sings that 'The spring blows from the East.'

Gorbachev clearly understands that to change the image of his country he will have to confront some of the more unpleasant aspects of the history of Soviet dealings with its Western neighbours. He also understands that the credibility of General Jaruzelski's Communist Party depends on its capacity to dissociate itself from the legacy of brutality and anti-Polish big-power policies of the Soviet Union. Hence the idea of a joint commission of Polish and Russian historians set up in 1987 to examine the 'dramatic episodes' in their nations' history. Hence also the idea to start with Stalin's dissolution of the Polish Communist Party in 1938 and the disappearance of its leaders in the gulag. There can be no better way to suggest that the Communists are not really Soviet agents, that they really do belong to the nation, than by presenting the Polish Communists as the first Polish victims of Stalin. But that, on its own, will not do. So Jaruzelski has suggested, in an astonishing article published (in August 1987) simultaneously by *Nowe Drogi* in Warsaw and by *Kommunist* in Moscow, that such a re-examination should deal with Stalin's policies towards Poland during the war, including the most sensitive period of the Stalin–Hitler Pact from 1939 to 1941. Jaruzelski, while avoiding a direct reference to Katyn, mentioned the deportation, after the Soviet invasion of September 1939, of 'thousands of Poles into the depths of the Soviet Union'. The actual figure was 300,000 but, judging by recent public discussions in Warsaw, anything short of an apology for Katyn will not do. 'When Molotov described Poland as "that bastard of the Versailles treaty", wasn't he challenging the very idea of an independent Polish state?' asked one Pole at a recent public discussion of the so-called 'blank spots' in the official version of history. And why, another participant demanded, must we listen to all this rubbish about Stalin signing the pact with Hitler in order to buy time, when everybody knows that Russia was still unprepared when the German tanks poured over its borders in the summer of 1941?

Polish historians point to the limits of the current official efforts to revise history. There is a tendency to deal only with those crimes that can be laid directly at Stalin's door and to avoid questioning anything to do with Soviet policies at the end of the war. So, one can refer to deportations of 1939–41 but must avoid mentioning the deportations of 1944–5. That would be questioning the very legitimacy of the Soviet-sponsored post-war regime. Thus in January 1988, Andrei Gromyko, the former chief of Soviet diplomacy and, admittedly, not the most daring champion of *glasnost*, reminded Mr Rakowski, a visiting member of the Polish leadership, that after the war Stalin 'fought like a lion' to make Poland a Communist state tied to the Soviet Union.

Not surprisingly, Polish intellectuals feel that the reassessment of the history of Polish–Soviet relations is too serious a matter to be left to the Communist states. An open letter from sixty leading Polish intellectuals was addressed to a wide cross-section of the Russian intelligentsia, including Andrei Sakharov and Bulat Okudzhavas, as well as leading personalities known for their liberal stance. The letter proposed a dialogue of 'free and independent people, not hampered by official guidelines and diplomatic considerations. We are ready to undertake such a dialogue with all the nations of the Soviet Union.' The Polish signatories, who include Lech Walesa, film director Andrzej Wajda and Adam Michnik, stated that, in order to 'change radically' the relationship between the two peoples, 'the truth about the Katyn murders must be told out loud. . . . We desire relations removed of all servility, lies and the threat of force.'

It might be too much to ask that Gorbachev reverse a pattern established over two centuries. But it would be no small achievement if by venturing into the 'unknown' territory of history he could help dispel the continuity thesis between Tsarist and Soviet Russia. In order to gain credibility for the present, he must be prepared to come clean about the past. The question is: how far can one challenge the history of the imperial relationship without, at the same time, undermining it?

3 The German Mirror

No one can understand the Germans who does not appreciate their anxiety to learn from and to imitate the West; but equally no one can understand the Germans who does not appreciate their determination to exterminate the East.

(A. J. P. Taylor, 1945)

In 1871, Nikolai Danilevsky, a friend of Dostoevsky and a socialist turned Slavophile, published an influential book entitled *Russia and Europe* in which he argued that, after periods of Roman and then German domination, the time had come for Slavic domination. Russia was to be the centre of an emerging Pan-Slavic force in Europe. The Pan-Slavic dream eventually came true under Stalin.

Running parallel with Russian Pan-Slavic ambitions regarding the small nations of Central Europe were rival Pan-German ideas of German hegemony in the region. The latter were not just held, as one would expect, by turn-of-the-century nationalists, let alone, in the 1930s, by advocates of a German *Lebensraum* in the east. They were also typical of the German socialist tradition, even in the period leading up to German unification.

Marx and Engels' views, as expressed during and in the aftermath of the revolution of 1848, are of particular interest, considering the lofty place of those two thinkers in the post-Second World War official ideology of the countries concerned. Identifying the spread of civilization and progress with that of German influence, Marx and Engels not only dismissed the national aspirations of the small nations of Central Europe, they questioned their very right to exist: 'Isn't their very existence already a protest against a great historical revolution?' they asked in 1848. Their fate, in the face of

German-sponsored historic progress and revolution, would be 'denationalization'.

Some of the statements by the inventors of 'scientific socialism' bordered on outright racism. Engels predicted that the Germans and the Hungarians would 'wipe out these petty hidebound nations, down to their very names'. 'The next world war will result in the disappearance from the face of the earth not only of reactionary classes and dynasties, but also of entire reactionary peoples. And that, too, is a step forward.'

Once the fervour of the 1848 revolution had subsided, the hostility towards the Slavic nations of Central Europe acquired a more analytical, more 'Marxian' tone. It was the steam engine (not just Germany) that was to destroy the Austrian Empire, together with the Czechs and other Slavic nations, because the railroad would destroy 'the granite walls behind which each province had maintained a separate nationality and a limited national existence'. In the well-known 1852 articles published by Marx in the New York *Daily Tribune*, the incorporation of the area in a German sphere of influence was presented as being in line with social and economic development: the backward, rural, Slavic nations were to be absorbed by the industrious and culturally more advanced Germans.

Even the Poles, otherwise worthy of support because of their antagonism towards reactionary Russia, were not completely spared. Marx recalled that in 1848 the question had been raised: 'Should whole tracts of land, inhabited chiefly by Germans, should large towns entirely German, be given up to a people that as yet has never given any proof of its capacity of progressing beyond a state of feudalism based upon agricultural serfdom?'

The Czechs were supposed to be the best illustration of the argument and the prime candidates for extinction, despite the recent events of 1848:

> As often happens in history, dying Czech nationality, dying according to every fact known in history for the last four hundred years, made in 1848 a last effort to regain its former vitality – an effort whose failure, independently of the revolutionary considerations, was to prove that Bohemia could only exist henceforth as a portion of Germany, although part of her inhabitants might yet for some centuries, continue to speak a non-German language.

The fact that the Czech lands became one of the most industrially advanced regions of Europe and that, despite attempts at Germanization and later Russification, Czech is still spoken there, simply goes to show that this summary dismissal of the Czechs was yet another unfulfilled Marxist prophecy. Clearly, in looking for the origins of the conflict between a universalistic (Communist) ideology and national realities or aspirations in contemporary Central Europe, one does indeed have to go back to the 'founding fathers'.

The current search for a Central European identity, as an alternative to the Sovietized present, tends to put emphasis on ascertaining the area's otherness from Russia. The tragedy of Central Europe is seen as having come from without. But the problem of Germany – the other power which has shaped the history of Central Europe – does not allow such a convenient evasion; it forces us to confront the tragedy that came from within. Stalin would never have conquered Central Europe if Hitler had not been let in first. Thus the other side of the 'Russian question' (Soviet domination over half of Europe) is the German question (a divided nation which ultimately cannot accept that Europe remains partitioned).

The rediscovery of Central Europe is more than nostalgia, more than the 'invention of a tradition', in Hobsbawm's phrase. It is above all an attempt to rethink the predicament of the area beyond official Marxist clichés as well as nationalist stereotypes. It is an attempt to reclaim a world that is lost, a legacy that is fundamentally pluralist, the result of centuries of interaction between different cultural traditions.

The playwright Odon von Horvath, author of the famous *Tales from the Vienna Woods* (1930), gave himself as a typical example of the Central European mix: 'If you ask me what is my native country, I answer: I was born in Fiume, grew up in Belgrade, Budapest, Pressburg, Vienna and Munich, and I have a Hungarian passport; but I have no fatherland. I am a very typical mix of old Austria–Hungary: at once Magyar, Croatian, German and Czech; my country is Hungary, my mother tongue is German.'

Czeslaw Milosz writes movingly about the ethnic and linguistic mix of his home town before the war: 'The Poles say Wilno; the Lithuanians, Vilnius; the Germans and the Byelorussians, Wilna. The inhabitants of the town spoke either Polish or Yiddish; the other languages – Lithuanian, Byelorussian, Russian – were spoken only by small minorities.' Though the city was predominantly Catholic, there were also Jews, Calvinists and Russian Orthodox: 'two enormous Orthodox churches with their inflated domes, a reminder of the solicitude the tsarist regime had for the mental health of its expatriated officials' (Milosz).

Prague, the birthplace of Franz Kafka and Jaroslav Hašek (the author of *The Good Soldier Schweik*), was a meeting ground of Czech, German and Jewish cultures, the Jewish community often acting as a bridge across the Czech–German divide. Kafka's father's mother-tongue was Czech while his son wrote in German; to make things even more complicated, Czechs often had German names and vice versa.

'I am "hinternational",' wrote Johannes Urzidil in his *Prager Triptychon*, reminiscing about his Prague childhood. 'One could live behind nations [*hinter* is German for behind] and not just below or above them.... Whether a ball broke a Czech, German, Jewish or an Austrian aristocrat's window was irrelevant.' Urzidil, of course, later amends his idyllic picture by noting that his father, though married to a Jewish woman, was anti-Semitic and anti-Czech.... Prague as a cultural frontier, writes Central Europe's leading literary historian Claudio Magris, was 'felt by its inhabitants in their bodies as a wound'.

A bridge and a divide: similar observations about Gdansk (Danzig) can be found in the novels of Günter Grass, particularly *The Tin Drum*. The city was a place of contact between Poles, Germans and the Katchubs (one of the oddest and most ancient of Central European minorities surviving on the margins of two worlds).

From Prague's Charles University founded in 1348 to the University of Czernowitz founded in 1875 in the far-off Austrian province of Bukovina, the universities too became bridges between cultures, At Czernowitz, German was the academic language, but the students included Jews, Romanians, Ukrainians, and Magyars. Königsberg, now Kaliningrad, was the town of Kant and Hannah Arendt.

Polish writer Adam Zagajewski was born in Lwow–Lemberg–Lviv in 1945 just as the Red Army moved in, and of the three possible ways of spelling the name of the city only one, officially, remains. Though too young to remember the cultural diversity that characterized his home town, he writes about his Polish family's departure from Lwow with the same sense of loss for the vanishing pluralist world of pre-war Central Europe as writers from the previous generation.

It has been argued that the artistic and intellectual creativity of Central Europe was related not just to the ethnic diversity, but to the interaction and even the rivalries between the various national cultures. This is what Hungarian composer Béla Bartok had in mind in his important essay on 'Race and Purity in Music'. Written in 1942, the essay transcended the problems of musicology *per se*. In sharp contrast to those for whom folklore was a means to exalt the supreme virtues of national particularism, Bartok stressed the 'continuous give and take of melodies' among the Hungarians, Slovaks and Romanians over the centuries.

> When a folk melody passes the language frontier of a people, sooner or later it will be subjected to certain changes determined by the environment and especially by the differences of language. The greater the dissimilarity between two languages in terms of accents, metrical conditions, syllabic structure and so on, the greater the changes that, fortunately, may occur in the 'emigrated' melody. I say fortunately because this phenomenon itself engenders a further increase in the number of types and sub-types. . . .

Thus in the process of migrating musical elements (but one can, of course, extend this observation to other spheres of cultural life) music becomes richer, more complex, offering new possibilities of artistic creativity. Bartok argued that the richness of Central European folk music was 'the result of uninterrupted reciprocal influences', and concluded that 'racial impurity' was therefore 'definitely beneficial'.

The implications of Bartok's viewpoint might help explain the explosion of intellectual and artistic creativity in Central Europe which centred on turn-of-the century Vienna. In addition to the interaction of emerging and competing national cultures, there was also a genuinely supranational or cosmopolitan outlook, often identified with the Jewish community. Many of the great names associated with Viennese *fin de siècle* cultural life were Jewish and not originally from Vienna: Freud, Mahler, Musil and Husserl came from lands that are today part of Czechoslovakia. Joseph Roth, the author of one of the finest novels about that period, *The Radetzky March*, came from Polish Galicia. Budapest, Prague or Cracow were not 'suburbs' of Vienna, but rather part of a cultural network strongly connected with Vienna.

The novelist Hermann Broch suggested that, at the turn of the century, an 'enlightened' Jewish bourgeoisie had replaced the Catholic aristocracy as the main force behind the development of a cosmopolitan Central European culture. The baroque tradition had been implanted in the far corners of the Habsburg Empire, at least as regards architecture and music. Now the bearers of a common, German-speaking culture were middle-class and Jewish (caught between the Empire and the emerging nations); but the context had changed and a culture that was often German in form but universalistic in content was eventually to give way to the rise of nationalisms.

The current rediscovery of that Central European culture entails an implicit rejection of its reverse side: ethnic nationalism (and its by-product of anti-Semitism). This interest has little to do with the superficial nostalgia for an embellished imperial past illustrated by the popularity of the Viennese exhibition 'Traum und Wirklichkeit' ('Dream and Reality'). For the Czech writer Milan Kundera, as before him for Stefan Zweig, author of *Memories of a European, finis Austriae* – the disintegration not only of a supranational state but also of a pluralist culture – foreshadows the coming European crisis. It is a metaphor for a vanishing Europe whose spirit survives today only in the memory of those 'unhappy few' Central European intellectuals recovering from a double hangover: that of nationalism followed by that of Communism.

This also accounts for the fact that the revival of the cultural and political concept of Central Europe, which started in Budapest and Prague, has now also reached Vienna and Berlin. The West German writer Karl Schlögel points this out in an essay appropriately called 'The Middle Lies in the East'. The dissolution of borders in our minds is understandably a highly attractive theme in a divided country in search of its identity.

In the late 1980s the reinterpretation of German history became the focus of a major political and intellectual debate. To reassess modern German history in European terms implies, according to Schlogel, seeing it as part of the history of Central and Eastern Europe. German history is the history of an eastward expansion. 'One can deal with the history of Prussia only in connection with the history of Poland, and vice versa; with the history of the University of Leipzig founded in 1409 only in connection with the earlier developments at the University of Prague; the founding of Berlin as part of the German settlement policy in the East: civilizing and Germanizing trends, both fruitful and catastrophic.'

For all these historical reasons (as well as contemporary political ones), German intellectuals tend to be on the whole more familiar and more involved in the Central European debate than their counterparts in London, Paris or Madrid. Moreover, revising German history and reclaiming a Central European heritage raises questions about the motives involved, even (or especially) when they are not clearly stated. Many Eastern neighbours must have wondered what Peter Glotz, a leading spokesman for the Social Democratic Party, meant when he advocated (in *Neue Gesellschaft*, January 1986) that West Germany should act as 'guarantor [*Machtgarant*] of Central European culture'.

Meanwhile the East Germans have been busily rehabilitating the Prussian tradition from Frederick the Great to Bismarck. Between the Luther anniversary in 1983 and the 750th anniversary of Berlin in 1987, the two Germanies seemed engaged in parallel yet rival exercises in selective reappropriation of their national past. Selective it must remain not just for ideological reasons: it is not easy, for instance, to speak of Kaliningrad (formerly Königsberg) as a centre of German culture. For the East German population this dilution of ideological orthodoxy is welcome. The success in East Berlin of Hamel's play *The Prussians Are Coming* is an indication of that. But from Warsaw this reclaiming of the Prussian past is seen differently. Poles still remember Bismarck's statement that 'for Germany to survive, we must first destroy Poland'.

Schlögel's and Glotz's observations, like the new, positive East German view of Prussia, reflect the two traditional faces of German influence in Central Europe: a long history of interaction and the tendency to seek hegemony. This duality (with the emphasis on the latter) is also present in Central European perceptions.

Two Czech historians, Jan Kren and Vaclav Kural, authors of a major (though unpublished) study of the subject, speak of a 'community of destiny', often bringing conflict, between the Germans and the Slavic nations of East-Central Europe. If one of the features of Central Europe is national fragmentation, the inadequacy of ethnic and state boundaries, then Germany too is an integral part of it. In this perspective the German minorities (*Volksdeutschtum*) are both an important component of the Central European space and an integral part of the German nation (*Gesamtvolk*).

In their eastern neighbours the Germans evoked a mixture of fear and attraction, a threat and a model. On the one hand, the threat of Germanization was very real. In the Habsburg Empire under Joseph II, it was assimilation through 'enlightenment': the German language gained supremacy in schooling and administration. In Poland, Germanization was carried out by the much more ruthlessly implemented Prussian *Kulturkampf* of Bismarck and later that of Hitler.

On the other hand, the German presence was at the same time identified with modernization, the development of towns and the spread of Western civilization. In the words of Kren and Kural, 'Just as France has long been identified with the idea of revolution, Germany represented in Central Europe a development model of industrial capitalism as well as its socialist alternative.'

The Germans share with the other nations of Central Europe a similar pattern of nation-building: a *Kulturnation* in search of a

political identity. Hence some of the common features of Central
European nationalism were a feeling of insecurity revealed in recurrent debates about the national character, and the tendency for
nationalism to invade social and cultural life. But whereas in the
German case the nation-building process in the nineteenth century
led to the unification of Germany, for the Slavic nations from the
Baltic to the Balkans it was centrifugal, leading to political fragmentation.

Although the nationalism of the Slavs developed in reaction to
the rise of German (and Hungarian) nationalism, its content often
mirrored the German pattern: it was Romantic and ethno-linguistic
and influenced by the philosophy of Herder. A nation was defined
by *ethnos*, by language, and by an often mythified version of its
history. Guiding the initial phase in the early nineteenth century
were ethnographers (such as Vuk Karadzić, expert on the folklore
of the South Slavs and author of a famous ethnographic dictionary
published in 1818), linguists (such as Josef Jungman, who compiled
the first Czech dictionary) and Romantic poets (Poland's Mickiewicz
was perhaps the most widely admired).

The conflict between these adverse – but in some respects also
similar – nationalisms eventually brought about the destruction of
Central Europe as a pluralist and multicultural society. The process
culminated in two stages which coincided with the two world
wars.

In the first stage, the very idea of Mitteleuropa as defined in
Friedrich Naumann's influential book published in 1915 became
merely a code word for a German sphere of influence from the Rhine
to the Danube; even today the German word remains associated for
many Poles with the *Drang nach Osten* (expansion to the east).
This indeed was Masaryk's reading of German intentions; the 'New
Europe' of independent nations which he and R. W. Seton-Watson
conceived of in London during the First World War was precisely
meant as an alternative to a German-dominated Mitteleuropa.

The new Central Europe of 1918–38, conceived of not only
without Germany but also against it, acted as a pro-Western buffer
zone between Soviet Russia and Germany. It was made possible
only through exceptional circumstances; the power vacuum created
by the simultaneous collapse of Germany and Russia. And it lasted
only as long as these exceptional circumstances did.

In the 1930s Hitler used the German minorities to challenge
the Versailles settlement and seek a new *Lebensraum* in the East.
Conversely, when German domination was replaced by a Soviet one,
Stalin used the idea of protecting the Slavic nations against the

common German enemy to legitimize his conquest. A policy of de-Nazification – identified with de-Germanization – became an instrument of Sovietization in Central Europe.

The inter-war concept was a Central Europe without Germany; the post-war concept was a Central Europe without Germans. The expulsion (or 'transfer', as it was called at the Potsdam Conference in 1945) of over ten million Germans was the main result of this policy: six million when Poland's borders were shifted to the west (to include Pomerania, Silesia and East Prussia); nearly three million from the Czechoslovak Sudetenland; and several hundred thousand from Hungary, Romania and Yugoslavia. In Hungary, the German transfer was considered secondary to the Transylvanian question (the Hungarian minority in Romania) or the proposed population exchange with Slovakia. The Hungarian Primate, Cardinal Mindszenty, expressed doubts about the wisdom of the expulsions. But in Poland and Czechoslovakia, following the terrible suffering inflicted by the Germans during the war, the expulsions had the support of the overwhelming majority of the population. They were seen as a painful yet necessary outcome of a centuries-old conflict of which Hitler's barbarism was merely the culmination. The method was by no means an elegant one, but it was thought to be the price for future peace in Europe.

Munich (1938) and Potsdam (1945) provide two landmarks, two faces of the break in the relations of Central European nations with Germany. Not just the Poles and the Czechs, who were the first victims of Nazi Germany's *Drang nach Osten*; the trauma extended, albeit differently, to the nations whose nationalism compromised itself with Germany. Hungary's territorial claims against Romania helped turn it into the last, if reluctant ally of Hitler. Romanian claims on Soviet-annexed Bessarabia led them to fight alongside the SS on the Eastern Front. Anti-Czech nationalism among the Slovaks and the anti-Serbian separatism of the Croats led them to seek 'independence' under the sponsorship of Nazi Germany.

Thus the war and the ensuing Soviet domination brought with it both a Stalinist 'final solution' of the German problem and the end to the 'private civil war' waged between Central European states since 1918. The method, as the common wisdom of the day had it, might not be the most elegant, but it seemed the necessary price to pay for future peace in Europe.

More than forty years later, the main problem in Central Europe is less a German than a Russian one. This fact, as well the current re-examination of nationalist ideologies of the past, has encouraged a reassessment of the trauma of 1945. Jan Josef Lipski, in a lucid and courageous analysis of Polish nationalism written at the height of the Solidarity period, invited the Poles to rethink their relationship with their neighbours. The expulsion of the Germans is for him an 'injustice', at best 'a lesser evil' sanctioned only by 'the necessity to organize the life of millions of Poles forced to leave their country [the Eastern territories, now part of the Soviet Union]'. Lipski summed up the Polish–German relationship as follows:

> For centuries we have held many grudges against the Germans: German emperors used to invade our country to keep it in submission; the Teutonic knights were the nightmare of the Prussians, the Lithuanians, the Pomeranians and the Poles; Prussia, Russia and Austria divided the First Republic. National and religious persecutions in the lands occupied by Prussia already foreshadowed what was to come during the Second World War. We shall not dwell on the enormity of Hitlerian crimes in Poland. Despite all this, since we identify with Christian ethics and European civilization, somebody had to come and say concerning the Germans, 'We forgive and ask for forgiveness.' In the dependent situation of our country, it was the highest independent moral authority which said it: the Polish Church. Despite all our resentments, we must make this sentence ours.

Czech soul-searching over the expulsion of the Germans is both more tormented and farther-reaching in its conclusions. The issue was cautiously raised during the Prague Spring of 1968 but the real debate was only launched a decade later, with a *samizdat* essay by a Slovak historian, Jan Mlynarik, entitled 'Thesis on the Expulsion of the Czechoslovak Germans'. It focused on three issues challenging the hitherto accepted orthodoxy.

First was the moral question: by endorsing the theory of 'collective guilt' Beneš, and more generally the whole Czech post-war political elite, broke with Masaryk's humanist principles on which democratic Czechoslovakia had been founded in 1918. Next came a political problem. The expulsion of the Germans was the dubious centrepiece of Beneš' alliance with the Communists under Stalin's sponsorship. In the twentieth century, population transfers have been the speciality of two totalitarian great powers, Nazi Germany and Stalinist Russia. Mlynarik poses the question of whether by depriving its non-Slavic minorities of civic rights (including the right to vote) on ethnic grounds, newly restored democratic Czechoslovakia was not in fact succumbing to the logic of exclusion characteristic of its two totalitarian neighbours. In other words, was not the expulsion of the

Germans the first step in the slide towards the establishment of a totalitarian system in 1948?

Finally, there is the question of national identity. In his monumental *History of the Czech Nation*, Frantisek Palacky argued that the 'meaning' of Czech history was to be found in the interaction and rivalry of Czechs and Germans in Bohemia and Moravia. The expulsion of the Sudeten Germans put an end to that coexistence which went back to the thirteenth century, and thus represented a radical break in the nation's history. What was supposed to be the 'meaning' of Czech history, asked Czech historian Milan Hauner, now that its partner (adversary or interlocutor) had disappeared from the horizon? Was not, in this perspective, the expulsion of the Germans therefore a Pyrrhic victory for the Czechs?

The question applies not just to the Czechs, it holds for the whole of Central Europe. One of the essential features of Central Europe was the historic presence there of Jewish and German minorities. Hitler destroyed the Jews, using Poland as the base for the Holocaust. Stalin expelled the Germans. What is then supposed to be the meaning of Central Europe without two of its vital common denominators?

The complex Central European ethnic puzzle was 'simplified' through murder, migration and forced assimilation. What was left in 1945 was a series of ethnically 'pure' states incorporated into the Soviet empire. The great dream of right-wing nationalists finally came into being under the Communists.

Central Europe used to be national states that claimed to be multinational. It was then turned into multinational states that claimed merely to be national. Finally, it became a series of nation-states which actually were nation-states. As Ernest Gellner pertinently observed, Central Europe before the war resembled a painting by Kokoschka made of subtle touches of different shades; after the war it was turned into a painting by Modigliani, made of solid single colour patches.

In Central Europe since the nineteenth century the conflict between two ideas of the nation and of culture has been acute: the first, inspired by the ideas of the French Revolution, was the democratic, political definition of the nation as a community of citizens. The other was the German, Romantic, 'blood and soil' concept of the nation. Conversely, two ideas of European culture were at stake: a universalist, humanist concept of a European culture defined by Julien Benda as the 'autonomy of the spirit', versus a concept of culture as identity, a *Volksgeist*, unique to each nation.

The transition from the 'traditionalist', ethno-linguistic or cultural concept of the nation to the democratic idea of the political nation between 1848 and 1918, associated with the names of Masaryk, Oscar Jaszi or Pilsudski, was merely an apparent success. The non-correspondence of ethnic and political borders, the permanent state of insecurity, an almost pathological fear for the 'fate' of the national community, accounts for the persistence of a combination of defensive (against Germans) and aggressive (against minorities, especially the Jews) features of Central European nationalism. Thus the 'German hysteria', as Istvan Bibo described the rise of German nationalism in the period from the trauma of Napoleon's victory at Jena to the 1930s, also produced its Central European counterparts. In this sense Hitler, the Austrian, was also a product of Mitteleuropa.

Bibo, the Hungarian political thinker who became in the 1980s a key inspiration for independent-minded intellectuals in Hungary, wrote between 1943 and 1946 three seminal essays: 'The Reasons and the History of German Hysteria', 'The Jewish Question in Hungary' and 'The Misery of the Small Central European States'. These are indeed the three closely intertwined components of the 'tragedy of Central Europe'.

This tragedy did not start with the arrival of the Red Army in 1945 and the Sovietization that came with it. The Holocaust, the destruction of whole nations, had preceded the destruction of whole classes. It did not come just from without, from the East; it also came from within. In Central Europe in 1945 all, even apparent victors, were in some way vanquished.

Reflecting, in the late 1940s, on the meaning of the post-war partition of Europe, the Polish historian Oscar Halecki introduced a subtle distinction to the conventional wisdom about Eastern and Western Europe. In his study *The Limits and Divisions of European History* Halecki observed that the Soviet westward expansion into Europe had pushed Western Europe into a close association with the United States, creating a new Atlantic community. He interestingly compared that development with the period at the end of the first millennium when the Islamic conquest of Spain was offset by the extension of Christendom to Poland and Scandinavia. Halecki suggested that the Atlantic dimension which Europe gained after the war could be seen as a compensation for the loss of the Other Europe.

But Halecki's most interesting insight, forty years ago, concerned the cultural and historical divide within the Western and the Soviet camps. He distinguished between what he identified as West-Central Europe, consisting of the defeated German-speaking countries, and

East-Central Europe, comprising the lands between Germany and Russia. At the time the theory challenged, from an unusual perspective, the dominant 'bloc' approach.

Twenty years later it would probably have been dismissed on the grounds that the experience of socialism, in the form of an identical social, economic and political system, was thought to be steadily reducing the differences between the Soviet Union and its allies. And to distinguish sharply between Western and West-Central Europe seemed even more obsolete, now that old rifts had been healed by de Gaulle's partnership with Adenauer and the West Germans were behaving like model pupils of the post-industrial society and the American way of life.

Today, however, the validity of Halecki's insight seems easier to confirm. The differences between what Halecki called East-Central Europe and Soviet Russia are as great as ever. In terms of culture, way of life, even communication, the real Iron Curtain runs farther east than commonly assumed – along the Soviet border. The 1980s have also revealed a growing latent dissatisfaction in West Germany with its post-war Atlantic identity. The debates there on the Central European theme often combine anti-Americanism with a dose of *Heimat* provincialism. The renewed discussion of the German question and the priority given to relations with East Germany; the loosening of old-fashioned ideological stereotypes about the Eastern bloc, used too often as a negative legitimation for an insecure democracy; finally the 'Euro-missiles' controversy, with the two Germanies stockpiling weapons over which they have no control – all these developments have contributed to the continuing reassessment of the Germans' place in Europe. In this context, the German rediscovery of Central Europe, of cultural and economic affinities with their Eastern neighbours, becomes an alternative (or a compensation, a *supplément d'âme*) to a fast-eroding Western, Atlantic self-definition.

In 1987 the Friedrich Ebert Foundation, which is close to the Social Democratic Party, organized a conference entitled 'Mitteleuropa: Dream, Nightmare, Reality'. Pictured on the invitation was a map of the two Germanies, Poland, the Baltic countries and the former lands of the Austro-Hungarian Empire. Karl Schlogel, one of the speakers at the conference, says that the word 'Mitteleuropa' should be a 'provocation' in the face of 'the wall in our heads'. It certainly represents an unspoken farewell to the post-war settlements.

Here cultural trends very clearly blend with political aspirations. The interaction between East- and West-Central Europe is growing in at least two areas where the spill-over into politics is obvious: one is the growing concern over the environment; the other is the parallel search for alternatives to the Yalta-ordained partition of Europe.

Acid rain, the slow death of the Central European forests, the hotly contested plan to build two dams on the Danube between Hungary, Austria and Slovakia, and, last but not least, the fall-out from Chernobyl have brought into the open the scale of the ecological disaster facing the area as well as the realization that environmental issues are oblivious to borders. You don't need to be a weatherman to know what kind of wind is blowing from Chernobyl. The concern of the Green Parties in the two Germanies has spread to the whole of Central Europe, especially Czechoslovakia, Hungary, Austria and Slovenia.

One of the issues which have most inflamed public passions and also provoked the best organized opposition is the Gabcikovo–Nagymaros hydroelectric power station currently under construction. The whole landscape between the Slovak capital of Bratislava and Budapest is to be 'reshaped' – destroyed, say the Hungarian Greens. Their fears range from water pollution in Budapest to a flood threat posed to the city in the event of an accidental break in the dam. They also point to the likely disappearance of the Hungarian rural communities on the Slovak side of the Danube, and question the financial wisdom of a venture whose main purpose seems to be to secure cheap electricity for Vienna.

The unofficial Hungarian environmental movement, called the Danube Circle, gathered thousands of signatures between 1984 and 1986 protesting against the construction of the dam. The Danube Circle has now apparently been silenced. In the spring of 1986, the Hungarian police broke up a joint demonstration of Austrian and Hungarian environmental activists on the site of the planned power station. As one participant put it, 'Austria will provide finance and technology; Hungary, censorship and police clubs.'

The Greens' conception of grass-roots 'anti-politics', based on concrete issues, the distrust of party politics and circumvention of the state bureaucracy, appeals especially to young people who feel alienated from the regime but do not belong to the 'ghetto' of dissident intellectuals. The 'greening' of Central Europe is one of the major developments of the 1980s.

The second area in which the concerns of Europeans on both sides of the divide are starting to overlap is the relationship between disarmament and the issue of the partition of Europe. In the context of missile deployments in both East- and West-Central Europe in the first half of the 1980s, cooperation involved Western (particularly German) peace movements and dissidents from the Other Europe. It started as a debate about the meaning of détente, peace and human rights; it turned into a reassessment of Yalta, the Central European status quo and the German question.

Reflecting on the connection between Soviet domination of his country, Czechoslovakia, and the division of Germany, former Charter 77 spokesman Jiri Dienstbier wrote:

> Long after the war, the division of Germany served the internal consolidation of the Stalinist regimes. After the terrible experiences of the war, many anti-Communists accepted an anti-German and pro-Soviet political orientation as a lesser evil. . . . The events of 1968 dealt a heavy blow to this way of thinking, especially since, unbelievably and perhaps thoughtlessly, the East German army took part in the invasion, so that for the first time since the Second World War a German Army entered a foreign territory. . . . The unification of Germany is still a spectre which haunts Europe.

Since 1945, the Soviet bloc leaders have justified the division of Europe by conjuring up the bogey of the German threat. There were the good de-Nazified Germans building socialism in East Germany, and there were the bad Germans, in the Federal Republic, presented as nostalgics of the Third Reich.

Yet, however strong the anti-German feeling was initially, especially in Poland and Czechoslovakia, it gradually gave way to anti-Russian sentiment. There was also growing popular aversion to government manipulation of the German issue to justify the unjustifiable. The Warsaw Pact invasion of Czechoslovakia was presented as a prevention of a 'revanchist plot' (even the Russian soldiers clearly expected to fight the Germans). In Poland the repression of students in March 1968 was accompanied by denunciations of an alleged 'Germano-Zionist' conspiracy. There was an interesting innovation on the part of official propaganda: could waning anti-German feeling be propped up by anti-Semitism? Tadeusz Walichnowski, head of the Police Academy in Warsaw, obviously thought so when he published a book entitled *Israel and the FRG*, in which dubious parallels were made. Until 1967, Israel had been accused by the official propaganda of behaving like the German 'revanchists'. After the Six Day War the Germans were accused of behaving like Israelis.

The anti-German rhetoric died down, however, in the post 1968 atmosphere of détente and Chancellor Brandt's *Ostpolitik*. Following certain developments – the signing of treaties recognizing the Oder–Neisse border with Poland in 1970, Western recognition of the GDR in 1972, and a treaty with Czechoslovakia describing as null and void the Munich Agreement – and in view also of the fact that the Federal Republic was led by an anti-Nazi Nobel Peace Prize winner, the 'German threat' argument became out of date. And it is likely to remain so unless Chancellor Kohl's pre-electoral appearances at gatherings of Silesian refugees under the banner 'Schlesien bleibt unser' (Silesia is ours) gives unexpected ammunition to tired propagandists.

The German thinking behind *Ostpolitik* was that, in the aftermath of 1968, one had to accept the status quo in order to be able to transform it in the long run – accept the existing borders in order to make them more permeable. The inter-German approach was extended to the whole of Central Europe. Détente between Germany and East European states, it was assumed, would also help to bring about internal improvements in the Soviet bloc countries.

Note: gradual improvement and not fundamental change. The basic tenet of the German concept of détente in a divided Europe, was that inter-German relations constituted a model for the coexistence of the two Europes. Now the Central European idea is a useful extension of the model: it helps (as P. Hassner put it) to 'Europeanize' the German question or to Germanize the European question. Hence the idea of a web of mutual dependence and joint responsibility for peace in Central Europe. This, of course, has an economic dimension bringing trade and credits, of which the East Germans, but also the Hungarians in the 1980s, have been the prime beneficiaries.

The 'security partnership' is considered to be the centrepiece of this policy: the draft treaty on the ban of chemical weapons which was signed between the German Social Democrats and the East German Communist Party is presented as an example to be followed in the whole of Central Europe. The signing, in 1987, of a joint ideological platform for the two parties was the final stage in this development, representing the bridging of the historical divide between Communists and Social Democrats as a step towards overcoming the ideological partition of Germany and of Europe. In dealing with the ruling Communist Parties of Central Europe, the Social Democratic Party of Germany has now gone further than any Western Communist Party; it has a tendency to behave as a government in exile.

Another key element is the linkage between the German and the Russian question in Central Europe, between *Deutschlandpolitik* and

Sicherheitspolitik. The rapprochement between the two Germanies, between West-Central and East-Central Europe, depends on (and therefore always remains subordinated to) West Germany's good relations with the Soviet Union. This is the *sine qua non* for the prospect of a symmetrical withdrawal of American and Soviet nuclear and conventional weapons from Central Europe.

Finally, stability in the neighbouring lands of so-called 'real' socialism was and remains a vital precondition for these objectives, and the prospect of very gradual change – a change that would be so gradual that it would go almost unnoticed by the Communist Establishments themselves, not to mention, of course, Moscow.

The Gierek regime in Poland in the 1970s was often presented as the illustration of the low-key approach to détente at work. Whether or not the emergence of Solidarity was its paradoxical success, Jaruzelski's military coup certainly seemed to mark its demise. The eighteen months that shook Poland in 1980–1 were anathema to the German concept of détente. The Poles remember that on 13 December 1981, the prime concern of Helmut Schmidt and Erich Honecker was that General Jaruzelski's military coup should not spoil their progress in inter-German relations. The restoration of order and 'stability' in Warsaw was perceived in both Germanies as a prerequisite for the pursuit of *Deutschlandpolitik* and for East–West détente. Conversely, from this (German) perspective the prospect of crisis or social movements in East-Central Europe is associated with the threat of East–West confrontation.

There are two types of response in East-Central Europe to this German-centred concept of détente. Some are highly suspicious of the vested interest that the Germans have in condoning the internal status quo in its neighbouring countries. Others, aware of the fact that in the West only the Germans actually mind the East–West divide, share with them a search for alternatives to the partition of Europe and of Germany.

A New Rapallo?

Eastern Europe under the shadow of a new Rapallo? Can the spirit of the 1920s' treaty – an understanding between Russia and Germany at the expense of Polish freedom – be revived? This was the provocative question posed by Hungarian philosophers Agnes Heller and Ferenc Feher in an essay assessing the meaning of the neutralist drift of the German left for the countries of the Other Europe. According to their reading, the 'ecolo-pacifism' and neutralism of the left is merely German nationalism in disguise; the real goal is German unity at the price of 'self-Finlandization'. A drawing-together of the two Germanies in the context of a neutralized Central Europe implies American withdrawal from Europe. It can only be achieved on terms acceptable to the Soviet nomenklatura in Moscow (for geographical reasons there can be no real equivalence between American and Soviet withdrawals). Moreover, it would provide for the Soviets a 'necessary *cordon sanitaire*' around an unruly East-Central Europe. Such an approach has many drawbacks and few (very hypothetical) advantages: it could mean a 'Finlandization' or a 'Hong-Kongization' in the West, and better control in the East.

'A new Rapallo, why not?' asked Rudolf Bahro, the East German dissident, now active in the West German Green movement. For the German left the price of such an arrangement might well be acceptable, especially in the Gorbachev era. But, as Feher and Heller have argued, an inter-German and Soviet–German attempt to heal the wounds of Yalta would only be feasible 'over the heads' of the Poles, Czechs and Hungarians.

East and West German attitudes towards Solidarity and even more towards martial law have confirmed in Warsaw the suspicion that, as always in history, a German–Russian rapprochement could only be anti-Polish. The Polish opposition journal *Nowa Koalicja* (*New Coalition*), which favours cooperation of dissidents from all over Central Europe, prefers to set aside the German question. The journal tends to leave the GDR out of the 'new coalition' altogether, considering that 'the natural representative of the interests of East German citizens is the German Federal Republic'; in other words, that the Germans, even the East Germans, belong to Western and not Central Europe. Willy Brandt's visit to Warsaw in 1986 and his refusal to meet with Walesa only seemed to confirm, as the Solidarity underground leadership put it, that stability to the east of their borders, which the Germans claim is necessary to the improvement of inter-German relations, simply ignores Polish aspirations for freedom.

One of the first and more significant documents in the launching of the debate on the link between the German question and the overcoming of the divide in the heart of Europe was the 'Prague Appeal', published by Charter 77 signatories in 1985 on the eve of the fortieth anniversary of the end of the Second World War:

> We cannot ignore the existence of certain taboos. One of them is the division of Germany. If we cannot, in the perspective of the unification of Europe, deny anybody the right to unification, this

applies to the Germans too. This right should not be used at the expense of others nor should its use disregard their fears. Let us declare unequivocally that the solution cannot lie in any kind of revision of the present European borders. In the context of a European rapprochement, borders should become less important, and not provide the occasion for nationalist relapses. Let us nevertheless recognize the Germans' right to decide freely if – and under what form – they desire the union of their two states within their present borders. As an extension of Bonn's agreement with its Eastern neighbours and of the Helsinki Agreement, the signing of a peace treaty with Germany could become a significant instrument in a positive transformation of Europe.

The main idea of the 'Prague Appeal' is that Germany is no longer dangerous, while the partition of the continent into two antagonistic military blocs is. This became the basis for a dialogue between Western pacifists and Eastern dissidents which centred on the connection between peace and human rights, on détente between states and the relations between the state and society. The result was a joint document submitted to the delegations at the Third Helsinki Review Conference in Vienna in November 1986.

The document is remarkably revealing about East–West intellectual and political communication in the 1980s. The result of a trade-off between the concerns of Western peace activists and those of dissidents, the Appeal can be considered as the manifesto of the 'greening' of Central Europe. Its common starting point is the rejection of the Western habit of identifying Europe with the EEC and, conversely, of calling 'Eastern Europe' the countries that 'by geography as well as political and cultural traditions belong to Central Europe'.

The link between peace and human rights comes clearly from the dissidents: the idea of a détente 'from below' which would no longer be the monopoly of the states but involve societies as well. Indeed, the document suggests that the measure of East–West détente between states is proportional to the degree of détente between state and society. A long list of prerequisites for détente in the field of human rights follows.

The Western pacifists' input, as endorsed by the dissidents, is the symmetrical treatment of the two superpowers, one involved in Afghanistan and the other in Central America. Their military–industrial complexes are the source of conflict. Both should withdraw their troops and missiles so that Europe can break free from its bipolar straitjacket and become a place where all peoples and nations 'have the possibility to organise their mutual relations as well as their internal political, economic and cultural affairs in a democratic and self-determined way. It should be clear that the German question is a European question and therefore efforts to solve it should be part of a democratic programme to overcome the bloc structure in Europe.'

This manifesto was signed by leading dissidents from Czechoslovakia (Havel, Benda, Simecka, Uhl), Hungary (Kis, Konrad, Rajk, Haraszti, Demszky) and East Germany (Templin, Eppelmann, Poppe, etc.). Though, significantly, Kuron and Michnik have not signed, other Poles did, such as Solidarity spokesmen Onyszkiewicz and Romaszewski and Jan Josef Lipski, one of the founders of the KOR (Workers' Defence Committee) as well as the members of the Freedom and Peace movement led by Jacek Czaputowicz, which represents a younger, post-Solidarity generation of dissidents. It is the first joint document conceived across East–West and also East–East borders, and concerned not just with a protest or a commemoration of a particular event but with an alternative vision of Europe.

A Central Europe under the double ecological and military threats of two systems of domination: that seems to be the German Greens contribution to the Central European *Zeitgeist* of the 1980s – a central Europe where the military and ideological division imposed on the continent by the two rival superpowers is most strongly resented. The United States and the Soviet Union are increasingly perceived as external, non- or at most semi-European powers; 'what were once role models have become mere guardians,' says Peter Bender, the West German socialist, whose writings on Germany and Europe echo Gyorgy Konrad's farewell to Yalta.

Fundamental differences exist, of course, between Western 'peaceniks' and the dissidents in East-Central Europe. In his famous 1985 essay 'The Anatomy of a Reticence' Vaclav Havel discussed why the political naivety and utopianism of the former do not go down too well in a Central Europe long since grown allergic to any promises of a 'radiant tomorrow'. The very word 'peace', because of its place in the official ideology and propaganda, arouses, says Havel, 'distrust, scepticism, ridicule and revulsion' in the population – distaste not for the goal of peace but for its official association with the 'struggle against Western imperialism', which is a bitter joke in countries still occupied by the Red Army.

Other voices among the dissidents pointed out that the alleged symmetry between the two superpowers and the two political systems is based on false premises. Not only, as Janos Kis noted, is there no geographical symmetry between the USA and the USSR *vis-à-vis* Europe, but the two alliances cannot be compared either. Most importantly, protest possibilities are fundamentally unequal because of the different nature of the regimes in the East and West, a point made by Czech historian Vaclav Racek in a much discussed letter to European Nuclear Disarmament (END) leader E. P. Thompson.

Dissidents and pacifists differ also in their assessment of the very cause of the 'threat to peace'. For Western pacifists, the prime threat is the over-accumulation of nuclear weapons. In this view, the peace movement in the West and the dissidents in the East should simultaneously strive to become a counterweight to their respective military–industrial complexes. The right to survive must come first; other human rights will follow. The dissidents tend to emphasize that the root of the conflict lies in the totalitarian nature of the Soviet system. The more détente there is between a state and society internally, the more likely détente between states becomes. Similarly, the imposition of an internal 'state of war', as was the case in Poland in December 1981, increases the likelihood of an external tension or 'state of war'. To the extent that the existence of Solidarity was a measure of internal détente between state and society, Solidarity was indeed the most powerful 'peace movement' Central Europe ever produced.

Why then were so many dissident intellectuals prepared to put aside their 'reticence' towards the Western left and get involved in what might seem to be a dubious dialogue?

One pragmatic reason is that in the 1980s it was the only game in town. In the 1970s, calls for human rights were voiced within the Helsinki framework of East–West détente; in the mid-1980s they had to be presented in the context of the dominant East–West issue, the superpower arms race. After 'no détente without human rights', the slogan of the 1980s was 'peace and freedom are indivisible'.

And then there is the Central European predicament. As all attempts at genuine internal change in the region have failed (1956 in Hungary, 1968 in Czechoslovakia, 1980–1 in Poland) the focus of people's hopes has tended to switch to external factors. The loosening of the Soviet grip, the argument goes, is plausible only as part of a mutual disengagement from the centre of Europe by the two superpowers. The way to overcome the Yalta legacy is through the denuclearization of a 'neutralized' Central Europe.... Seen from Paris, this looks like a perfect nightmare, raising the spectre of German reunification. But seen from Prague, Budapest and above all from East Berlin, 'neutralism' is by no means a dirty word.

After the Central Europe of nostalgia for a historical and cultural identity, neutralism is the Central Europe of utopia. The Central European idea, the longing for the 'Europeanization of Europe', is not devoid of ambiguities and misunderstandings. All the main protagonists – the dissidents, the Germans and, of course, Mikhail Gorbachev – have their hidden agendas. In East-Central Europe it is primarily a quest for autonomy, for an emancipation from the Soviet empire. In West Germany, the new interest in Mitteleuropa is related to the search for a solution to the German question which entails greater distance from the United States, and the West. At the same time it implies a degree of understanding with the Soviet Union: a Mitteleuropa without America but consistent with the goal of a 'common European house' which Gorbachev is trying to promote. The fact that these different concepts of Central Europe, east and west of the political divide, are being rediscovered simultaneously does not imply that they are compatible, or even desirable.

Part 2
SOVIETIZATION

4 The Legacy of Yalta

> The Yalta Agreement does not stipulate the rule of the
> Polish United Workers' Party – that rule is merely the
> consequence of terror, rigged elections and Stalin's
> violation of the agreement.
>
> (Adam Michnik, *Letters from Prison*)

For the nations of the Other Europe Yalta is the 'original sin', the
founding myth of a divided Europe. It has become synonymous
with Sovietization and with the disappearance of the very notion of
Central Europe. The fate of the lands in between Germany and
Russia was decided by the Soviet Union and the United States.
Europe divided by non-European superpowers: that is the potent
myth of Yalta.

The Yalta Agreement of February 1945 thus became the modern
symbol for the European nations' recurring experience of not being
masters of their destiny. As Leszek Kolakowski put it forty years
after the meeting in the Crimea: 'Let us remember, Poland was in
no way represented at Yalta and the fate of millions was decided by
three old men: a bloodthirsty tyrant, a terminally ill statesman who
knew little about the issues, and a Realpolitiker of a declining
Empire.' The 'Yalta system' is still with us, says Ferenc Feher, 'in the
sense that the powerful of the world still feel themselves appointed to
make ultimate and supremely rational decisions for the rest of us'.

Finally, there is Yalta as the 'betrayal', as another Munich, another
Western attempt to appease a totalitarian dictator at the expense of
the nations of Central Europe.

At the time this feeling was most widespread among the Poles. It
has since been strengthened in the whole of Central Europe by the
spectacle of Western passivity during the violent suppression of the

Hungarian Revolution of 1956, of the Prague Spring of 1968 and of Polish Solidarity in 1981. 'Yalta' has become the code word for the East–West European status quo. Not surprisingly, bitter references to Yalta are heard each time this status quo has been challenged by attempts at internal change in Central Europe.

This connection between the East–West status quo and the internal 'status quo' of Central Europe was and remains the main point of contention over Yalta. The post-Solidarity controversy on the subject re-emphasizes that Yalta remains unfinished business. As if catering to popular misgivings about the Yalta legacy, official Soviet bloc propaganda has insistently referred to it in order to legitimize Soviet domination. In the aftermath of his military coup, General Jaruzelski argued that 'Poland is being regarded as a tool, as a lever for putting pressure on the Soviet Union, on the socialist community.... It has been allotted the role of a detonator under the edifice of the peace founded on agreements signed in Yalta and Potsdam which cannot be separated from each other....'

While for most Europeans, both East and West, Yalta is seen as the prime cause of the partition of Europe, both Moscow and Washington have rejected such arguments (admittedly for opposite reasons) and called for better observance of the Yalta Agreement. A pamphlet, published jointly in 1985 by the Polish and Soviet Embassies in Paris, concluded that 'the cause of evil in the post-war world does not lie with Yalta but rather in the departures from it'. Meanwhile President Reagan also called for 'full compliance' with the Yalta Agreement: 'We see that agreement as a pledge by the great powers to restore full independence to and to allow free democratic elections in all countries liberated from the Nazis after the Second World War. There is no reason to absolve the Soviet Union or ourselves from this commitment.'

There was, of course, some irony in Reagan's defence of Roosevelt's record at Yalta which, since the late 1940s, has been a favourite target of conservative Republicans, who attack it as a 'sell-out' of half of Europe to the Russians. But there was more cynicism than irony in the reference to Yalta by a general who had declared war on his own nation in order to save the 'edifice of peace' founded at Yalta.

What then was the reality behind the much used and abused myth of Yalta? Does Yalta deserve its reputation?

The answer, of course, depends on the extent to which one is prepared to separate the general statements of principle from their actual implementation. As far as the general principles are concerned, there is little to argue about. The Declaration of Liberated Europe adopted by the big three has no hint of a partition of the world among the great powers. On the contrary, it contains a clear endorsement of democratic principles, including the holding of 'free and unfettered' elections in the countries liberated from the Nazis. Considering the overwhelming presence of the Red Army on the ground this endorsement of democratic principles has sometimes been presented as a major Western achievement. It was Stalin's subsequent violation of these principles in East-Central Europe that became the prime cause of the breakdown of the wartime alliance which led to the Cold War. Thus, the argument goes, it is not the Yalta Agreement as such which was at fault, but its implementation (or rather the lack of it) by the Soviet Union. In that case the supporters of democratic change in the Soviet bloc ought to be pressing for a return to the letter of the Yalta Agreement.

But what about the spirit of the agreement? The Polish question was a concrete test of what the lofty words in the Declaration of Liberated Europe meant to the signatories. First, they confirmed the agreement reached at Teheran on shifting the Russian–Polish border westward to the Curzon Line (the truce line suggested by Lord Curzon in 1920 at the time of the Polish–Soviet war). To Roosevelt's feeble attempt to raise the question of the city of Lwow, a matter of great importance to the Poles, Stalin replied that he could not be any less pro-Russian and pro-Ukrainian than Lord Curzon.... Then came the crucial move from the question of Poland's territory to that of its new regime. Ever since the Teheran Conference, Churchill had pleaded with the Polish government-in-exile in London to accept concessions on the territorial question in return for guarantees of post-war independence. The Poles refused, possibly weakening their bargaining position with Stalin, while virtually ceasing to be on speaking terms with Churchill. It could indeed be argued that by concentrating their intransigence on the issue of frontiers, the London Poles made it more difficult for the British and Americans to stand firm against the Soviets in defence of the London government as the proper basis of a future administration in Warsaw. Had that been the basis of the new government, Polish politics in the immediate post-war period might have resembled more closely those of Hungary or Czechoslovakia, rather than leading straight into civil war. Instead, Roosevelt and Churchill accepted Stalin's proposal that the Communist-controlled Lublin Committee should become the basis of Poland's future government. To be sure, the Committee would be 'enlarged' to include a few exiled democratic politicians, but the decision amounted to a *de facto* repudiation by the West of the legitimate Polish government-in-exile and thus represented a fundamental break in the continuity of Polish institutions and of Polish political representation, over which, after all, the West had gone to war.

So free rein was given to Molotov – who shortly after the signing of the 1939 pact with Nazi Germany had declared of Poland that 'one blow from the German Army and another from the Soviet Army will put an end to this ugly product of Versailles' – to discuss at Yalta who were the true 'non-fascist and anti-fascist' parties entitled to take part in Polish elections. The only provisions concerning the implementation of the democratic principles of the Declaration were 'measures for the carrying out of mutual consultation' among the Allies. In other words, there were no institutional guarantees, merely a reliance on Soviet goodwill, for the future of democracy in Central Europe.

The decisions concerning Poland had broader significance for the whole area. If the Western powers were unable to defend the future of democracy in an Allied country over which they had gone to war, what could be expected in the case of former proto-fascist allies of Hitler? There is an ambiguity to the Yalta exercise which gives an odd flavour to the lofty words of the Declaration of Liberated Europe. As Adam Ulam put it, 'How can you turn a country over to a foreign power and yet demand that it be done through free elections and in accordance with high principles of morality and democracy?'

Stalin's interpretation of the message was very clear indeed. Immediately after the Crimean conference he sent Vishinsky, his favourite judge in the show trials of the late 1930s, to Romania to issue an ultimatum to King Michael and install a Communist-controlled government. Meanwhile a Polish delegation representing the non-Communist Home Army resistance went to Moscow to help prepare the post-war settlement, and was arrested upon arrival. In a letter – drafted but never sent – to Roosevelt, Churchill came nearest to stating plainly the connection between the words of Yalta and the events that followed: 'If we do not get things right now, it will so be seen by the world that you and I, by putting our signatures to the Crimea settlement, have underwritten a fraudulent prospectus.' He was right. Yalta failed not because of some mythical dividing up of the world – nor, strictly speaking, because of Western inability to restrain Soviet designs on East-Central Europe; it failed mainly because the agreement rested on the dubious assumption (or pretence) that Stalin and the Western leaders could give the same meaning to words like democracy, sovereignty or independence, and because the concrete meaning given to these words in the provisions

for the future government of Poland came close to a Western acceptance of Soviet double-talk concerning the 'peoples' democracies'.

Speaking at a dinner at the end of the Yalta Conference, Stalin
told his hosts: 'I, as a naive man, think it best not to deceive my ally
even if he is a fool. Possibly our alliance is so firm just because we
do not deceive each other.' Stalin did not really deceive the leaders
of the West. If anything, they deceived themselves.

Yalta was not a conspiracy to divide Europe, but it contributed
to the legitimization of Soviet control in East-Central Europe in
exchange for promises that were never kept, nor were meant to be.
In this sense the Soviets got something for nothing (unless, like
Roosevelt, we consider as relevant counterparts the Soviet declaration of war on Japan or Stalin's apparent support for the idea
of the United Nations as a 'universalist experiment with world
government', to use Arthur Schlesinger's phrase).

Yalta thus illustrates two general problems: the weakness, or more
often the absence of Central Europe as a consideration in Western
thinking about post-war Europe, and second, the inherent contradictions of policies based on mistaken assumptions about Stalin
and the Soviet system. These were made by statesmen who convinced themselves that during the war the Soviet Union reverted to
being good old imperial Russia; they were also made by intellectual
elites and public opinion, which had been mobilized to support the
alliance with a new, positive image of the Soviet Union conveyed
through favourable media reports and films such as *Mission to
Moscow*.

America's senior wartime diplomats Charles Bohlen and Averell
Harriman later argued that a confrontational attitude at Yalta over
the Polish question would not have been understood by Western
public opinion. On the other hand, it was also out of the question in
1945 completely to ignore democratic principles with regard to East-
Central Europe (even though they could not be upheld in practice,
given Soviet military control of the area), because people in the
West identified the war effort with those values and with Poland in
particular. In other words, public opinion made it impossible simply
to 'give away' Poland (or, by extension, Central Europe), but it made
it equally impossible to adopt a firm anti-Soviet stand.

This duality reflects the basic ambivalence of Western policy
towards East-Central Europe after 1945: verbal refusal to accept
the Sovietization of the region, without having the means or the
determination actually to oppose it. This, realists such as George
Kennan have argued, was one of the main ingredients in the origin
of what became known as the Cold War.

Yalta, in this respect, was neither as evil nor as crucially important for the fate of Central Europe as it was made out to be. And the 'demonization' of Yalta downplays other, more important factors in the Sovietization of the area, namely the primacy of military power at the end of the war and the internal factors which played a part in the Communist takeovers in East-Central Europe. Much more significant for the fate of Central Europe was the absence of any clear concept in Western strategic thinking at a time when things were still in a state of flux – that is, between 1941 and 1943. The meeting of the British and American Chiefs of Staff on the eve of the Teheran Conference of November 1943 confirmed this lack of concern: with the Second Front postponed until May 1944 the Americans dismissed the British suggestion of an offensive in the Balkans, which would have given the Allies their only other chance of influencing developments in Central Europe.

Teheran was the real turning point. There the Western leaders first openly confronted the likelihood of the Soviet Union's becoming the dominant power in East-Central Europe after the war. Following Churchill's remark to that effect, Stalin asked whether the British thought he was going to 'swallow Poland up'. Eden replied that he did not know 'how much the Russians were going to eat. How much would they leave undigested?'

In retrospect, Yalta appears as a belated, if not very successful, exercise in damage limitation. A similar argument could be made about Churchill's often criticized spheres-of-influence deal with Stalin in October 1944. The British Prime Minister gave a very matter-of-fact description of what remains the most explicit acknowledgement of the inevitability of Soviet dominance in the countries occupied by the Red Army at the end of the war (though, significantly, Poland and Czechoslovakia were left out):

> The moment was apt for business, so I said, 'Let us settle about our affairs in the Balkans. Your armies are in Romania and Bulgaria. We have interests, missions, agents there. Don't let us get at cross purposes in small ways. So far as Britain and Russia are concerned, how would it do for you to have 90 per cent predominance in Romania, for us to have 90 per cent of the say in Greece, and go fifty–fifty in Yugoslavia?' While this was being translated, I wrote out on half a sheet of paper: Romania: Russia 90%, others 10%; Greece: Great Britain (in accord with USA) 90%, Russia 10%; Yugoslavia 50–50%; Hungary 50–50%; Bulgaria: Russia 75%, the others 25%.
>
> I pushed this across to Stalin, who had by then heard the

translation. There was a slight pause. Then he took his blue pencil and made a large tick and passed it back to us. It was settled in no more time than it takes to set it down.

This, however, was not quite the whole story. The next day Molotov presented Eden with a claim for 75 per cent influence in Hungary (an ally of Hitler on the Soviet border) and for 90 per cent in Bulgaria. Since the Soviets already had a dominant position in Bulgaria, their demand for 90 per cent control was clearly meant only as a bargaining tool in wrangles over Hungary. Still, curiously enough, Eden was prepared to back down on Hungary against the promise of Anglo-American participation in the Allied Control Commission in Bulgaria.

As Vojtech Mastny put it: 'For the sake of an ephemeral role in a country for which Churchill felt little but disgust, they resigned themselves to the status of a passive bystander in Hungary, perhaps the most Anglophile nation in all of East-Central Europe.'

It is easy, of course, to adopt a moralizing posture towards the mixture of ignorance and cynicism displayed in Western dealings with Stalin over the fate of the lands of the Other Europe. It certainly would be fascinating to know what an alleged 10 per cent influence in Romania or a 25 per cent influence in Bulgaria was supposed to mean. Yet, in retrospect, the 'percentage deal' can be seen, much like Yalta, as an attempt to cope 'realistically' with the single most important consideration concerning Soviet influence in East-Central Europe: the primacy of the military factor. 'The map of Europe,' said Charles Bohlen, 'would look very much the same if there had never been the Yalta Conference.' More than any amount of diplomatic manoeuvring, the overwhelming and unchallenged presence of the Red Army shaped the post-war predicament of Central Europe and the Balkans.

From Hitler to Stalin

'Whether we like it or not,' wrote Sebastian Haffner in 1977, 'today's world is the work of Hitler. Without Hitler no divided Germany and Europe; without Hitler no Americans and Russians in Berlin.' And without Hitler, one is tempted to add, no Sovietization of Central Europe. The discussion over what could have been done to stop Stalin in 1945 has to start with the question of what had not been done to stop Hitler after 1935.

After Stalingrad, there was little to prevent the Red Army from filling the vacuum left in Central Europe by the German retreat. Ironically, between 1941 and 1943, Stalin had been constantly pressing the Western Allies to open up a second front; had that actually happened, it would undoubtedly have spoiled his expansionist ambitions in Central Europe. Instead, as we have seen, the area never featured prominently in Western strategic thinking during the War. At the end of the summer of 1943, Anglo-American military planners informed the Czech and Polish governments-in-exile that. even if a second front were opened, Western troops would not penetrate as far as their countries. In other words, they were already destined to be Soviet territory.

There were a number of reasons for this, including understandable concern for the risks and the human cost involved. Crucial, too, were America's 'Pacific first' policy and the more debatable reluctance on the part of Roosevelt to make the connection between the military and the political outcome of the war. Averell Harriman, who was his main adviser at the time, later explained: 'In 1941–43 we were not interested in what Stalin's peace policies might turn out to be. We were at war with Hitler. We were interested in Stalin's war policies, and that was enough to keep us busy.' Roosevelt was also keen to inform Stalin at Yalta of his intention to bring US troops back home within two years. Given the predictable decline of British power after the war, this was another way of saying to Stalin that he need not worry about his control over East-Central Europe. This assurance of Roosevelt's, incidentally, goes a long way towards refuting the 'revisionist' thesis which attributes Stalin's Sovietization of East-Central Europe to his alleged security concerns in the face of American military might. Astonishingly enough, quite the opposite was the case: despite its overwhelming military superiority there is no evidence – not even the explosion of the nuclear bomb during the Potsdam Conference – to substantiate speculations that the United States ever actually used that superiority to influence the situation in East-Central Europe at the end of the war.

Stalin, in contrast, understood perfectly what the consequences of victory were to be: almost as soon as the Normandy landings brought Western troops to the continent, he launched the Communist-led Lublin Committee, which was to become the provisional government of Poland.

The ultimate illustration of American reluctance to think in Clausewitzian terms (war as politics through other means) was the liberation of Prague. The Americans were stationed (on the Budejovice–Plzen–Karlsbad Line) merely an hour from the Czechoslovakian capital when a spontaneous insurrection broke out there on 5 May 1945. The Red Army was still several days away. While the insurgents launched desperate pleas on Prague radio for help against the Germans, Eisenhower instructed Patton to observe the 'spheres of liberation' agreed with the Russians. 'We should have gone on to the Molldau River,' Patton wrote in his memoirs, 'and if the Russians didn't like it, let them go to hell.' It apparently did not occur to President Truman, concerned only with winning the war, nor even to Eisenhower, the most political of American generals, what a difference, politically, an American liberation of Prague would have made.

More than a failure of Western diplomacy, what happened between 1943 and 1945 reflected a failure of Allied strategic thinking on Central Europe. The failure of Yalta concerns the legitimacy of Soviet domination in Central Europe. The primacy of the military factor accounts for its feasibility.

Only three days after the end of the war, surrounded by an atmosphere of euphoria, Churchill wrote a most lucid assessment of the political significance of the Soviet military presence in the heart of Europe. In a message to President Truman the British Prime Minister expressed his concern over:

> the combination of Russian power and the territories under their control or occupied, coupled with the Communist technique in so many other countries, and above all their power to maintain very large armies in the field for a long time. . . . An iron curtain is drawn down upon their front. We do not know what is going on behind. There seems to be little doubt that the whole of the region east of the line Lübeck–Trieste–Corfu will soon be completely in their hands.

The 'iron curtain' phrase was not the product of the Cold War; it was coined the very moment the war ended. The result of the war was the greatest conquest made in Europe since the days of the Ottoman Empire. In addition to annexing the lands that had been part of the Tsarist Empire, the Soviet Union extended its grip to half a dozen European countries comprising 100 million inhabitants. Stalin's great achievement was his capacity to integrate into the Soviet empire the great diversity of countries ranging from Catholic Poland to Protestant Prussia, from Allied Czechoslovakia to enemy Hungary and Romania, from agrarian Bulgaria to industrial Bohemia.

The Red Army's vital contribution to the defeat of Nazi Germany served to justify Soviet claims to a buffer zone against any future German threat – hence the Soviet claims to turn East Germany into a truly anti-fascist socialist state. Hence also the recurrent argument about the big Slavic brother protecting the small nations of East-

Central Europe against the bogey of West German 'revanchism'. The trouble was, as it turned out, that the Soviets could not conceive of security without political control, nor accept the idea of friendly yet unSovietized governments on their western borders.

Western distinctions between security and control were, from the Soviet point of view, purely academic. Stalin tried to convey this to Churchill at the end of April 1945:

> Poland is to the security of the Soviet Union what Belgium and Greece are to the security of Britain.... I do not know whether a genuinely representative government has been established in Greece; or whether the Belgian government is a genuinely democratic one. The Soviet Union was not consulted when those governments were being formed, nor did it claim the right to interfere in those matters, because it realizes how important Belgium and Greece are to the security of Great Britain. I cannot understand why in discussing Poland no attempt is made to consider the interests of the Soviet Union in terms of security.

In other words, it was clear – to anybody who had cared to observe Soviet behaviour in the occupied Baltic countries in 1940 – that Stalin's 'security' concerns went beyond a traditional territorial concept of spheres of influence towards the goal of political control. For security reasons you create a buffer zone stretching a thousand kilometres west of your borders, and since the conquest is likely to breed resentment and thus 'insecurity' you put in charge only 'trustworthy' governments which, by definition, are those run by Communists. In this way military presence led to political and ideological absorption. As Stalin explained at the time to the Yugoslav Communist Milovan Djilas: 'This war is not as in the past; whoever occupies a territory also imposes his own system as far as his army can reach; it cannot be otherwise.'

War and Revolution

If Stalin had really wanted to, he could probably have incorporated the lands of East-Central Europe into the Soviet Union at the end of the war. Militarily speaking, there was little to stop him. However, in order to sustain the 'spirit of Yalta' and a degree of cooperation with the West, he opted not only for the preservation of at least formally sovereign states but also for an intermediate phase of coalition politics. In Bulgaria, Romania and most blatantly Poland, these were essentially bogus coalitions dominated by the Communists and some token opponents (or fellow travellers). But in Hungary and Czechoslovakia, for nearly three years the Soviets tolerated genuine coalition governments reflecting the results of democratic elections. By 1948, of course, the end result was the same, and the Communist monopoly of power was established as soon as Stalin had decided to consolidate Soviet-style socialism not just in one country but in one empire. Yet this post-war quasi-democratic interlude raises important questions about the diversity of the conditions and methods of imposition of a Soviet-type system in Central Europe as well as about the domestic ingredients at work in the process.

In what remains probably the most clear-sighted analysis of what he called the East European Revolutions, Hugh Seton-Watson distinguished three main phases in the Communist seizure of power. The first stage was the genuine coalition: several political parties (committed to the joint programme of what was called a National Front) competed for power. Freedom of the press and of association were observed, though inhibited by the Soviet factor and, of course, by Communist control of key ministries such as Defence or the Interior. In Bulgaria and Romania this phase lasted merely a few months. In Hungary it survived till the spring of 1947; in Czechoslovakia until February 1948.

The second stage was the bogus coalition. Non-Communists were still in the government but they owed their posts less to the power of their parties than to their personal subservience to the Communists. Peasant parties and 'bourgeois' parties were driven into opposition. Poland and Yugoslavia, which had skipped the first stage, experienced only a brief acquaintance with the second. It came to an end everywhere in the aftermath of the Cominform meeting at Szklarzka Poreba in September 1947.

The third and final phase was the establishment of a monolithic Communist regime: all opposition was suppressed and its representatives arrested (e.g. Maniu in Romania, Petkov in Bulgaria) or forced into exile (Poland's Mikolajczyk). The socialists were purged and then forcibly merged with the Communist Party. The February 1948 coup in Czechoslovakia was the most drastic transition from the first to the third stage.

Within these three main stages of coalition politics one can detect a series of common ingredients used in all of the Communist takeovers.

(1) The use of the military situation, or the position acquired during the resistance, to eliminate the most serious rivals and opponents. This could take the form of physical elimination (especially in the Balkans), of preventing the rivals to return from

exile (Poland) or of sending them into exile (Bratianu in Romania). A very broadly defined anti-fascism can also serve as a justification for the ban on rival parties: the National Democracy, Poland's largest pre-war party, was banned. The same applies to the largest pre-war Czechoslovak parties, the Agrarian and the People's Party in Slovakia.

(2) The takeover of all key levers in the state apparatus, namely the army, the police, and communications. As former Budapest police chief Bela Kopacsi explained in his memoirs, in the fairly open initial phase in Hungary many appointments were open to discussion, but not that of the head of Security. After its 1945 election victory (57 per cent) the Smallholders' Party in Hungary asked for the post of Minister of the Interior. Voroshilov, the Soviet head of the Military Control Commission, imposed his veto because of Soviet 'security' concerns.

(3) The temporary abandonment by all the Communist Parties, in order to promote coalition politics, of their revolutionary programme ('the dictatorship of the proletariat'). Each initially adopted a relatively moderate 'people's democracy' programme. Hungarian Communist leader Erno Gero declared at the end of the war: 'Some Communists think that the order of the day is the establishment of socialism. This is not the point of view of the Hungarian CP. It is not correct to urge the construction of socialism on the rubble of defeat.'

(4) The use of economic measures to weaken opposition forces and to introduce the foundations of a new economic system: agrarian reform, confiscation of German or collaborationist property, nationalization of key sectors of industry, etc.

(5) The claim that the Communist Party is the best possible intermediary between the society and the Soviet overlord. The Communists have 'access' and do get things done. Criticism of the Soviet Union is taboo everywhere.

(6) The 'salami tactic' (so called by Hungary's Rakosi), whereby the Communist Party constantly increased its demands on its allies, on various groups in the society, in order to remove 'slice by slice' all the elements deemed undesirable. This meant isolating and gradually disposing of the main adversary or the hostile faction in another party and letting others believe that if they condone this process and eliminate the 'difficult' elements the coalition politics will remain viable. Eventually, of course, these others end up sawing off the branch on which they are sitting. In Hungary this meant detaching from the non-Communist bloc all the potential allies of the Smallholders' Party. In other words, the Communists encouraged the political fragmentation of their opponents. They fostered the creation

of a variety of small groups or parties in order to weaken the dominant position of the Smallholders' Party in the national front. All this makes sense, of course, only as long as there are relatively free elections: the East German local election in 1946, the general election of May 1946 in Czechoslovakia, in Hungary in 1945 but not quite in 1947 (when there was large-scale fraud).

(7) Related to this approach was the infiltration of rival political parties. This proved useful in the case of the Polish Socialist Party or in that of the left parties and the trade unions in Czechoslovakia. This is where the fellow travellers of the Party get a chance to contribute to the cause and, of course, to enhance their own careers (Osobka-Morawski, the Polish socialist leader; Z. Fierlinger, Czechoslovakia's first Prime Minister; or Petru Groza in Romania).

(8) The tactic whereby the Social Democrats are for ideological reasons to be used (but also feared), and eventually eliminated as an autonomous force. They were usually first split between right and left, and the latter then merged with the Communists; the first merger was the creation of the SED (German Socialist Unity Party) in the Soviet zone in Germany in 1946; it was followed in 1947 by Bulgaria and Romania and finally in 1948 by Poland, Hungary and Czechoslovakia.

(9) Police fabrication of plots to discredit political rivals of the Communists. This is how in early 1947 the leader of the Hungarian Smallholders' Party Béla Kovacs was arrested by the Russians in Budapest when he was implicated in a so-called 'anti-democratic conspiracy' which eventually decimated the leadership of his party.

(10) The imposition of an officially binding version of how the takeover actually took place. The rewriting of history became part of the historical process itself. The takeovers were not presented as 'revolutions' on the Bolshevik model, but as the natural evolution of the nation's history. Democracy was liquidated in the name of the 'acceleration' of the democratic process, its superior form.

Though the outcome (and many of the ingredients) were remarkably similar, the differences in the implementation of the common pattern were significant. The charade of coalition politics in Poland and Yugoslavia accounts for the fact that the interaction between war and domestic civil war is still for historians there the key question concerning the legitimacy (or the lack of it) of the regime. In contrast, the democratic interludes in Hungary and Czechoslovakia remained an important point of reference, if not a model, for those who wished to democratize the existing socialist system in 1956 or in 1968.

The three-stage pattern of seizure of power tends to stress the unscrupulousness of the Communists' methods (their 'salami tactic') in the early stages, and their use of terror in the last. It was, of course, made possible by the Soviet presence, but that presence alone does not satisfactorily explain the relative weakness of resistance to the Communist takeovers. The answer varies with the political culture of each country: the legacy of pre-war authoritarian patterns, the relative weakness of the civil society, the appeal of Marxist ideology among the intellectuals (or the discrediting of conservative or liberal alternatives), and, of course, the indigenous base of the Communist Parties. But the crucial factor was the impact on these societies of the war itself. The Nazi occupation and the agonies of liberation represented a radical breach in the social and political structures and helped to create the conditions for post-war Communist takeovers.

Hannah Arendt wrote that 'wars and revolutions have determined the physiognomy of the twentieth century'. Nowhere has this been more true than in East-Central Europe – not only, as one might expect, in the countries which had collaborated with the Axis powers prior to Hitler's defeat. Moscow did not draw too fine a distinction between the Allied and the enemy countries it liberated. Hungary, Hitler's last ally, was given more leeway than Allied Poland. All in all, the 'victorious Allies' received from the Soviets as a 'reward' what others received as a punishment. But the really crucial legacy of wartime upheaval lies in the collapse of the *ancien régime*, be it pre-war democracy or a variety of authoritarianism: the physical destruction of intellectual and political elites, the disruption of the social fabric. The result is a power vacuum which, as George Schöpflin observed, was one of the main preconditions of the Communist takeovers: 'Effectively the Communist revolution was made possible by Nazi Germany and its wartime ideological allies, like the Arrow Cross in Hungary, Ljotič in Serbia or the Iron Guard in Romania.'

In Hungary the Horthy regime was already disintegrating when Eichmann and his troops moved in. The fascist coup led by Salasi in October 1944 (while Horthy's emissaries tried to negotiate in Moscow) gave the final *coup de grâce* to the *ancien régime*. After the lengthy siege of Budapest Hungarian society had reached a point of no return. It was ready for radical change, leaving the Communists in a strong position to offer their version of change and to implement it. In Hungary, as in the rest of East-Central Europe, the Soviet Union did not create the need for fundamental change; it simply tilted the balance in favour of one particularly brutal version of it.

In Romania, the collapse was closely connected with Antonescu's wartime military dictatorship, which had sent troops to the Eastern Front to fight for the Germans. Despite a skilful change of sides at the eleventh hour, there was little room for manoeuvre once the Red Army approached Bucharest. But it can be argued that the war merely completed a process of disintegration which went back to the late 1930s. In his memoirs (*Les Moissons du solstice*, Paris, 1988), Mircea Eliade, one of Romania's leading intellectuals, traced that process back to King Carol's imposition of an authoritarian dictatorship in 1938 to halt the rise of Crodeanu's Iron Guard. For Eliade, Carol's dictatorship was not only a break with what was left of inter-war Romania but anticipated all that was to happen seven years later after the Communists and their associates took control. 'Carol's only originality', says Eliade, 'was his confidence that he could afford to do anything because "the people" would remain without response.'

The connection between war and Communist revolutions was if anything even stronger in countries that belonged to the victors. The experiences of Poland, Yugoslavia and Czechoslovakia are very different indeed, yet in all three cases the German invasion, which had destroyed the old political structures, represents the crucial turning point. In Poland, Red Army liberation turned into Sovietization and war into civil war. In Yugoslavia (and Albania) more than anywhere else the 'double war' was connected with the transition to a Communist regime with only limited Soviet involvement. Czechoslovakia and Hungary enjoyed a 'democratic interlude' and a more gradual process of Sovietization. But even in Czechoslovakia, it could be argued, the 'elegant' takeover of 1948 was merely the tail-end of a process begun in 1938.

Yugoslavia: Revolutionary War

Two features distinguished the Yugoslav (but also the Albanian and, despite its failure, the Greek) revolutionary model from the dominant pattern in Central Europe and in the rest of the Balkans. First, the Communists assumed a leading role in the resistance against the Axis powers and emerged from the war as the dominant political force. They therefore felt confident enough to skip the initial coalition phase in Yugoslavia and Albania and step straight into the 'third phase' of Communist hegemony. Secondly, the Communist Parties in these two countries owed their dominant position (and eventually their ability to seize political power) to the achievements of their wartime resistance rather than to Soviet military might. In contrast to other Communist Parties, only the Yugoslav and the Czechoslovak parties had a strong indigenous base in the country at the end of the war. Drawing on all of these factors, the prevailing contemporary interpretation of the Yugoslav takeover stressed Marshal Tito's personal ability, his charisma, his independence *vis-à-vis* Stalin and, above all, his ability to represent, in 1945, the only cohesive political movement in a country deeply divided by nationalist feuds which the war had brought to a paroxysm of murderous hatred.

The transition from war to revolution in Yugoslavia was thus presented as logical, as the only available solution for the war-torn country and, at the same time, because of its independent nature, as the root of Tito's conflict with Stalin, as the real origin of the distinct Yugoslav model of socialism. This interpretation derived its strength not only from its consistency, but also from the fact that it was simultaneously put forward both by official Yugoslav historiography and by numerous Western admirers of Tito, particularly British conservatives. However, since Tito's death in 1980, Yugoslav historians have been able to give us a more complex and accurate picture of the connection between war and revolution in Yugoslavia.

In a book published in Belgrade in 1985, described by the chairman of the Serbian Committee for Sciences as being 'without precedent' in Serbian historiography, Veselin Djuretić confronted the supreme founding myth of Titoism: the claim that the Communists were *de facto* the only genuine force in the resistance and therefore the only ones with legitimacy to determine the political orientation of the country after the war. There was not just one resistance movement in Yugoslavia, there were two: Tito's partisans and that of the Serbian royalists, led by Draža Mihajlović. The latter were usually lumped together with the Croatian fascists (Ustasha), who in their ideology, their methods and indeed their wartime allegiance were totally subservient to the Nazis.

The historians' rehabilitation of Mihajlović created a sensation in Belgrade. It cast doubt on the Party's claim to a monopoly and thus on its decision to prevent the King and the government-in-exile from returning to Yugoslavia. But no less important were the revelations about Tito's wartime priority of fighting his Serbian political opponents, even if that meant a pause in the struggle against the Germans (sometimes even at the cost of hitherto unmentionable negotiations with them, as was the case in March 1943). Finally, as

Djuretić shows, Tito's triumph was made possible only by the fact that he enjoyed the logistic and strategic support of both Moscow and London. Churchill's decision at the end of the summer of 1943 to shift British support to Tito at the expense of Mihajlović helped to seal Tito's victory.

In Yugoslavia the civil war caused more deaths than the brutality of German repression. This includes the nationalist ('tribal') warfare of the Croatian Ustashas against the Serbs; it also includes Communist partisans and Serbian Chetniks against the Ustashas and against each other. By the end of the war and in its immediate aftermath Tito had already eliminated most of his political rivals. Unlike in the rest of Europe where, in line with the instructions of the Communist International, resistance was to be based on a broad 'national front' coalition, in Yugoslavia (and also in Albania and Greece) Communist-inspired liberation fronts were formed in opposition to other resistance movements. Even Stalin wondered in March 1942: 'Are there really no Yugoslav patriots apart from Communists and Communist sympathizers?' Tito obviously thought not. As early as November 1943 (while the Teheran Conference was meeting), he proclaimed his Council of National Liberation as the provisional government. Clearly, regardless of Stalin's diplomatic concerns, Tito had no intention of sharing power.

Yet a compromise was reached at the end of the war and the Yugoslav Communists withdrew from what could have been a straightforward revolutionary dictatorship in favour of an admittedly brief phase of limited pluralism. Hence the parallels with the other so-called 'people's democracies'. The importance of this period has been reassessed by two Belgrade academics, Vojislav Kośtunica and Kosta Ćavośki, in a recent study appropriately entitled *From Pluralism to Monism*.

First to be eliminated were those opponents who did not fit into the Communist-led People's Front: 'He who is against the People's Front is our enemy, which means he is the enemy of his own people,' was the slogan of the day. Splits were organized in political parties reluctant to toe the Communist line. By September 1945 Foreign Minister Šubašić and Milan Groll, the former leader of the Democratic Party, resigned from the government with this bitter comment on parliamentary activity: 'A reasonable man shudders at an assembly where all the proposals are passed unanimously and with acclamations.' Shortly after, *Democratija*, the only independent newspaper, ceased publication after only seven issues, allegedly because printers refused to print it. The Front was a *pro forma* coalition meant to conceal the Party's real drive for hegemony. There could be no alternative programme to that of the Front; the opposition was confined to criticism of its implementation. Even in Slovenia, where the wartime Liberation Front had come close to resembling a genuine coalition, Josip Vidmar, a leading fellow-travelling intellectual, asserted in 1945 that:

> In Slovenia there is no place for any other party or for any other political organization, because there is only one united people's movement in Slovenia and that is the Liberation Front. The invaluable merit for all this goes to the most progressive party that has ever existed in Slovenia, that is the CPY [Communist Party of Yugoslavia]. What it has achieved with its tireless eduation of us non-Communists and with its tireless enlightening of the masses of Slovenia ... is that people have moved towards complete unity and will never again want any other kind of party in the future, but only the unified will of the people.

After the elimination of those opponents reluctant to join the Front, the remnants of pluralism within the Front itself were disposed of. Most of the Communists' opponents within the Front called for abstention in the November 1945 elections. But even that effort was promptly neutralized. The paper *Politika* claimed that 'the people who did not go to the polls do, in fact, vote because they have made it possible in advance for the candidates whom the majority vote for, to be elected'. In other words, even those who abstained in order to oppose the Front were 'objectively' voting for the Front.

The final stage in the elimination of the opposition came in July 1946 when Dr Dragoljub Jovanović, the leader of the Serbian Peasant Party, who had been a strong supporter of an alliance with the Communists (even helping the Communist Mosa Pijade to draft the programme of the People's Front), criticized the new law on cooperative farms, the excessive powers given to public prosecutors and the complete alignment with the Soviet Union. A month later he was expelled from his Party for having 'sabotaged' the struggle against the enemy during the war, and for his 'shameless attack on the Soviet Union – on Mother Russia, on that which is held most dear and most sacred by every one of us'. Two years later, people would be sent to jail for writing in such a pro-Moscow vein. But in the meantime it was Jovanović who was sentenced to nine years.

At the end of the war, Yugoslav Communists were, if anything, too unabashedly Stalinist in their behaviour even for Stalin's liking. They demonstrated that a Soviet-type political system can be introduced without an actual Soviet presence. By the time the Red Army reached the Yugoslav border, Tito's Communists had imposed their own administration and security apparatus on two-thirds of the territory. And it was precisely Moscow's attempts to penetrate these instruments of 'Sovietization', and their failure, which became one of the main causes of Stalin's break with Tito.

The Polish Path: From Katyn to Lublin

Nowhere in Europe did the war represent such a dramatic destruction of the old society and such a radical breach in the political continuity of the nation as in Poland. 'God's playground', as Norman Davies called it, Poland was also Europe's killing-ground. The country lost over a sixth of its population, more than any other country in Europe (proportionally to the pre-war population, this meant twice the number of German war losses, and more than both Yugoslavia and the Soviet Union, whose wartime demographic losses can by no means be attributed only to the war). It is estimated that more than half of the pre-war 1.2 million inhabitants of Warsaw were killed between 1939 and 1944. After Hitler and Stalin jointly invaded the country in 1939, they followed parallel, complementary policies aimed at the eradication of resistance to totalitarian rule. Besides massacring civilians, both followed a policy of systematic destruction of the nation's elites. According to special provisions of the September 1939 secret protocol of the Nazi–Soviet Pact, the Gestapo and the Soviet NKVD were to cooperate in liquidating any 'agitation' that could have spilled over into the other's zone. There were, of course, differences of emphasis. The Nazis exterminated on racial grounds, making the Jews their prime targets; the Soviets deported Poles to the gulag on a 'class basis'.

But their common aim was the destruction of the intelligentsia. Thus, in the spring of 1940, while some five thousand members of the educated classes were killed by the Gestapo, the NKVD liquidated a similar number of Polish officers at Katyn. They were part of a total of fifteen thousand murdered officers. When their graves were uncovered by the Germans in 1943, the Poles immediately understood this atrocity for what it was: a deliberate attempt to decapitate a nation, to eradicate potential opponents. To this day the inscription on their graves at the military cemetery in Warsaw declares that these were the victims of Hitler. But every Pole knows they were the victims of Stalin. The men murdered at Katyn were among the first casualties of Soviet expansion into Central Europe; they were also the first victims of the Communist lie. Thus from the very first day the resistance of Polish society against Soviet domination has been the struggle of memory against forgetting.

Demographic engineering was the prelude to post-war social engineering. Here again the process had been started by German wartime resettlement schemes in West Prussia (750,000 Poles were expelled) and by mass deportations to the Soviet Union. The post-war westward shift of Poland's boundaries pushed about one-third of the population from the rural east to the largely destroyed industrial towns of the west. Danzig (now Gdansk) was considered by the Russians to be a German city and so they razed it completely. Meanwhile, the exodus of the German population was set into motion by the advance of the Red Army, of which Christa Wolf, the East German novelist, gave a powerful autobiographical account in her novel *Kindheitsmuster* (the first book in East Germany to deal honestly with this sensitive topic). The new Poland was to be ethnically different from the old: without Germans, Ukrainians or Byelorussians. And without Jews.

Most of the Polish Jews, who accounted for nearly 10 per cent of the pre-war population, had been exterminated in the Nazi death camps of Auschwitz, Treblinka and Maidaneck. The Final Solution of the Jewish question was an integral part of Poland's tragedy. Yet it was a separate tragedy. Poles and Jews experienced side by side, yet separately, the double onslaught of two totalitarian powers against their country. More than three million Poles and as many Polish Jews were killed. Two defeated Warsaw insurrections symbolized these parallel catastrophes in the respective collective memories. For the Poles, the Warsaw Uprising of August 1944 represents the heroism of their nation. For the Polish Jews, the Warsaw Ghetto Uprising of April 1943 is the symbol of the destruction of their community, just as Auschwitz remains identified with the Holocaust of European Jewry. As if even death on both sides could not bring Poles and Jews closer, as if one should distinguish even 'Two Deaths', as suggested by the title of a poem by Wladyslaw Szlengel, written from within the Warsaw Ghetto:

> Your death is a death by bullets
> for something, for the Fatherland...
> our death is trash-heap death,
> Jewish and disgraceful...

The novelist Jerzy Andrzejewski, author of *Ashes and Diamonds*, echoed this observation, saying that 'the Polish nation could look straight in the face of Polish men and women who were dying for freedom. Not in the face of Jews dying in the burning ghetto.'

One way to start coming to terms with this double tragedy is to recognize that on one hand Poland had suffered more under German occupation than any other country in Europe; on the other hand, there was the fact that the extermination of European Jews by the Nazis took place in a country which witnessed widespread anti-Semitism not only before but even during the war. A report of 30 September 1941 sent by General Grot-Rowecki of the Polish Home Army to the government in London is quite explicit on the subject:

> Please take it as an established fact that the overwhelming majority of the population is anti-Semitic. Even the socialists are no exception. There are only tactical differences about what to do. Hardly anybody advocates imitating the Germans. German methods provoke compassion [sic], but after the merging of the two occupation zones, on learning how the Jews behaved in the East, this is now considerably reduced.

Anti-Semitism had been strengthened by the fact that many Polish Jews, like other minorities (Ukrainians or Byelorussians), had welcomed the arrival of the Soviet Army in the eastern territories in 1939. As Aleksander Smolar, editor of the Polish quarterly *Aneks*, observed in a profound and illuminating essay on Polish–Jewish relations, Poland had no Pétain or Quisling. In Poland under Soviet occupation 'Jews themselves were seen as quislings.' The second unique feature of the Polish situation was that in contrast to the rest of Nazi-occupied Europe, where anti-Semitism was abhorred as the ideology of the enemy and of its collaborators, 'Poland was the one paradoxical country where anti-Semitism was compatible not only with patriotism but also with democracy. The anti-Semitic National Democratic Party was represented both in the Polish government in London and in the structures of the underground state in Poland. Precisely because Polish anti-Semitism was not tainted by any trace of collaboration, it could prosper. . . .' – and not only in the wartime resistance but even after the war. The anti-Jewish pogrom of Kielce in 1946 is a tragic reminder of that.

In the West the Holocaust represented a trauma, shock at the discovery of the irrational side of our civilization. In Poland, as Smolar observed, it did not provoke a similar shock:

> both the war and the post-war experience tended to confirm the patriotic legitimacy of anti-Jewish feelings. . . . The Poles, having suffered much heavier losses than the countries of the West, and entering now another era of foreign domination, had little time

to worry about the crisis of civilization or indulge in the Christian–European remorse with regard to the Jews.

More generally, it could be argued that anti-Semitism was a by-product of Polish nationalism, which since the nineteenth century had helped the Poles survive as a nation in the face of foreign domination. The Polish blend of Catholicism and nationalism helped to create a fairly homogeneous political culture, highly resistant to external totalitarian domination but by no means only democratic or pluralistic.

The slide from war to civil war, from Nazi domination to Sovietization, has reinforced the siege mentality and perpetuated the Polish–Jewish estrangement so vividly experienced during the war. Paradoxically, it is only now, with no Jews left in Poland, that society has regained some of its autonomy from the regime, and that it feels self-confident enough to re-examine its past, including the darker, intolerant sides of its nationalist ideology.

The 1952 Polish Constitution states that 'the historic victory of the USSR over fascism liberated Polish soil, enabled the Polish working people to gain power'. Thus the role of the Red Army in the Communist seizure of power is proudly acknowledged. It started in September 1939 with the Soviet annexation of half the territory of the Polish state (as well as of the Baltic states and Romania's Bessarabia. The deportation of 1.25 million Polish citizens to the Soviet Union gives some indication of the scale of the repression involved. What is less known, but no less revealing of the nature of Sovietization, is the decision to organize in the territories of the Western Ukraine and Western Byelorussia, within a month of the invasion, the first Soviet-style elections in East-Central Europe. This was no small achievement, as documented by historian Jan Gross in *The Revolution from Abroad*:

> In a backward foreign country plunged into chaos, the Soviet conquerors undertook to elicit from every adult the simultaneous performance of a specific series of acts on demand. It is a wonder but they managed. On 22 October 1939, the date of the elections, the authorities knew and monitored the whereabouts of almost every adult citizen in Western Ukraine and Western Byelorussia, even temporary residents. The overwhelming majority actually performed the rites which were expected. Most of those who failed to do so were identified, which means that their behaviour was monitored as well.

The overwhelming majority of the population apparently had no idea what the purpose of the election was. As in all the post-war elections, mobilization and control were more important than the apparent legitimation of the new regime and Soviet annexation. The first pseudo-election of the Communist era in East-Central Europe was not about the transfer of sovereignty from one state to another but rather, as Jan Gross observed, 'the transfer of individual sovereignty from each person separately to a state. And this was a process that took place in instalments, every time people visibly yielded to coercion and surrendered some control over their lives' – a telling description of the slide into totalitarianism experienced by all the nations of East-Central Europe.

A similar pattern of Sovietization to the one experienced in the eastern territories between 1939 and 1941 was resumed and extended to the whole country in 1944–5. Along with the Red Army came the NKVD, whose task was to disarm non-Communist resistance groups and purge recalcitrant elements. Only trusted elements acceptable to the Lublin Committee were put in charge of the new administration. With their memories of 1939 and Katyn, and given the spectacle of a completely exhausted society subjected to a ruthless pattern of Sovietization, is it altogether surprising that, although grateful that the Nazis had been driven out, most Poles failed to welcome the Russians as true liberators?

The ultimate attempt to avert an imposed solution and give the home resistance a chance to influence the country's political future was the Warsaw Uprising launched on 2 August 1944, a week after the establishment of the Communist-led Lublin Committee. For two months the Poles fought desperately against the Germans as the Red Army looked on from the other bank of the Vistula. While a quarter of a million civilians died Stalin refused to give the orders to help the insurgents, and described its leaders as 'a handful of power-seeking criminals'. The defeat of the Uprising was the crucial turning point in the emergence of Communist Poland. As Norman Davies put it: 'It was the end of the old order in Poland. After that, the Home Army was broken and no one was left to challenge the Communists effectively. The Nazis had done the Soviets' work for them.'

'What kind of Poland would not be anti-Soviet?' asked the Polish Communists' chief ideologist Alfred Lampe in September 1943. This was by no means a rhetorical question. In a confidential paper (which was smuggled out of the Warsaw archives in the 1970s), Lampe analysed various alternatives, only to conclude that Poland's traditionally anti-Russian upper classes must be deprived of power. Unable to find a respectable yet pro-Soviet partner, 'a Polish Beneš', Stalin too concluded that only a Communist-led regime would be reliable. This meant rebuilding the Polish Communist Party which

Stalin himself had disbanded and ordered to be physically liquidated
in 1938. The politicians who were available were either pre-war
Communists who, like future Party chief Wladyslaw Gomulka, had
the luck in 1938 to be sitting in a Polish jail or, as one of the survivors,
Roman Werfel, put it, 'débris, people whom Stalin did not have the
time to finish off, third-rate cadres of the KPP'. The Party was rebuilt
in the wake of Hitler's attack on the Soviet Union, re-emerging
under a new name as the Polish Workers' Party. The Party and
its Soviet advisers in turn controlled a Moscow-based umbrella
organization called the Union of Polish Patriots as well as the Polish
Armed Forces in the Soviet Union, the embryo of Poland's post-
war armed forces. This is where the future General Jaruzelski
received his early training. At no point did these Soviet-controlled
structures envisage cooperation with the London government and
the Home Army. Yet the Communists remained a minuscule group
in Poland. Since, as veteran Polish Communist Roman Werfel put
it, 'there were no partners for the Soviet Union, except the Communists', because all the parties were hostile to the Russians, only
coercion could do the job.

This is now admitted by the senior post-war Polish Communists
(most of whom remained unreconstructed Stalinists) interviewed in
the 1980s by journalist Teresa Toranska. Stefan Staszewski, former
Minister of Agriculture, recalls that terror started the very day war
ended:

> There is nothing to compare with the period of violence, cruelty
> and lawlessness that Poland experienced in 1944–47. Not
> thousands, but tens of thousands of people were killed then. The
> official trials that were organized after 1949 were merely an
> epilogue to the liquidation of the wartime resistance, of activists,
> of independent parties, and of independent thought in general.

In other words, Stalinism in Poland did not start after 1948 with the
arrest of Gomulka and the 'nationally minded' Communists, but had
begun already in 1944.

It is only in this context of a doubly defeated society that one can
try to assess the nature of post-war pseudo-coalition politics, or the
credibility of Gomulka's indignation when he said: 'We completely
reject the accusation made against us by the reactionaries that we
will impose a one-party system', or Stanislaw Mikolajczyk's hopeless
struggle to rebuild the Peasant Party as a new focus of opposition,
or the dilemmas of the socialists, weakened by internal divisions,
torn between their socialist ideals, hopes for change and Soviet-style

practice. What, under such conditions, could be the meaning of elections?

Asked by Toranska about the Yalta provisions concerning free elections, Werfel replied: 'Oh, come on, don't be silly. One thing was agreed at Yalta: the frontier between the great powers lay along the Elbe. The rest was mere decoration.' Former Politburo member Jakub Berman admits that the elections had to be rigged because otherwise the Communists would have lost; as they would lose now. 'So what's the point of such an election?' he asks. 'You can't be honest if you want to stay in power.'

Czechoslovakia: If You Can't Beat Them, Join Them

Czechoslovakia represents the most striking contrast to the Polish pattern of Sovietization. The origins of the contrast go back to 1938 when the Western powers abandoned Czechoslovakia to Hitler only to go to war over Poland the following year. The betrayal at Munich also helps account for at least two features which distinguished post-war Czechoslovak politics from the situation in Poland, or indeed in the rest of Central Europe. Munich led the Czech political elite from distrust of the West into the warm embrace of the Slavic East: the Soviet Union was perceived as the future guarantor of Czechoslovak statehood. It also helped to establish the patriotic credentials of a Communist Party which emerged from the war as the dominant force in Czechoslovak politics.

For President Edvard Beneš, the trauma of Munich was equal to that of Katyn for the Poles, but with foreign-policy implications that were just the opposite. Katyn determined the resolutely anti-Soviet posture of the Polish resistance and caused the break between Moscow and the Polish government-in-exile. But even during the period of the Nazi–Soviet Pact, Beneš was already convinced that Russia would eventually join the Allies and play a dominant role in Central Europe after the war. Consequently to ensure the future of Czechoslovak statehood, Beneš reasoned, it would be necessary to reach an agreement with the Soviet Union. The more friendly the Czechs were to the Soviet Union, the more leeway they would be likely to gain for themselves internally.

Beneš' approach might be considered as a lesson in political realism, or as making a virtue out of necessity, relying on Czech-style prudence and adaptability in order to avoid the Polish impasse at all costs. A closer examination of Beneš' December 1943 dealings with Stalin and the Czechoslovak Communists, however, suggests something more: a deliberate attempt to secure the insertion of Czechoslovakia into the Soviet sphere of influence and to grant to the Communists a dominant position in internal politics.

It is not so much the 'friendship and cooperation' treaty itself as the spirit in which it was signed in Moscow in December 1943 which sheds a strange light on Beneš' role in Czechoslovakia's smooth 'transition to socialism'. The transcript of his talks with Stalin and Molotov provides a fascinating illustration of the theme, 'how democracies perish'.

It was Beneš, not Stalin, who requested Soviet interference in Czechoslovakia's internal affairs: 'I would like your government to put pressure on ours to demand the punishment of all those people in Slovakia who have been guilty of the war against the Soviet Union. I wish you'd put a friendly request to us to punish those guilty of having declared war [on the Soviet Union] or of having collaborated with the Germans.' At first even Molotov found it a bit excessive to 'throw the Slovaks in the same bag as the Germans and the Hungarians'. So Beneš had to explain that it was for internal political reasons (namely the Slovaks' hostility to Beneš and the Prague centralism he represented) that he needed Soviet help against those in Bratislava who had overplayed the German card. 'I understand,' Molotov said finally, 'you need Soviet help against the Slovaks. Who are the ones that you want to punish . . .?' The item was approved and Beneš' aide did not even need to draw up a list of names.

Perhaps the most important issue for Beneš was the plan to expel the Sudeten Germans, 90 per cent of whom Beneš considered to be Nazi supporters who had contributed to the break-up of the First Republic. Here again Beneš sought Stalin's support by linking the national question with the promise of socialization: German land, property and banks were to be confiscated, that is 'put under state control', 'nationalized'. To the Soviet Union's surprise, he added that the wealth of large-scale Czech capitalists would be expropriated as well.

Nationalism, it has often been argued, is what gave the exaggerated, intransigent edge to Polish relations with Moscow. In the Czech case, on the other hand, nationalism – bitter, petty, obsessive nationalism – is precisely what drove Beneš into the Soviet orbit. In Moscow, in December 1943, the exiled President chose to settle his scores with those who had betrayed the Republic in 1938: the Sudeten Germans and the Slovaks. And instead of trying to envisage new possibilities for Central European cooperation in the shadow of the Soviet Union, despite the failures of the past, he advised Stalin (of all people) to be tough with what Churchill called the 'grabbing nations' (i.e. the Hungarians and the Poles), who, as soon as the Munich verdict dismembering Czechoslovakia was announced, had been prompt to snatch chunks of their neighbour's territory.

As if to reciprocate, Beneš said in Moscow that he was anxious to see that the Red Army did not leave the occupation of Hungary to the Anglo-American forces. In answer to Stalin's question 'Where can one find any Poles one can talk to?' Beneš recommended Miko-lajczyk but, to his hosts' amazement, he also ventured to predict that events in Poland were likely to follow the course already evident in Yugoslavia: 'A new government will be formed on Polish territory which will have nothing to do with the government in London.' And in addition to Beneš as the inventor of the Lublin Committee there was Beneš as lecturer in Marxism for the benefit of Stalin and Molotov: 'The condition for coexistence with Poland is the dis-appearance of the aristocratic and feudal caste.'

In the three memoranda which he presented to Stalin on the occasion of his visit to Moscow, Beneš asked for Soviet assistance in bringing about the expulsion of the Germans from Czechoslovakia, in equipping the Czechoslovak Army and shifting the country's trade from West to East. In short, Czechoslovak leaders did not wait for Yalta to push them into the Soviet orbit. They prepared it, for their own reasons, with extreme care and zeal long before the war ended.

Naturally, Beneš' favourable assessment of the future Soviet role in Central Europe and his view that Communism was becoming 'national' also shaped his relations with the Czechoslovak Commu-nists. After he had established such a rapport with Stalin, no less could be expected from his partnership with Klement Gottwald. The Communists understood Beneš' psychology very well. They began their December 1943 meeting by reminding him that they had been right on the mark about Munich and about the Soviet Union being the only genuine ally of little Czechoslovakia. Playing on Beneš' Munich complex was a shrewd move. But was the Communists' patriotic record as immaculate as they made out?

At first sight the contrast between Beneš' capitulation, under strong Western pressure, to Hitler's demands for the Sudetenland and the adamantly patriotic stance of the Communists is striking. In a speech in Parliament on 11 October 1938 Gottwald stated:

> In front of the whole world we declare that the government
> had neither the constitutional right nor the political right to
> capitulate. The people wanted to fight. The whole nation
> wanted to defend its country by all available means.

Munich represents a decisive turning point in Czechoslovak politics. The political and moral failure of Beneš to defend the state which he had helped to create contrasted with the paradoxical spectacle of a Communist Party – formed in reaction against the Masarykian patriotism of 1918 – presenting itself to the nation as the most fervent protector of the Czechoslovak state.

It is true, of course, that the Communists did not advocate armed resistance after Munich, and the Gottwald leadership left Czechoslovakia for Moscow in October–November 1938, that is, six months before the German occupation of the country. But whatever doubts one could have about the likelihood of Soviet aid to Czechoslovakia in 1938, or about the low profile of Communist activity between Munich and the summer of 1939, the official line nevertheless called for the restoration of the Czechoslovak state.

The Nazi–Soviet Pact of 23 August 1939 provoked a complete turnabout in the Communists' attitude towards Czechoslovakia. Following the Comintern line, Gottwald sent the following message to allegedly 'disoriented' comrades in the home underground: 'The present war is an unjust imperialist war in which all parties share equal responsibility. . . . In no country should the working class support this war. . . . The distinction between fascist states and democratic ones has lost all significance.' The main task, Gottwald added, was to oppose the war and 'develop everywhere an offensive against the policy of betrayal of social democracy'. In a later message Gottwald gave the following advice to Communists in Prague: 'Be cautious, don't let yourself be dragged into premature action. Our time will come. In all circumstances, have confidence in our great fatherland.' In September 1939 the 'fatherland', for Gottwald, was the Soviet Union. Understandably, not everybody in the home Communist underground shared Gottwald's view. The Pact caused, in fact, one of the first divides between the leadership in Moscow and the home resistance, which would culminate at the end of the war in May 1945 with the astonishing elimination of the latter from political life. Both Beneš and Gottwald made sure that none of the leading figures of the home resistance would make it into the government.

The logical follow-up to the Nazi–Soviet Pact was the Soviet Union's recognition of the Slovak state. The Slovak Communists were quick to abandon the defence of Czechoslovakia for what seemed to them a more attractive and realistic prospect of a 'Soviet Slovakia'. Adapting to the new Stalinist line they advocated that 'following the example of the Baltic countries [annexed by the USSR], Slovakia should be attached to the Soviet Union, thus propelling the revolution westward'. This was the first time that Communists in Central Europe had suggested that the socialist revolution should be carried out through Soviet military expansion. Even Gottwald apparently had some difficulty in swallowing that. Clearly, the autonomy the Slovak Communists had *de facto* acquired during the war had also moved towards political autonomy. The seeds of future conflicts between Prague and the Slovak Communists had already been planted. By the spring of 1940, Gottwald seemed to have come to terms with Slovak interests; as he explained to the comrades operating in what was then called the Protectorate of Bohemia and Moravia:

The slogan of the 'reconstitution of Czechoslovakia' now hides imperialist anti-Soviet aims. I insist that our Party defend the nations' right to self-determination for Czechs and Slovaks; the right to have a separate state. In the Czech lands we struggle for the renewal of national and state freedom. In Slovakia we struggle for the full sovereignty of the present Slovak state. The right to self-determination is what distinguishes our path from that of world imperialism and of Beneš.

This willingness to sacrifice the integrity of the Czechoslovak state in 1940 separated the Communists from Beneš and the democratic underground. It also in a way ought to have cancelled the moral and political capital the Communists had gained during the Munich crisis of 1938. Almost overnight the very concept of Czechoslovakia had vanished from the platform of the Communist Party. Its defence then rested in the hands of Beneš and his entourage, i.e. in the hands of a political leadership that had already failed in that task at Munich. It is a tragic paradox of Czechoslovak politics that after the Soviet entry into the war in 1941 the new concept of post-war Czechoslovak statehood was to be conceived and worked out precisely by those leaders who had failed to defend it at times of crisis for the nation: Beneš in 1938, Gottwald at the outbreak of the war in 1939.

Just as with Stalin, Beneš thought he could outwit the Czechoslovak Communists ('swallow and digest' them was his phrase) by bringing them out of their ghetto into mainstream Czechoslovak politics. But if that was the rationale, in practice Beneš went much further: 'You will emerge as the main force of the new regime,' he announced to the Communist exiles in Moscow, and with breathtaking speed promised them the premiership as well as the key levers of the state: the ministries of Defence, the Interior and Information.

Beneš and the Communists also agreed to 'streamline' post-war political life by excluding political parties compromised by their post-Munich behaviour. Among these happened to be the two largest pre-war parties: the Czech Agrarian Party and the Slovak Catholic People's Party. The leading force of the ruling coalition would be a 'socialist bloc' of Communists, Social Democrats and Beneš' National Socialists.

In order to avoid a 'Polish solution', Beneš put all his eggs in the Soviet basket and thought it preferable to have 'his' Communists well surrounded by democratic parties. Would the democratic environment change the Communists or would it be the other way round? Encouraging the Communists to take an active part in democratic institutions, the argument went, was the only chance to have any such institutions at all and thus be able to afford the leisure of even asking such questions. Besides, Stalin sounded so reassuring in his farewell toast to Beneš, who was on his way back to Prague in April 1945:

> The Soviet Union will not interfere in the internal affairs of its allies. I know that some of you have your doubts. Perhaps even you [he turned to Beneš] doubt a little, but I assure you that we will never interfere in the internal affairs of our allies. Such is the Leninist neo-Pan – Slavism which we Bolsheviks follow. There can be no talk of any hegemony of the Soviet Union...

The result of Beneš' consultations was that the political system set up in Prague was marked by homogenization and a shift to the left. The programme of the Kosice government (presented by the new administration upon arrival on liberated Czechoslovak territory in April 1945) could just as easily be called the Moscow programme. It had been drafted there by the Communists and merely amended by Beneš in a few minor points on his second visit to Moscow in March 1945. The programme claimed Czechoslovakia's foreign-policy alignment with the Soviet Union but also promised that 'the government will act in harmony with the Soviet Union in all fields, military, political, economic and cultural'.

There was, in Czechoslovakia, as in the rest of Europe at the end of the war, a strong and widely shared desire for change. Heda Kovaly, a survivor of Auschwitz, the widow of Rudolf Margolius who was executed in the Slansky trial of 1952, was a dedicated young Communist at the end of the war:

When the war was over in May 1945, people started coming back from the concentration camps and all of them, partisans, freedom fighters, people who were in any way persecuted during the Nazi occupation, were looking forward to starting life all over again. We did not want this kind of society any more, we expected something much more beautiful, something we have given so much for. What we wanted was not, in a way, very realistic, but the resentment, the bitterness of what we had had to suffer for this end was overwhelming. The need for change was everywhere.

Politically, this meant a shift to the left, as was happening in the rest of Europe. In Britain, Churchill – the man who had won the war – suffered an electoral defeat at the hands of the Labour Party. In France and Italy the Communist Parties emerged as a dominant political force thanks to their role in the resistance.

The Communists in Czechoslovakia successfully took advantage of the wish for a clean break with the past. After the First World War the new state of Czechoslovakia, like Poland, had avoided the Central European tide of revolutionary radicalism that swept through the defeated Germany and Hungary in 1919. The 'national revolution' had defused the social revolution. The radical tide in Central Europe was not as powerful in the wake of the Second World War, but it was strongest in Czechoslovakia because it combined a wave of nationalism with the undercurrent of popular support for socialism.

The Czechoslovak democratic interlude after 1945 was based on an unlikely convergence: the democrats claimed to be in favour of socialism, while the Communists presented themselves above all as patriots and democrats. All the non-Communist parties accepted the idea of a transition to socialism and differed only on the pace or the means of achieving it. The social democrats were undoubtedly the radicals of the day, and the Communists were behaving like moderate reformists. The Social Democratic Party congress in October 1945 adopted a resolution drafted by F. Tymes: 'Our goal was not and is not to reform the capitalist order, but to abolish this order as the prime cause of all the poverty the population suffers' ('of all the ills of mankind' was the initial phrase in Tymes' speech). Beneš himself explained that the time was ripe for a 'new democracy' reorganized 'in a socialist sense'. Meanwhile, the Communists were putting forward a comparatively moderate programme. They too wanted a 'new democracy', a 'people's democracy' which on no account was to be confused with socialism. In fact they had to resist pressing offers of merger from the social democrats and from Beneš' Czech

Socialist Party. Gottwald felt called upon to argue for the preservation of pluralism, 'the possibility for each and every one to
belong where his convictions and his heart lead him' (12 May 1945).
In view of the forcible merger of the Communist and Social Democratic Parties three years later the socialist pleas for union in 1945
sound pathetically naive.

Shortly before returning to Prague from Moscow, Gottwald
explained to his comrades that 'in spite of the favourable situation,
the next goal is not soviets and socialism, but rather carrying out a
really thorough democratic national revolution'. And, abandoning
one of the basic tenets of Leninism, Gottwald argued that the road
to socialism need not entail the phase of the 'dictatorship of the
proletariat', i.e. the Soviet pattern. The Czech Communists even
billed themselves as the true disciples of Masaryk, the founder of
the Czechoslovak state at the end of the First World War. In a
speech for public consumption in March 1946 Kopecky, the leading
Party ideologue of the day, said, 'We continue Masaryk's historic
work, we adopt his living values and above all his democratic and
humanistic ideals which we implement in new form.' However, only
one month earlier the same Kopecky had said, at a closed session of
the Central Committee: 'The historical truth is that Masarykism is
out of date; it cannot be the ideology of the new Czechoslovakia.
The spirit of Masarykism capitulated at the worst possible moment
in the face of Berlin and Hacha [the Czech Quisling]. Of course, we
cannot speak out so openly against it.'

The key to the strength of the Communist Party in Czechoslovakia
was its unabashed use of nationalism. Not even Beneš was a match
for them in this area. The aim was clearly to capture and channel
the vehemence of the anti-German feeling at the end of the war:

> We are claiming and implementing the most national programme
> possible.... We are correcting the errors of history and driving
> the Germans out of our Czech fatherland.... We have extended
> our living space [echoes of *Lebensraum*?] into the border
> mountains. We will Czechize [*počeštujeme*] all the border regions
> and create there, at the expense of the Germans, great new
> wealth, new strength, new development possibilities. We are
> building a new Czechoslovakia as a state without Germans and
> Hungarians, as a nation-state of Czechs and Slovaks.

Needless to say, such views had little to do with Masaryk, but were
no doubt a convenient means of winning popular support and playing
on the most basic emotions of the people after six years of humiliation
by Nazi Germany. The expulsion of nearly three million Sudeten

Germans cemented the alliance of Beneš and Gottwald under Stalin's sponsorship. Here again nationalism and socialism could be joined to good purpose: the expulsions and the confiscation of German property constituted the first step on the road to the nationalization of large sectors of the economy. There was also a powerful means of building patronage: it was the Communist Minister of Agriculture who was in charge of redistributing confiscated German lands. In this way the Communists attracted a clientele from among the lowest strata of society, people whose eagerness to move up in the world brought them to the freshly deserted border regions and who were grateful for the chance.

An essential component of the Communist Party's post-war ideology was Soviet-inspired Pan-Slavism. Stalin had created a Pan-Slav Committee in Moscow in 1941 with the aim of providing a pseudo-nationalistic legitimation for the Communists and other allies in Central Europe and in the Balkans after the war. The Pan-Slav idea had little success in Poland, but in Czechoslovakia and Bulgaria it was used extensively:

'As Slavs we are proud that the victorious teaching of freedom, democracy, progress and socialism came from Slavic Russia,' Kopecky declared to enthusiastic applause at the VIIIth Party Congress in March 1946, 'whereas Germany has only produced Nazi barbarity.... As Slavs we must deeply identify with the teaching of Lenin and Stalin, and strive, following the example of Soviet theoreticians, to rid Czech thought of detrimental German influences....

Before the war the politics, economy and culture of Czechoslovakia had been incontrovertibly Western. At the end of the war, while President Beneš still toyed with the idea of Czechoslovakia as a bridge between East and West, the Communists used a distorted nationalist argument to proclaim *ex orionte lux*, the light was coming from the east. In Poland the Communists' identification with the Soviet Union was an overwhelming handicap for the credibility of their policy of following a 'national road' to socialism. But in Czechoslovakia the Russian connection was, at least for a while, considered an asset. The Red Army had been welcome liberators who had the good sense to leave the country before the end of 1945.

Thus, as the rapid growth in their numbers shows, the Czechoslovak Communists succeeded in exploiting popular aspirations for change while at the same time using and abusing the appeal of nationalism. Whereas pre-war Party membership levelled off at around 40,000, within weeks of the end of the war it reached

500,000 and grew to 1.3 million, as much as all the other parties put together, by the end of 1947. To the surprise of some of its coalition partners the Communist Party emerged as the strongest party in the general election of May 1946. With 38 per cent of the vote (40 per cent in the Czech lands and 30 per cent in Slovakia) the Czechoslovak Communists achieved the best showing ever by a Communist Party in a free election. Immediately after his electoral triumph Gottwald announced his party's new goals: 'to win the majority of the nation'.

In contrast to Poland, a democracy with free elections and a free press had been restored in Czechoslovakia in 1945. But it was a self-limiting democracy. The National Front coalition comprised a fixed number of government parties and the idea of a parliamentary opposition as a possible alternative to the government of the day was taboo. The election results could affect the balance of power within the government, but not alter its basic tenets. A democracy with no opposition eventually (as soon as a major political conflict developed) became a blocked democracy, leaving the outcome of the crisis to be decided by those who controlled the means of coercion.

The deterioration in the climate of East–West relations in the spring of 1947 and the related changes in Soviet policy towards East-Central Europe precipitated a crisis in the hitherto quiet waters of Czechoslovak politics. The Soviet reaction to the Marshall Plan was the first turning point. In some ways, it was a test case for the Czechoslovak democrats and a warning of worse things to come.

Poland and Czechoslovakia had initially accepted their invitation to take part in the Marshall Plan conference in Paris, to discuss American aid for Europe's post-war recovery. Immediately, however, a delegation of the Czechoslovak government including Gottwald and the politically unaffiliated Foreign Minister, Jan Masaryk, was summoned to Moscow and told by Stalin in no uncertain terms that the American aid offer was an attempt to undermine the Soviet Union's role in Europe. On 10 July 1947 the Prague government issued a communiqué reversing its original decision. 'I left for Moscow as Foreign Minister of a sovereign country,' said Jan Masaryk to Hubert Ripka, 'I return as Stalin's vassal.' Neither Beneš nor Jan Masaryk tried to voice publicly his opposition to Soviet interference.

Time was clearly running out for the advocates of the theory of 'separate paths to socialism'. In these early days of the Cold War Stalin opted for the formation of a unified, homogeneous socialist bloc. The effect of the expulsion of the French and Italian Communists from their governments was to discredit the parliamentary path to socialism in the eyes of Stalin and his most vociferous backers on this question, the Yugoslav Communists.

The decisive policy shift came after the founding meeting of the Cominform (Communist Information Bureau, the successor to the Communist International), convened by the Soviets in September 1947 at Szklarska Poreba in Polish Silesia. There Zhdanov, the leading Soviet ideologue, presented his 'two camp' view of the world and of the Soviet–American conflict: 'the anti-democratic imperialist camp on the one hand, and the anti-imperialist democratic camp on the other'. Zhdanov said pointedly that the Soviet victory over Nazi Germany had helped to bring about 'the complete victory of the working class over the bourgeoisie in every East European land except in Czechoslovakia, where the power contest still remains undecided'. The way was clear for criticism of the Czechoslovak Party for dithering over the task of seizing power.

Rudolf Slansky, the Czechoslovak representative at the Cominform meeting, promised a change of strategy, which would 'unmask the reactionary elements' and 'eliminate them from the National Front parties'. Upon his return to Prague Slansky presented to the Party leadership a detailed outline of how to proceed. It included the consolidation of the Party's role in the security forces, which were to play an increasingly active part in the struggle against the non-Communists, whose activities, according to Slansky, could no longer just be labelled as 'reactionary', but rather had become 'simply treasonable'. The National Socialist Party and the Slovak Democratic Party were singled out as the prime targets; but there was also a need to crack down on alleged 'anti-state' groups such as teachers, students, priests, civil servants, officers. Thus, concluded Slansky, 'as in the international field, we have gone on the offensive on the domestic front as well'.

The first stages of this Communist offensive, in the autumn of 1948, did not prove very successful. First, Gustav Husak's attempt to use a fabricated plot of American and Vatican agents in Slovakia to destabilize the Democratic Party failed in November 1947. A few days later the Communists tried to take over the Social Democratic Party at the Brno Congress but their candidate, the long-standing fellow traveller Zdenek Fierlinger, was defeated in his bid for party leadership by Bohumil Lausman, who remained attached to the independence of his party. From then on the pro-Communist wing of the Social Democrats (Fierlinger, Evžen Erban, Jiři Hájek, later Dubček's Foreign Minister) dropped the pretences and started behaving like a party within the Party, faithfully echoing the Communist line. Deeply divided, the Social Democrats helped tilt the balance in favour of the Communists during the Communist seizure of power in February 1948.

While the non-Communist parties were unable to conceive of political struggle outside the existing institutional framework of the National Front, the Communists mapped out a three-pronged strategy that completely bypassed this framework. It combined 'mass mobilization' from below, infiltration of rival parties and the stepping-up of the pressure on them through the security forces. The 'masses' played the minor part of a Greek chorus, called in only during the very last days of the confrontation to demonstrate popular support for the Communists. More important was the subversion of rival parties. A Department for Work in Non-Communist Parties was set up in the apparatus of the Central Committee. It was headed by Ota Hromadko, who twenty years later, during the Prague Spring, described its operation with great candour. Besides the already mentioned infiltration of the Social Democratic Party, he said, 'the main job was to subvert the National Socialist Party':

> Contacts were made with various groups and individuals who for one reason or another had been at loggerheads with the new Party leadership.... All these groups and persons were gradually brought together by conspiratorial methods.... The same aim was served by the proposal to call a nationwide conference of the opposition groups in the National Socialist Party, by the issue of a single edition of an illegal National Socialist opposition periodical and so on.... This kind of splitting activity, which the Communist Party practised even before the war, was the only line that promised success.

This is how, during the February crisis of 1948, the Communists had been able to set up the famous 'action committees', i.e. crypto-Communist splinter factions within all rival parties. It also explains how the Communists had no trouble finding substitutes for vacant government posts once the non-Communist ministers had resigned. In 1968 a National Socialist MP, A. Neumann, recalled the meeting he and a Catholic MP had with Gottwald during the Cabinet crisis:

> Gottwald began by telling us that the Communist Party had decided to prevent a reactionary putsch. At the same time he told us that the National Front coalition should continue in the government, but there was no question of accepting back the Ministers who had resigned. The National Front could only be regenerated with the help of honest people who stood by the side of the working class. Finally, Gottwald told us he had

discussed things and that the two of us could be included in the new Cabinet. He said he had seven portfolios to assign and we could choose whichever we liked. Petr [Catholic Party MP] chose Transport, and I asked if I could be in charge of Justice.

As Hromadko explained, there were various ways of creating agents in the other parties. The simplest was corruption: a third-rate politician would be promised a post in the Cabinet. Then there was blackmail: people with a dubious wartime record were easy targets for the Communists, who controlled the police. Finally, there were the ideologically motivated converts who wished to join the CP, but were asked instead to stay and work as Communist agents. Thus Evžen Erban, the Social Democratic trade-union leader, accepted this role provided his Communist Party card was kept for him in a safe at the Party headquarters.

General Ludvik Svoboda, wartime commander of the Czech Army in the USSR and appointed Minister of Defence in 1945, was perhaps the most important case in point. He recalled the story of his deceit at a Party Central Committee session in September 1969:

In April 1945 I was again summoned to Moscow, where a government had been put together. I was included and given the post of Minister of Defence. . . . I said to Gottwald: 'Tell me, Clem, why don't you have me as a Party member now?' Clem was smoking his little pipe; now he took it out and said with a laugh: 'Ludvik, do you know what parity means?' (laughter in the audience). 'Yes, I know what parity is, but what has it got to do with me?' He took his pipe out again and said: 'It's got a lot to do with you!' Then he explained just what would happen if they took me into the Party, how every time they had a 'militant vote' in the Cabinet they would lose one vote, mine, and a second one, Nejedly's [Minister of Education]. . . . It was in May 1945 that we came back to Czechoslovakia and finished this struggle successfully. And at that time Gottwald said to me: 'Don't apply to join the Party any more now. When the time comes we'll invite you in, but meanwhile we shall be counting on you.' I was a faithful and disciplined member of the Party. And when February 1948 came along I was in a better position to help the Party and the state than I was with one battalion or one brigade, or with my own body come to that. Now it was the whole brand-new Czechoslovak Army.

The Communists controlled not just a 'brand-new army' but also brand-new police and security forces. These had been established, with the help of the Soviet NKVD, in the immediate aftermath of the war. Special security departments were created to purge all the institutions, from local level up to the government, of Nazi collaborators. They were set up and operated by the Communists independent of the legal framework of the Ministry of the Interior. Although all the political parties had agreed not to politicize the security services, a Communist Party Central Committee Commission supervised the work of its faction within these organizations. A Registry Department was set up by Rudolf Slansky and Karel Svab to provide intelligence on other political parties. Among the politicians deserving the special attention of the Communists were, ironically, many of the leading fellow travellers – just in case they had come to have doubts about where their loyalties ought to lie. In 1946, Slansky and Svab extended their operation with an illegal unit which interrogated Germans, especially imprisoned officers of the Gestapo and of the Sicherheitsdienst, questioning them not just about their political rivals but also about the Communist resistance. The information was first used for political blackmail and a few years later as evidence in the show-trials of the 1950s. Both Slansky and Svab eventually became the victims of such trials.

All these security and intelligence operations were, from the outset, run in close cooperation with the Soviet NKVD. Karel Kaplan, a Czech historian and former Party official who in 1968 had unprecedented access to the Party archives on this subject, described these ties:

> The network of Soviet agents was in general very dense, including among senior Communist Party functionaries Bruno Kohler, Vaclav Kopecky and Vaclav David, and even denser among the lower-level functionaries. Collaborators even turned up among the non-Communist parties, as for example Jan Sevcik of the Democratic Party and Vojtech Erban of the Social Democratic Party. Two intelligence officers at the Soviet Embassy in Prague directed this network of Soviet agents.

Throughout the winter of 1947–8 the Party-controlled 'provocations division' in the security services stepped up its activities by sending parcel bombs to democratic politicians (such as Petr Zenkl and Jan Masaryk) and by unmasking fabricated plots supposed to incriminate the non-Communists. And it is this issue of the rise of the Communist police state which eventually brought about the clash of February 1948, the 'elegant takeover'.

On 13 February 1948, the Minister of Justice, Prokop Drtina, asked on behalf of the non-Communist ministers that the Minister of the Interior, Vaclav Nosek, reinstate the eight senior non-Communist police officials who had just been replaced by Communists. As the decision of the government had not been implemented by 20 February the non-Communist ministers handed in their resignations. The aim was to provoke the fall of the government, focusing the subsequent election on the issue of the Communist police state. In other words, they wished to treat a regime crisis as a mere Cabinet reshuffle. As a result they failed on both scores. Even in their own terms the non-Communists played a self-defeating game. They did not make sure that the Social Democrats, or independent figures such as Jan Masaryk, would fall into line. Only twelve out of twenty-six ministers resigned. There was therefore no constitutional reason (assuming the game was still to be thought of in these terms) to form a new government. A mere replacement of the ministers who had resigned would do. No wonder that Gottwald was over the moon: 'At first, I couldn't believe it would be so easy. But then it turned out that this is just what happened they had handed in their resignations.... I prayed that this stupidity over the resignations would go on and that they would not change their minds.'

The non-Communists did change their minds, but too late. While the Democrats played out a hopelessly incompetent parody of an old-fashioned pre-war government crisis, the Communists used a more varied strategy combining mobilization from below, the threat to use force, and political diplomacy with President Beneš. On the day of the resignations they called for an 'immediate mobilization of the working people in support of Klement Gottwald's government which stays in office... and will take all the necessary measures to ensure security, calm and order in the state'. This was not quite the Bolshevik seizure of the Winter Palace October 1917-style.

The main tools of 'mobilization' were the Communist-controlled trade unions. A congress of the works councils gathered in Prague – a 'people's parliament', said Gottwald, as opposed to the actually elected one. Its role was that of a pressure group supposed to scare the 'bourgeois' politicians and especially Beneš. It threatened strike action, but also expressed concern for inflation and, curiously enough, for the plight of the 'impoverished holders of small savings accounts'. Most significantly, it identified trade unionism with police activity. To attack the security organs, said the trade-union leader Zapotocky, was to attack the working class, since policemen were all unionized.

The unionized policemen were very busy indeed helping the working class to win its 'final struggle'. They helped to initiate the 'action committees' of the National Front, which were essentially

Communist-controlled organs set up within government institutions. They took over the headquarters of non-Communist parties,
banning their leadership meetings or the distribution of their newspapers. Meanwhile, in Slovakia, Gustav Husak transferred all the
posts in the Board of Commissioners held by Democratic Party
members to the Communists. The supreme symbol of the fusion of
the mobilization of the 'masses' and of the police was, of course, the
People's Militia. The militia, a totally illegal organization, was the
Communist Party's private army. It numbered 20,000, a third of
whom were based in Prague. It was run by Josef Pavel (Dubček's
Minister of the Interior in 1968), who during the Prague Spring
recalled its close ties with the Party and the police as well as the
limits of its role:

> When the crisis had been going on for four days, ten thousand
> rifles and two thousand automatics were brought up on seven
> lorries from the Brno arms factory through Sling's good offices.
> Was it fear or caution that made us leave the automatics in their
> cases and only hand out the rifles to the workers – practically
> without ammunition – on the last day of the crisis?

Given that the Communists already controlled the army and the
police, the only danger with the militia was overkill, especially since
the rival side proved unable to organize any serious opposition.
While the Communists gathered eight thousand delegates for the
works councils meeting in the capital, the democratic politicians
decided to tour their provincial constituencies. Petr Zenkl, the leader
of the National Socialist Party, left for the town of Lanskroun where
he was to be made an 'honorary citizen'. The local Communists
barred his entry into the town, so he decided to spend the weekend
with friends in Moravia. On Saturday, 21 February, the Communists
rallied 100,000 people to the Old Town Square to hear Gottwald's
ultimatum to President Beneš. The National Socialist Party merely
organized a ball where, according to witnesses, the atmosphere was
'excellent'.

If there was need for little more than a decorative role for the
People's Militia, there was even less need for the Red Army. Valerian
Zorin, Soviet Deputy Foreign Minister, suddenly arrived in Prague
on 19 February with an offer of Soviet military assistance. Gottwald
declined the offer, arguing (quite wisely) that he had the situation
under control. But that of course might not have been Stalin's point.
Were not his offers usually meant to be taken as orders? This indeed
was the only instance, since he had 'bolshevized' the Party twenty
years earlier, when Gottwald chose to differ from him.

On 25 February Gottwald, Zapotocky and the Minister of the Interior Vaclav Nosek faced President Beneš with their ultimatum and their list of names for the new government. They used thinly veiled threats of unpredictable radical outbursts ('the pressure of the street'): 'A single man cannot oppose an avalanche,' said Zapotocky, while a quarter of a million demonstrators gathered in the centre of Prague. Beneš' farewell to Czech democracy was a pitiful one:

> I do not intend to complicate things for you. It's only so that I could save, not the appearances, that's not the right word, but a decent, honest position and create a situation that would leave the way open for you . . . . I will not create unnecessary difficulties. You know that this is not in my character.

Indeed, it was not in Beneš' character to 'create difficulties' for those who threatened to take by force what he would not concede voluntarily. The Communists were, of course, aware of that, as Gottwald recalled a month later: 'We saw with our own eyes that his first gesture was "I will give it [the list] back to them, I will not accept it." But we knew, because we know him, that he has one good side, which is that he knows what strength is, and this led him to evaluate this [situation] realistically.'

As soon as Beneš had complied, Gottwald rushed to bring the good news to the 250,000 people gathered in the Old Town Square and spell out for them the meaning of their great victory: 'We now return again to our work, to our construction work for the completion of the Two-Year Plan.' The passive revolution was over.

So, in 1948 events in Czechoslovakia completed the Communists' seizure of monopoly political power in East-Central Europe, which had been begun in Poland. The roots of this process of Sovietization, however, are to be found in the dialectic of war and revolution. Czechoslovakia has often been described as the exception that confirmed the rule of a much more sudden and brutal Sovietization on the Polish model. Our intention is not to dismiss the democratic interlude of 1945–8 in Czechoslovakia – or that between 1945 and 1947 in Hungary – but to suggest that it was made possible only because the most radical changes had already occurred by 1945. The 'elegant takeover' of 1948 was made possible because the Communists (with Beneš' approval) peacefully acquired the control of the state and of all the means of coercion. They did not yet have a political monopoly, but in 1945 they held all the key levers of power. The events of 1948 were merely the tail end of the destruction of Czech democracy during 1938–45.

Munich and the Nazi occupation represent the deepest breach in modern Czech political history. 'The years 1938–45', wrote Pribram, a Czech historian, in an essay circulating in *samizdat*, 'were a test – and the nation failed it. . . . How could a nation and its political leadership, which had striven for decades for an independent state-hood and a democratic political system, abandon them without even putting up a fight?' True, perfectly rational explanations were given for the capitulation, namely the hopelessness of military resistance after Czechoslovakia had been abandoned by her Western allies on whose support her existence had depended since its very inception. But neither this, nor the attempt to confine the blame to the weakness of the political leadership, seems sufficient to explain not only the failure of nerve in 1938 but also the weakness of resistance in the period that followed. Wartime resistance was limited primarily to the intelligentsia (which was decimated by the Germans) and its scope cannot be compared to that of the Polish Home Army or that of the Yugoslav partisans. 'The Nazi occupation,' says Pribram, 'which the nation allowed without resistance in order to preserve itself, deprived it of its identity.'

It was only after the Soviet occupation of 1968 that Czech historians openly confronted these issues and attempted to do for their nation what Marcel Ophuls' film *The Sorrow and the Pity* did at about the same time for the French. The essence of their enquiry could be summed up in the words of one of the most courageous of them, Dr Jan Tesar, who served seven years in jail during the 1970s precisely for refusing to collaborate with another occupation regime: 'the spiritual content of the period lay in the conflict between sub-servience to oppressors and the emerging subservience to the future liberators'.

In 1945 Czechoslovakia, not unlike France after the fall of Vichy, the post-Munich 'capitulation complex' was compensated (some-times over-compensated) for by radicalism which combined the most chauvinistic brands of nationalism with a socialism identified with that of Stalin's Soviet Russia. Under the façade of a restored con-tinuity with the democratic Masarykian heritage and in the name of a slogan shared by all ('Munich must never repeat itself'), a manifold break with the pre-war political tradition took place.

First, as already discussed, despite all Beneš' talk about building bridges between East and West, we know today that between 1943 and 1945 Beneš himself – with the support of all the main political forces – had not just accepted but positively encouraged a complete integration of Czechoslovakia into the Soviet sphere of influence.

Secondly, the Communist Party was given control in 1945 of the army and of the security forces, which it reshaped according to the Soviet model.

Thirdly, in the name of eliminating political parties compromised after Munich, the two largest political parties (the Czech Agrarian Party and the Slovak People's Party) were banned. More importantly, the National Front, in which the Communists were granted the dominant role, operated as a coalition of democratically elected parties but without the right to form an opposition. By shrinking the size of the political spectrum and curtailing its *modus operandi*, Beneš and the Communists also reduced the scope of political democracy.

Fourthly, the 'transfer', in 1945, of nearly three million Sudeten Germans out of Czechoslovakia cemented the Beneš–Gottwald–Stalin alliance. Though understandably perceived by the population as the logical response to centuries of German oppression which had finally destroyed the young Czechoslovak state with the active help of its own German minority, the deeper significance of this historical break with a Czech–German co-existence in Bohemia that goes back at last to the thirteenth century is now questioned by Czech historians. In the twentieth century population transfers were associated with the emergence of Nazi Germany and Stalinist Russia. Was not Czechoslovakia's freshly restored democracy in danger of submitting to the totalitarian logic of her two neighbours? It was a meagre consolation for those who ended up in labour camps after 1948 for political or religious reasons to know that some of the camps had been created in 1945 for the Germans. The 1945 principle of exclusion on national grounds paved the way for exclusion on political grounds in the Stalinist era.

Finally, pluralism was simultaneously curtailed in the labour movement: the neutralization of the works councils in 1945 and the formation of a single Communist-controlled trade union operating on the principle of 'democratic centralism'. The best illustration of the same trend was the 1945 plan to merge the three parties committed to 'socialism': the Communists, the Social Democrats and the National Socialists. The request came from the latter two – a pathetic confirmation that the non-Communist left had no independent concept of socialism from that of the Communists, i.e. the Soviet model. The lines between Stalinism and democratic socialism became blurred; the former paying lip-service to the latter, and the latter eventually capitulating to the former.

In December 1929 Gottwald had expressed his utter contempt for 'bourgeois democracy' and his total subservience to Russian Communism in a memorable speech in Parliament:

We have no stake in your capitalist state, we would be ashamed
if we had. . . . You say that we take our orders from Moscow. . . .
We are the Party of the Czechoslovak proletariat and our supreme
revolutionary headquarters are in Moscow. And we go to
Moscow to learn, you know what? We go there to learn from the
Russian Bolsheviks how to twist your necks. And as you know
the Russian Bolsheviks are masters at that!

On 10 May 1945, the National Socialist MP Frana Zeminova, to
whom Gottwald's words had been personally addressed in 1929, met
with Rudolf Slansky, the Communist leader, to offer him the merger
of her party with his. A similar offer was made on behalf of the Social
Democrats by Bohumil Lausman. The Communists had politely
refused, arguing that the time was not yet ripe for such a merger. A
few years later Frana Zeminova was asked to serve as a witness in
the first of the great Stalinist show-trials against her own party leader
Milada Horakova. Horakova, with eight others, was sentenced to
death; President Gottwald, faithful to his promise of twenty years
earlier, refused clemency. Beyond the horror, the Kafkaesque absurdity of these events, the tragedy of Czech socialism was rooted in its
unconditional intellectual and political capitulation to Communism
during the war.

The February 1948 seizure by the Communist Party of the monopoly of political power was neither a 'revolution', as the victors
claimed, nor merely a *coup d'état*, as the defeated politicians claimed
in exile. A regime's latent conflict between its democratic and authoritarian components was brought into the open by the Cold War
and the Soviet push for total control of the 'bloc', but it was also the
conclusion of a deeper process of alteration of a democratic culture
which had started with Munich. In this broader sense, Beneš' capitulation to Gottwald's ultimatum in February 1948 was the follow-up
to his submission to the Munich *diktat* in 1938. The Communist
conquest of the political monopoly took place in a country without
Soviet troops, with substantial popular backing and without
encountering serious resistance from the democrats. These were
tamed revolutionaries and 'reactionaries' without reaction. If there
is such a thing as a Czechoslovak 'model', then it must surely be the
national and 'peaceful' road to Stalinism.

The contrast between the Polish and Czechoslovak roads reveals the
spectrum of Sovietization in East-Central Europe. The Poles, with
Katyn on their minds, remained resolutely anti-Soviet, whereas the
Czechs, with Munich on their minds, tried to accommodate the

Soviet dictator. Both earned, for opposite reasons, the displeasure of the West. After the war Poland was promptly Sovietized while Czechoslovakia toyed for nearly three years with a closely watched experiment in self-limiting democracy. The Polish case came to be regarded by the West as the touchstone of Soviet behaviour and, as such, became the cause of the Cold War. In contrast, the Communist takeover in Czechoslovakia was rather the consequence of Europe's slide into the Cold War. The Poles saw themselves as the victims of Yalta, while the Czechs pretended to thrive on it and 'build bridges' between East and West. Two approaches, two itineraries, but in the end the result was all too similar.

The Communist seizure of political hegemony completed the formation of a monolithic Soviet bloc in East-Central Europe and thus put the final touch to the partition of Europe. It demonstrated the constant interplay between domestic forces and the logic of the post-war international system. Several months before the Czechoslovak coup George Kennan, the father of the doctrine of 'containment', gave a striking interpretation of its meaning:

> The halt of the Communist advance in Western Europe has necessitated a consolidation of Communist power throughout Eastern Europe. It will be necessary for them, in particular, to clamp down completely on Czechoslovakia. As long as Communist political power was advancing in Europe, it was advantageous to the Russians to allow the Czechs the outer appearances of freedom. In this way, Czechoslovakia was able to serve as a bait for nations farther West. Now that there is a danger of a political movement proceeding in the other direction, the Russians can no longer afford this luxury. Czechoslovakia could too easily become a means of entry of really democratic forces into Eastern Europe in general.
>
> The sweeping away of democratic institutions in Czechoslovakia will add a formidable new element to the underground anti-Communist political forces in the Soviet satellite area. For this reason the Russians proceed to this step reluctantly. It is a purely defensive move. . . . It is unlikely that approximately 100 million Russians will succeed in holding down permanently, in addition to their own minorities, some ninety million Europeans with a higher cultural level and a long experience of resistance to foreign rule. One of the most dangerous moments to world stability will come when, some day, Russian rule begins to crumble in the East European area.

Kennan's analysis foreshadows some of the main issues which

have shaped the Central European predicament for more than four decades. As such it suggests several observations. First, the margin of manoeuvre tolerated by Moscow in its satellite countries remains directly related to its foreign-policy objectives *vis-à-vis* the West. When the internal dynamic threatens to get out of hand, or the overall context of East–West relations becomes unfavourable to such foreign-policy goals in Western Europe, tight controls are promptly imposed. Secondly, such a move is interpreted by the West (in Kennan's case even before it actually happened) as 'defensive'. The same argument was heard in 1956, and especially in 1968 when the Russian tanks crushed the Prague Spring. The point is that in a system which identifies security with control the distinction between 'offensive' and 'defensive' moves becomes virtually irrelevant. Finally, what might be presented as stabilizing in the short term remains inherently destabilizing in the long run: not just for East-Central Europe as such but for the whole East–West balance in Europe. The recurrent crisis on the western periphery of the Soviet Empire, especially in Poland, shows precisely how potentially unstable the 'Yalta system' has become.

5 Stalinism: The Ice Age

Many people would like to sacrifice Stalin in order to save Stalinism.

(Yuri Afanasiev, *Literaturnaia Rossia*, 17 June 1988)

'I demand the death sentence for all the accused. Let your verdict become an iron fist, without the slightest pity. Let it be a fire which burns out the roots of this shameful abscess of treason. Let it be a bell ringing through the whole of our beautiful country, for new victories, on the march to the sunshine of socialism' (Prague, November 1952).

The rhetoric of Prosecutor Josef Urvalek in the greatest of the show-trials of the Stalinist era in East-Central Europe captures the spirit of the times: terror in the name of the 'sunshine of socialism'. Whole societies were plunged into a state of fear amid staged displays of popular enthusiasm. Hundreds of thousands of people were sent to labour camps while youthful poets demanded 'a dog's death for the dogs'. Both the terror and the smiling faces confidently looking to a 'radiant tomorrow' were part and parcel of the Soviet style of socialism.

It was not just that Stalin wanted to extend 'socialism in one country' into socialism in one empire (that could be taken for granted even before 1948); now it was to be a single, Soviet, brand of socialism. Stalinism, to paraphrase Lenin, could be described as 'Ivan the Terrible plus electrification'. A system which was the product of the Russian experience and environment was imposed on societies with a radically different tradition and political culture. The Sovietization of East-Central Europe meant total control of society by each country's Communist Party, but also total Soviet control of the Communist Parties themselves.

In order to achieve this aim, the Soviet Union inflicted on the lands of East-Central Europe a crash-course in Stalinization. Between 1948 and 1953, these countries were put through all the major phases of the Soviet experience: they experienced 'dual power' and the defeat of their 'Kerenskys', the Five-Year Plan and forced collectivization, the irresistible rise of the Party bureaucracy and the show-trials. They even had their own mini-Stalins.

'It is not enough,' says Wolfgang Leonhardt, 'to determine or influence policy, to work together with other groups, no, total control of the economy, politics, armed forces, social problems, ideology, culture; total control, nothing less. This was the Stalinism now being imported into the countries of East-Central Europe.'

Speaking from personal experience as a Moscow-trained German Communist who returned to Berlin with the Red Army in May 1945, Leonhardt stresses the importance of Marxism–Leninism as the ideological justification for the 'total revolution':

> We were convinced at the time that this was the only scientific outlook. All these other groups, Social Democrats, Liberals, Conservatives, they have opinions; but we Marxist–Leninists have a scientific world view; it's like mathematics or physics. Nature, society, history are governed by laws and only Marxist–Leninists understand these laws. Other (bourgeois) people might be better in this or that practical question, but we know better because we know the 'laws'. There might be some setbacks or some mistakes but history is on our side. And therefore you had the feeling of security and of superiority.

By 1948 the 'laws of history' had been established in Moscow for the whole socialist camp. *Bolshevik*, the theoretical journal of the Soviet Party, proclaimed that 'the general laws of transition from capitalism to socialism, discovered by Marx and Engels and tested, put to concrete use, and developed by Lenin and Stalin on the basis of the concrete experience of the Bolshevik Party and the Soviet state, are binding upon all countries.'

The first 'binding' Stalinist law was that 'class struggle intensifies in the course of the construction of socialism'. In other words, the worse, the better; the more enemies you unmask, the closer you must be to socialism. And if that is the case then the security apparatus becomes the true vanguard of the vanguard Party. If post-war Stalinism in Central Europe was concerned above all with the massive transfer of a technology of power, then the technology of repression was clearly its centrepiece. It is also the most lasting legacy of that era; today, the methods are more subtle, but the technology of repression springs into action in any major crisis.

This technology of repression reached its peak in the late 1940s and early 1950s. It first focused on the control of society; in a second phase it was applied to the ruling Communist Parties themselves. In Poland and in Bulgaria the first phase started earlier and was particularly brutal, which perhaps accounts for the fact that the second phase, the extension of repression within the Party, was somewhat less widespread than in Hungary and in Czechoslovakia.

The 'inner Party' in charge of repression was located in the cadres section and the Control Commission of the Communist Party, on the one hand, and in State Security, on the other. Both were placed directly under the supervision of Soviet advisers. Beyond extensive surveillance of the population, the technology of repression rested on two complementary principles. The first was the permanent purge of all institutions: government offices, the administration, the army, etc. 'Unreliable' elements were either prosecuted or simply demoted into the working class. It is striking that a regime that claimed to be the workers' paradise considered sending somebody to work in a factory a particularly nasty form of punishment.

The second, related feature was the selection process for filling jobs at every level, in all areas of life. This ensured the promotion of hundreds of thousands who would become the new, loyal social base of the regime. The gradations of political reliability thus established a new social stratification. At the top were the Party people screened to work in the ministries; at the bottom of the pyramid were those who could only hold manual jobs in the factories. The 'new lumpenproletariat' (often belonging to formerly middle-class or intellectual families) was made up of people who were not allowed to live in the capital (or any other big city) and who had to work either in the steel mills or in coal mining.

The relationship between the Stalinist apparatus and the working classes was an ambiguous one. Although the 1948 Communist takeover in Czechoslovakia was a prototype of a 'revolution from above', the working class had been a willing accomplice. Post-1948 Stalinism crushed any form of autonomous workers' organization and more than a third of the political prisoners in the 1950s were workers. But at the same time upward mobility among the workers increased rapidly. Large sections of the working class were co-opted into the ranks of the new Communist bureaucracy. Between 1948 and 1953, an estimated 300,000 workers were promoted from the shop-floor into state administration: 100,000 into economic and industrial management; 30,000 into the various branches of the political apparatus; some 50,000 into the army, the security services, the judiciary and the diplomatic service. In 1952, for instance, these newcomers accounted for 86 per cent of the officer corps of the Czechoslovak Army.

Meanwhile, a substantial part of the country's intelligentsia experienced downward mobility. According to official statistics in 1951 alone the authorities fired some 77,000 intellectuals who were then to be 'retrained' in the industrial sector. Despite the hasty instruction organized for the new apparatchiks, the lasting consequence of the Stalinist policy of 'positive discrimination' was, among other things, complete mismanagement of the economy. In 1962, the year of the great economic collapse in Czechoslovakia, there were, according to official data, half a million people in decision-making positions for which they were not qualified. At the end of the 1960s, official statistics still indicated 182,470 people without higher education and some 300,000 people without secondary education occupying positions requiring such qualifications. The social policies of the Stalinist era account in part at least for the relative passivity of the workers during that period; but they were also responsible for the scope of the economic disaster which could only be fully measured in the following decade.

The fact that Communists themselves were eventually caught in the grip of their own police state should not obscure the fact that the first victims of the Stalinist repression were non-Communists. Jozsef Kovago, the former mayor of Budapest, recalls:

> The atmosphere of the Stalinist period was really almost indescribable. Everybody lived in fear. Family members suddenly disappeared, nobody heard about them. I was arrested in 1950, vanished from the scene, and my wife did not hear about me for another three and a half years. She received the first message that I was still alive only after Stalin's death. In the meantime she was told: If you declare that your husband betrayed the 'people's democracy' then you might get a job. She refused and never got the job. I was accused of being a spy, naturally. I was supposed to have been the head of a large-scale military conspiracy because eleven generals had been arrested at the time. My real crime was that I was an independent-minded man and there were people who respected me. I wanted to rebuild Budapest with Western aid and maintain the city's ties with the West of which she has always been part.

I. Nyeste had been active in the anti-Nazi resistance in Hungary. After the war, as a leader of a youth organization, he refused to join the Communists:

The difference between the Nazi and the Communist secret police – I am one of the happy few who experienced both – does not rest in the degree of brutality and cruelty. The torture chamber in the Nazi jail is the same as in the Communist jail. The difference lies elsewhere. If the Nazis caught you as a political dissident, they usually wanted to know what you did, who your friends were, what were your plans, etc. The Communists did not go in for that. They already knew, when they arrested you, what kind of confession you were going to sign. But you didn't. I had no idea that I was going to become an 'American spy'!

Torture was the prime means used in obtaining confessions: beatings, electro-shock treatment and 'an old Hungarian sword, kept red-hot in the oven, with which they handled your back'. After his trial Nyeste was sent to the Resz labour camp where he stayed until 1956:

Imagine working very hard (at breaking stones) for twelve hours in wintertime and sixteen hours in the summer. The guards beat us every day; but the worst is a permanent state of hunger. You can be hungry for a few days, but being hungry for a year or two years is something I cannot describe.... But when I heard later what my wife and friends who remained 'free' went through I feel in a way lucky to have spent the entire Rakosi era behind bars. They were very poor; but you can take that. You can do a menial job, have little to eat or manage with poor clothing. But what you cannot digest is to have to stand up, applaud and shout long live Stalin. And they had to do this every week, sometimes every day. I am glad to have been spared that.

The first targets of this repressive onslaught were the former non-Communists. Imre Nagy, in his remarkable first speech of the post-Stalin era (in June 1953), spoke of 'several hundred thousand people subjected to the legal proceedings of the courts, or simply of the police'. Official Hungarian statistics show that nearly 700,000 people were sentenced between 1948 and 1953. For the year 1952 alone the figure was 144,743, of which some 77,000 had to serve prison terms. Hungarian historians today estimate that, at one point or another during the Stalinist period, one family in three had one of its members in jail, and that every other family had some dealings with, or at least threats from, the secret police. The whole society was subjected to arbitrary repression and terror.

In all countries, the first targets were real, potential or simply imaginary opponents of the Communists: former officials of other political parties, Christians, members of independent youth associations, the Boy Scouts, 'Sokol' sports associations, etc. The first Czechoslovak show-trial was that of Milada Horakova and thirteen other leaders of Beneš' National Socialist Party and the Social Democratic Party. The defendants included Zavis Kalandra, a Marxist intellectual who had split with the Communists in 1936 precisely over the Moscow show-trials. A Prague magazine at the time published an ironical comment on the event: 'The boot of our vigilant GPU [Stalin's secret police] has crushed this nest of vipers. This is the end for these disgusting reptiles. The Trotsko-terroristic nihilists have been convicted for their crimes. The depraved bandit estranged from any patriotic fervour, Záviš Kalandra, has confessed!' Fifteen years later Prosecutor Urvalek concluded his summation with these words: 'Now Záviš Kalandra is unmasked before this court in all his nakedness as a traitor; and there are no words harsh enough to describe his crimes with sufficient precision. For such obstinate criminals, unique and revolting, there is no room in our society.' The 1936 joke turned into tragic reality in 1950. Kalandra and Horakova were executed.

Theirs were by no means isolated cases. From 1948 to 1952, the same court passed 233 death sentences, of which 178 were carried out. But the Horakova and Kalandra trial stands out as the symbol of the liquidation of Czechoslovak democracy. The legal murder of Kalandra, an independent intellectual and pre-war associate of the surrealists, left the Prague cultural milieu in a state of shock. In Paris, André Breton, the leading figure among the surrealists, wrote an open letter to the poet Paul Eluard (who knew Kalandra well and whose words might have carried some weight with the Communist establishment) to intercede on behalf of the Czech writer. Eluard replied with a memorable excuse: 'I am too busy defending the innocent who claim their innocence to deal with guilty people who claim their guilt.'

The Horakova trial was significant in another way. According to data revealed in 1968, it had a follow-up in the form of some 300 political trials related to the same central plot which were conducted in provincial towns between May and July 1950. A total of 7,000 former members of Horakova's National Socialist Party were sent to jail. Czech historians estimate that between 1948 and 1954 there were close to 150,000 political prisoners in Czechoslovakia.

The big show-trials were meant to inspire fear and mobilize the public behind the Party; local trials were meant to control and 're-educate' society. Ota Ulč was a judge in a small town at the time and recalls how the whole legal system had been adapted to suit Party control even at the local level:

The jury system was abolished and replaced by the Soviet pattern of 1 + 2, that is, the professional judge presiding with two lay assistants, the so-called 'people's judges'; the three had an equal vote, so that Party control would be guaranteed (though I always tried to find ways to outwit them). The Party interference depended on the type of adjudication. In the political trials the control was total. In criminal cases it was sporadic, but it was not absent in civil adjudication either; and that was my field. I would say that there was Party interference in about 5 per cent of these cases; but here again, how many people do you need to spit in your bowl of soup to dislike that particular dish? It affected your entire outlook. You became your own censor, your own apparatchik and you ended up behaving like a cow behind an electrified fence.

The 'class approach' was prescribed in the economy, in cultural life, in schooling. Class justice meant that particular groups were singled out as prime targets of Communist attacks, as Ulč describes:

After the seizure of power you go after the visible targets, the political opponents, people who used to hold public office. Then repression shifts to the 'class enemy', former capitalists, stockbrokers, the real-estate agents. During the collectivization of agriculture you go after the so-called 'kulak'; in the early 1950s Church people, etc. After de-Stalinization the crackdown was on the emerging dissidents (though in those days we did not call them 'dissidents'). Nowadays in Prague they're even hunting the jazzmen. So it depends on the season.

The class origins of people often influenced the judgements made against them in court:

For instance, there was the felony of non-delivery of agricultural quotas. If for some reason (bad harvest or whatever) you were unable to deliver the fixed quota, then the consequences of that failure were strictly dependent upon class determination. If it was a so-called small farmer, then it was a misdemeanour or a nominal fine; if it was a 'kulak' it was judged as sabotage and your life might be at risk.

An example of local 'class justice' in reverse:

There was a case involving a member of the Central Committee of the Party who in one village wanted to evict a family so that the vacated premises could be turned over to newlyweds. The tenants were classified as 'class enemies', and the court had to okay this manifestly illegal measure. For me the dilemma was a very uncomfortable one: if I did not comply I would lose the confidence of the toiling masses represented by this particular comrade; and if I did comply I would feel very miserable about myself. So I postponed the decision and left. Not an admirable action, but under the circumstances I really did not know what to do.

While society in East-Central Europe was being subjected to repression and rigid Party control of all spheres of social and cultural life, Stalin pressed for direct control of each Party-state. The Yugoslav crisis provided the opportunity. The Communist purge of society was to spill over into the parties themselves.

The ideological hierarchy which Stalin wanted to establish within the Empire was meant to justify the complete subservience of the bloc to Soviet economic needs and the Soviet bid for direct control. The Yugoslav–Soviet rupture both exposed and accelerated this process. It was Yugoslavia's eventual resistance in the face of Soviet infiltration of the media, of economic institutions, even of the Central Committee apparatus and the intelligence service, which precipitated the crisis. The Yugoslav Communist Party had, in the inimitable phrase of the Cominform resolution condemning it, 'placed itself outside the family of the fraternal Communist Parties'.

Stalin obviously presumed that no Communist power could survive without Soviet backing. 'If I lift a finger, Tito will fall,' Khrushchev quoted him as saying. Yet the hysterical campaign launched against Tito, the 'fascist dog', did not succeed. A military intervention was prepared, but as General Kiraly, commander of the army which was supposed to invade Yugoslavia, later disclosed, the Korean War and the United States involvement in it made Stalin think twice.

The Yugoslav defection was the first major split-off from the Moscow centre since the creation of the Communist International in 1919. But the setback was immediately put to good use. For Stalin, it was proof that besides the external 'enemy', the Western 'imperialist' bloc, there was an internal enemy lurking within the 'fraternal' Communist Parties. The anti-Tito campaign thus provided a rationale for establishing a tighter grip on all the ruling Parties.

When the war ended, the Communist Parties in most of the

countries in the Soviet sphere were small groups without much of a base in society. With the exception of Czechoslovakia and Yugoslavia, these parties were considered marginal to the nation. Most had been banned before the war and their leaders, sitting either in jail or in the Hotel Lux in Moscow, had little familiarity with the national realities of their countries. Since the 1920s the Communist Parties had favoured a policy of 'national self-determination up to separation' for minorities and had been used to recruit primarily among them. The Polish Party had a strong contingent of Ukrainians, Byelorussians and Jews. The majority of the members of the pre-war Romanian Communist Party were Hungarians and Jews. The mentor of the Romanian Communists in the Communist International was none other than Béla Kun, the leader of the Hungarian revolution of 1919. When the Russian tanks reached Bucharest in August 1944, the Romanian Party had less than a thousand members. Under these conditions the question was not whether Sovietization was likely but simply what form it would take.

Most of the Parties were divided between 'Muscovites' and 'natives'. They all shared an enormous debt of gratitude towards the Soviet Union, but the Muscovites, who had spent the war (or longer periods) in Moscow, were more directly part of the international branch of the Soviet Communist Party, or of the NKVD. After the dissolution in 1943 of the Communist International led by Georgi Dimitrov, the International Department of the Secretariat of the Central Committee of the Soviet Party (headed by the same Dimitrov) took over the supervision of the Communist Parties of East-Central Europe. The natives had spent the war in domestic resistance against the Germans. They were no less fervent admirers of Soviet-style socialism, but they simply failed to identify this with direct Soviet control. Another crucial difference was that the natives (as well as the Communists who had spent the war in the West) did not owe their position to a Soviet 'personnel officer'.

These contrasts were not immediately brought into the open precisely for the reason that the Communist Parties were desperately trying to 'go native' in a hurry. Each claimed all the 'progressive' traditions of its nation's history and sought to increase its membership as rapidly as possible. The Polish Party, which had boasted barely 20,000 members before the war, was up to 1.3 million at the end of 1948 (admittedly after absorbing the socialists). In Hungary there were an estimated 3,000 Communists in a country of 10 million at the end of the war; by March 1949 they were 1.2 million. The Romanian Party witnessed a similar, albeit not so spectacular, expansion. In the spring of 1948 the Czechoslovak Party reached the

2-million mark out of a population of 13 million. And the same figure was achieved in East Germany, where Erich Honecker, the first head of the Communist Youth organization (FDJ), declared that former members of the Nazi Youth were acceptable provided they repented and made a clean break with their past. Clearly, the policy of following a 'national path' to socialism coincided with a massive recruitment drive at the expense of Leninist purity.

However, once total monopoly of power had been gained and especially after the Stalin–Tito split, such a departure from the Soviet model became an embarrassment and all the Parties proceeded to purge their freshly enlarged rank and file. Thousands of examining commissions were set up to do the job, initiating the masses into the technique of 'criticism and self-criticism'. Czecho-slovakia held the record by reducing Party membership by 900,000 in 1948–51; in Hungary it was reduced by nearly half a million. It is estimated that, on average, one out of every four Party members was purged in each bloc country.

Even purged, the Communist Parties were already divided between the rank and file and the hard core. Members of the latter, who were issued with special cards, represented about one-tenth of the membership and were put directly in charge of the whole machinery of power. The supreme stage of the Stalinist terror was the purge of that very machinery, the highest echelons of the Party leadership.

The immediate consequence of the rift between Stalin and Tito was the elimination of would-be 'Titoists' from the leaderships of the other Parties. Who were the protagonists of these imaginary anti-Soviet plots which had to be unmasked with the help of the Soviet NKVD? Answer: all those whose 'biography' (a crucial term in Communist cadre policy) might suggest a *potential* for less than complete subservience to Soviet policy. The roster of suspects comprised Communists from the home resistance, veterans from the International Brigades during the Spanish Civil War, Communists who had spent the war in London rather than in Moscow and, last but not least, Jews.

Some of the 'national Communists', such as Patrascanu in Romania, Clementis in Slovakia or Gomulka in Poland, were obvious targets. They had identified with the 'national path to socialism' policy with excessive sincerity. In 1947 Gomulka, with surprising candour, expressed a lack of enthusiasm for the Soviet model. 'We have completely rejected,' he wrote in *Nowe Drogi*, 'the collectivization of agriculture. . . . our democracy is not similar to Soviet democracy, just as our society's structure is not the same as the

Soviet structure.' A year later such words had become utter heresy and Gomulka (along with several of his associates) was expelled from the Party and arrested, though not executed. The Polish Party leadership had already been liquidated by Stalin once before, only a decade earlier. The lesson had been learned in Poland, even by the staunchest of Stalin's disciples. Besides, the Communists had been too busy fighting a very real nationalist opposition to start a witch-hunt against imaginary enemies in their own ranks.

In Bulgaria the bloodbath unleashed against the opposition (100,000 people killed) was already nearly complete and what was to become the most faithful Soviet-bloc Party would refuse Moscow nothing. The Party leader was Georgi Dimitrov, the hero of the Reichstag fire trial staged by the Nazis in 1933. That made him a difficult candidate for a spectacular Stalinist show-trial. Not that the former head of the Comintern was unwilling to learn. Milovan Djilas recalls how Bulgarian and Yugoslav delegations met with Stalin in the Kremlin in February 1948 to hear Soviet opposition to the planned Balkan federation of Bulgaria, Yugoslavia and Albania. Stalin criticized Dimitrov so sharply that even the Yugoslav Communists felt embarrassed. Dimitrov: 'But, Comrade Stalin, we are still learning...' Stalin: 'What are you learning? You've been learning for fifty years and you are still at it. You do not even know how to cover your tracks, but keep on gossiping like an old woman.' Dimitrov was kept in Moscow, so Beria chose one of his close associates in the Bulgarian leadership, Traicho Kostov, as the 'Titoist' to be eliminated. The choice was all the more obvious since Kostov had been among the most vehement in denouncing the Yugoslav leader. In fact Tito himself paid undue attention to the Bulgarian Communist. In a speech in April 1949 Tito said:

> Kostov was arrested during the reign of King Boris together with a number of other Communists. Although he was one of the main leaders of the Party, his life alone was spared. Why?...
> Today we have proof that certain capitalist states have infiltrated their own agents into some Communist Parties.

Stalin could not have said it better. Kostov was arrested two months later and sentenced to death. Following the same twisted logic, the key witness against Kostov was a certain Hadji-Panzov, an anti-Tito defector from Yugoslavia turned appropriately into a Titoist agent.

The most important of all the anti-Titoist trials was that of Laszlo Rajk in Hungary. Rajk had fought in the Spanish Civil War and spent three years in internment camps in France, before returning to Hungary to join the resistance. Given the uncharismatic character of the leadership, known as the 'gang of four' (Rakosi, Gero, Revai, Farkas), Rajk was easily the most popular member of the Hungarian Communist leadership; that is, until he became Minister of the Interior. As such, he played an active part in liquidating the opposition and particularly in staging the trial of Cardinal Mindszenty in February 1949, which gave the signal for a massive onslaught on the Catholic Church. Rajk's biography made him an ideal candidate for the part assigned to him by the Soviets in the show-trial.

The Rajk trial was indeed the model for all others to come. First, it completed the Soviet takeover of the local State Security, the AVH. The trial was prepared under the supervision of General Byelkin, a Soviet 'adviser', and of Party leader Rakosi. The extravagant confessions of a Western imperialist–Titoist plot aimed at over-throwing the Hungarian regime were obtained through a mixture of torture and psychological blackmail. The torture was the job of the AVH. The indictment was written by Rakosi. The blackmail fell to Janos Kadar's lot.

Vladimir Farkas (the son of the Farkas in the Party leadership) was a senior AVH officer in charge of torture and interrogation in the Rajk case. This is how he remembers his training and role in the Rajk trial:

> I was told that it was high time I learned about interrogation work. And then I got Sandor Cseresznyes, Rajk's assistant, for interrogation. I asked my bosses (some of whom were lawyers) how one should start an interrogation like this. The answer was to just slap him in the face. As far as I remember it was very hard for me because this had never been part of my nature. But since I was considered a good boy in the AVH I smacked him in the face. In all his confessions Sandor Cseresznyes denies it, of course. Well, that was my first lesson. In the Rajk case the confession was to be obtained by terribly cruel beating, sometimes carried out in the presence of some members of the Politburo. This turned out to be a complete fiasco after six or eight weeks. So Rakosi asked Stalin for assistance and the experts from the Cheka, I mean the KGB, arrived. From then on the Soviet interrogation experts led by Byelkin were fully in charge. I don't mean to say that Rakosi no longer took part; he was in daily contact with Byelkin and there was a Hungarian investigator working with every Soviet expert. For example, in the case of Pal Justus – a defendant in the Rajk trial – I worked with a very pleasant major called Kremlov Kamenkovics. The actual indictment, however, came from Rakosi.

The final stage before the trial was to make sure the victim fully cooperated in the charade. Janos Kadar, an old friend of Rajk's and godfather to his son, took on himself this thankless task. He visited Rajk in his cell. Of course, Kadar said, the comrades in the Party leadership knew perfectly well how things really stood, but he begged Rajk to render the Party this ultimate service and accept his role as the Titoist spy. True, the verdict might be the death sentence, but that would be only for show. Rajk and his family would have the privilege of going to the Soviet Union to start a new life. Rajk accepted the deal as proof of his loyalty to the Party, and kept his part of the bargain at the trial. Kadar did not keep his. The tape of their last conversation was played by Rakosi at a Central Committee meeting in 1956 – a convenient way for the old Stalinist to shift the responsibility for the murder of Laszlo Rajk on to Kadar.

All the other victims received – and trusted – similar promises. György Hoddos, also arrested in the Rajk trial, describes the situation:

> Tortured into unthinking clumps of flesh only a few days before, they now eagerly embraced the possibility of demonstrating their devotion to the Party. If the Party could transform good Communists into abominable criminals, it could also return to them their lives and the meaning of their lives. The only choice appeared to be between the hangman and the certainty of rotting away in a prison cellar. Now miraculously a new choice was offered to them. At the price of a few more charges, a few more incriminations, their lives would be placed in the hands of the Party.
>
> They signed everything. The cellars were transformed into livable rooms. Gourmet food appeared three times a day from the excellent AVH kitchen. Cigarettes and books were distributed and the prisoners were permitted to write their first letters since their arrests. At night the warders wore felt slippers so as not to awaken their charges. In sunlit rooms upstairs, interrogators and victims worked together in friendly collaboration, setting up the carefully coordinated final statements.

On 24 September 1949 Rajk and two other defendants were sentenced to death. Their executions were carried out on 15 October. Béla Szasz, one of the survivors of the trial, described them as 'volunteers for the gallows'.

The Rajk trial in Hungary was a model for all the other show-trials. It was also conceived by Soviet security as merely one stage in the revelation of a vast imperialist plot with ramifications in several countries of the Soviet bloc. Noel Field, an American citizen based in Switzerland, had been involved in helping a number of Central European Communists during and immediately after the war. His arrest in Prague in 1949 provided useful evidence of American involvement not just in the Rajk trial but also in Poland and Czechoslovakia. Thus, while Field was being mentioned as a Soviet agent in the Alger Hiss case during the McCarthy hearings, he was simultaneously referred to as an American agent in the show-trials in Budapest and Prague.

On the eve of the Rajk trial the Soviets, and also the Hungarian and Polish comrades, stepped up the pressure on the Czechoslovak Communists, showing surprise at their reluctance to unmask the enemy in their own ranks. Rakosi's letter to Gottwald on 3 September 1949 is most explicit: 'In two weeks we shall begin the case of the first group accused in the Rajk trial. The indictment will be published in a week. In this connection, we come up against the difficulty that Czechoslovak names will appear by the dozen at the hearing, names which you also know. All these people are at liberty, they will protest vehemently about the things said in court and will try to undermine the credibility of the charges.'

While Gottwald dragged his feet, Party General Secretary Rudolf Slansky was eager to unmask the enemy from within. At the Cominform meeting in November he said that the 'weakness' of the Czechoslovak Party was its underestimation of the class enemy, its 'insufficient Bolshevik vigilance'. He complained about the sluggish pace at which 'saboteurs and spies' were being uncovered. At a public rally in the Lucerna Hall in Prague in December 1949 Slansky declared: 'Not even our Party will be spared from the enemy's attempt to place its agents in our ranks.... We therefore have to be all the more vigilant in order to unmask the enemy in our own ranks, since these are the most dangerous of enemies.' This implied, according to Slansky, unmasking the 'bourgeois nationalist face' of the spies, which provided the justification for a massive security purge in the upper echelons of the Czechoslovak Party. Having completed their task in Budapest, Soviet security Generals Makarov and Likhachev could move to Prague, where they engineered the most extravagant and the most murderous of the show-trials of the Stalinist era. It eventually destroyed even some of those, like Slansky himself, who had set the terrifying witch-hunt in motion.

Whereas the leitmotif of the Rajk trial was anti-Titoist, the 'trial of the anti-state conspiratorial centre headed by Rudolf Slansky' was resolutely 'anti-Zionist', i.e. anti-Semitic. Eleven out of fourteen accused were Jewish. Stalin's domestic foreign-policy priorities had changed since the Rajk trial. In 1949 the Yugoslav crisis appeared to the Soviet dictator as the main threat to the monolithic nature of his empire. Three years later, his fit of anti-Semitic dementia, exhibited in the 'doctors' plot' in Moscow and followed by the Slansky trial in Prague, also suited his new Middle East policy. After having supported the creation of the State of Israel the Soviet Union shifted its support to the Arabs. And there was no better proof of the sincerity of this shift than sentencing to death Jewish Communists as 'Zionist agents' who presumably were responsible for the previous pro-Israeli policy.

A combination of these themes is to be found in the indictment, and the accused sometimes had to wear more than one hat. Slansky was declared to be an American agent, also working for Ben-Gurion's government in Israel, while still in the service of Tito's 'fascist clique' as proved by an imaginary meeting with a Yugoslav Jewish Communist leader, Mośa Pijade. Prosecutor Urvalek said in his summation: 'The Zionist agents in Slansky's conspiratorial centre served, by their criminal activities, the efforts of American imperialists to dominate the world and to unleash a new war. Their cosmopolitanism and their bourgeois nationalism are indeed the two sides of the same coin minted on Wall Street.'

The Czechoslovak plot was presented as part of a worldwide conspiracy masterminded by American Jewish capitalists and the Israeli government of Ben-Gurion. The 'Zionist' label used against the accused simply stood for 'Jew'. In this shameless orgy of anti-Semitism, the 'guilt' of the accused was derived from their 'bourgeois' and Jewish 'origin'.

'I came into the workers' movement as a man of bourgeois origin,' is Slansky's opening line. His 'origins' are supposed to explain why he 'never became a real Communist' and eventually ended up as a spy and murderer. Bedřich Geminder was the only member of the Czechoslovak leadership to hold the Order of Lenin, the highest Soviet award. His testimony, prepared by Soviet ghost-writers, follows the same pattern: 'I had always been close to Slansky in the past. He knew my cosmopolitan, Zionist background, my ties with the West, and the fact that I always followed my personal, careerist interests. He expected that I would be a good partner for him.' André Simone, 'whose real name was Otto Katz', as the audience was reminded, was a leading journalist with wide international pre-war experience: 'I am the son of a manufacturer, educated in the spirit of bourgeois ideology. The working class was always alien to me. Therefore I always moved in circles close to my heart, among traitors of the working people, Trotskyites, right-wing Social

Democrats, and Jewish bourgeois nationalists.'

Asked to explain why he had such a hostile attitude towards Czechoslovakia's People's Democracy another defendant, Otto Fischl, replied: 'I am a Jewish bourgeois nationalist.' As if the constant reference to 'origins' were not enough to establish the anti-Semitic nature of the trial, the Prosecutor sometimes became more explicit:

Prosecutor: Accused Geminder, what is your nationality?
Geminder: Czech.
Prosecutor: Do you speak Czech well?
Geminder: Yes.
Prosecutor: Do you want an interpreter?
Geminder: No.
Prosecutor: Do you understand the questions and will you answer in the Czech language?
Geminder: Yes.

One does not expect such deep interest in linguistics, but it all falls into place when the Prosecutor asks the defendant to describe his 'attitude towards the Czechoslovak working people':

Geminder: I never identified myself with the interests of the Czechoslovak people. Their national interests remained alien to me. . . . I went to a German school. After finishing my studies, I lived in a petty-bourgeois, cosmopolitan, Zionist milieu, where German was spoken, and that's why I have not mastered the Czech language.
Prosecutor: And you never learned to speak Czech well, even after 1946, when you came back to Czechoslovakia and acquired a responsible position in the Party apparatus?
Geminder: That's right.
Prosecutor: And which language do you speak well?
Geminder: German.
Prosecutor: Do you really speak German well?
Geminder: I have not spoken German for a long time but I know the German language.
Prosecutor: Do you speak German as well as Czech?
Geminder: Yes.
Prosecutor: That means that you speak no language decently. You are a typical cosmopolitan!
Geminder: Yes.

This trial with its outrageous dialogue was taking place in Kafka's city. The accused was, like Kafka, a Czech Jew whose mother tongue was German. Like the rest of the co-accused, he confessed to the most absurd charges brought against him by his lifelong friends and associates.

> Ḳ. now perceived clearly that he was supposed to seize the knife himself, as it travelled from hand to hand above him, and plunge it into his own breast. But he did not do so, he merely turned his head which was still free to move, and gazed around him. He could not completely rise to the occasion, he could not relieve the officials of all their tasks; the responsibility for this last failure of his lay with him who had not left him the remnant of strength necessary for the deed. (Franz Kafka, *The Trial*)

The loyalty and faith in Communism of the accused were used to extract extravagant confessions and more. Thus André Simone concluded his testimony with a most stupefying appeal:

> There is a beautiful saying that the writer is an engineer of human souls. What kind of engineer was I who poisoned these souls? Such an engineer belongs on the gallows. The only service I can still render is to serve as a warning to those who, because of their origin, their character and qualities are in danger of going the same diabolical way as I did. The more severe my punishment, the more effective will be the warning.

This is closer to Dostoevsky than Kafka. One thinks of Raskolnikov following Sonia's advice to 'salute the people, kiss the earth and say loud and clear: I am an assassin'; or Dimitri Karamazov saying to his judges: 'You can all despise a scoundrel, I deserved it.' The Court granted André Simone's wish and sent him to the gallows.

On 27 November 1952 Slansky and eleven defendants were sentenced to death (Artur London, Eugen Lobl and Vavro Hajdu were given life sentences). They were executed in December and their ashes scattered on a country road near Prague.

The overt anti-Semitism of the Slansky trial was the original Czechoslovak feature of the show-trials which shook the whole of Central Europe. The Soviet advisers had been particularly active in playing up this theme. Likhachev was a notorious anti-Semite. And Boyarsky, another Soviet adviser, devoted a lot of time to persuading the Czechoslovak leaders of the dangers of 'an international bourgeois–Jewish conspiracy' against socialism. But the Soviets could rely on well-disposed groups in the Czech security services, particularly a certain Andrej Keppert, head of an 'anti-Zionist' department in the police. Artur London, one of the survivors of the trial, had this to say on the subject:

The Jews played (not for the first time) the part of scapegoats.
The trial was meant to channel mounting popular discontent. It
was as if the Party told the people, 'it's the fault of the imperialists
and their Titoist–Zionist agents' who had seized temporarily the
leadership of the Party. They tried to awaken popular anti-
Semitism, which was strong in Russia and in Poland, but which
had almost vanished in the Czech lands.

Into a country whose first President, Tomáš Masaryk, had
launched his political career with a campaign against anti-Semitism
and whose pre-war republic established a climate of tolerance and
understanding between Jews and non-Jews, the Communists tried
to import anti-Semitism along with other features of a totalitarian
system.

The word 'confession', like 'gulag' or 'normalization', is part of the
original contribution made by Communism to the modern political
vocabulary. all three words refer to the technology of repression. In
Stalin's day it had reached its most paranoid stage, as seen from the
evidence produced by the Piller Committee in Czechoslovakia in
1968 (the same pattern applied throughout the bloc):

> From the middle of 1949 a very paradoxical situation emerged:
> at the initiative of leading officials of the Central Party apparatus
> a unit was created inside the security organs in order to search
> for enemies within the Party ranks; and operating parallel to that
> was a unit like the Party Control Committee which, using security
> methods – i.e. confessions, torture – aimed at uncovering enemies
> among the Communists inside the security apparatus.

'Orwellian' is almost an understatement in describing this Central
European initiation into the technology of repression. The mutual
purging of its two branches (the security services and the Party
Control Commission) accounts for the sudden changes that turned
yesterday's accusers into today's accused in the show-trials. But the
whole process was part of the bloc's total and lasting subordination
to its Soviet masters. The 'new man' of the socialist era was not the
one heralded by the ideologues but the one who was screened,
purged and capable of acting as the faithful instrument of Soviet
control. More than the ideology it was the special Communist mentality which not only needed 'enemies' to prosper but which con-
doned and invited Sovietization, even in its most extreme forms.
The role of Soviet advisers was decisive, says the 1968 report, in
the purges: 'their authority was great, their advice, directives or
decisions carried the weight of orders.' These advisers informed

Moscow about 'the situation and the direction of the investigations of persons who might be suspected of political deviation or enemy activity', including the 'leading figures of the Party and the state, officials of the political, military, security, economic and diplomatic apparatus'.

The Sovietization of East-Central Europe went hand in hand with a 'war psychosis', the militarization of all the societies of the region and their economies. This meant giving absolute priority to the 'military–industrial' complex, the coal and steel gigantomania of the Stalinist period, and expanding the role of the army in society. The effects were also felt in education, publishing, the film industry, etc.

According to the Czech historian Karel Kaplan, who in the 1960s had unique access to Party archives, by 1950 the Soviet leadership considered that a military conflict with the capitalist world was inevitable and estimated that, militarily speaking, the situation would remain potentially favourable for three or four years for a rapid blitzkrieg conquest of Western Europe. According to the testimony of Alexej Cepicka, Czechoslovak Defence Minister (and Gottwald's son-in-law), this option was put forward by Stalin in January 1951 at a crucial meeting with Soviet bloc leaders in the Kremlin. Only First Secretaries and Defence Ministers were invited. On the Soviet side were several Politburo members, led by Stalin and Molotov, surrounded by a group of generals. Based on his perception that the United States was demonstrating relative military weakness in the Korean War, this is how Stalin presented his intentions:

> No European army is capable of seriously opposing the Soviet Army, and one can even assume that there will be no resistance. The current military strength of the United States is not very great. The Soviet camp thus enjoys a temporary superiority in this field. But it is only temporary, for three or four years. After that the United States will have at their disposal rapid means of transport to bring troops to Europe and could exploit fully their nuclear superiority. It will be necessary therefore to make good use of this short period to complete the systematic preparation of our armies by devoting to them all the economic, political and human means at our disposal. During the three or four years to come the whole of our domestic and international policy will be subordinated to this goal. Only a total mobilization of our resources will allow us to seize this unique occasion to spread socialism to the whole of Europe.

The next day details of implementation were worked out and a protocol was signed with the Party leader and Minister of Defence of each country. Whether or not Stalin actually believed in the 'window of opportunity' *vis-à-vis* Western Europe, he certainly used the 'inevitability of war' argument to accelerate the Sovietization and the militarization of all the countries of East-Central Europe.

Sovietization thus meant the imposition of a single political system of totalitarian control and of an economic model based on the concentration of decision-making in the hands of the Party-state. It could be argued that, in the initial phase (1945–7), the Communists tried sometimes successfully to mobilize society for reconstruction, land reform and social change. In the ensuing Stalinist phase, society was 'mobilized' merely for political purposes while it was subjected to total control. Much like Chigalev in Dostoevsky's *The Possessed*, the Communist intellectuals, at first attracted by the utopian promise of the 'perfect society', discovered that 'starting with unlimited freedom, [they] ended up with unlimited despotism'.

While Western Europe was trying to heal its war wounds and restore continuity with the pre-war period, a radical caesura was experienced in the other half of Europe. It is this traumatic experience, which accompanied the formation of two military and ideological blocs, that cleft the two Europes. The whole of the Other Europe became a world apart, a homogeneous Soviet zone, decorated with the same banners, with the same slogans coming from their loudspeakers, the same statues of Stalin erected by the local Soviet satraps.

Part 3
TOTALITARIANISM IN DECAY

6 The Party-State: 'Them'

The cause of the Party's defectiveness must be found. All
our principles were right, but our results were wrong. . . .
Our will was hard and pure, we should have been loved
by the people. But they hate us. Why are we so odious
and detested?

(Arthur Koestler, *Darkness at Noon*)

On coming to power the Communist Parties of the Other Europe
claimed to be 'parties of a new type'. This was an understatement.
A party is meant, by definition, to be merely a part of the political
spectrum. By monopolizing the spectrum, the ruling Communist
Parties ceased to be political parties in the proper sense of the term.

By the same token they have abolished the distinction between
'right' and 'left'. Are Jaruzelski, Ceausescu or Honecker supposed
to be on the right or the left? For most people in Central Europe,
the question has become utterly irrelevant. It also explains why
leading dissident intellectuals such as Adam Michnik, Vaclav Havel
or György Konrad resent the use of Western political labels to
describe the politics of their countries, including dissent.

None of the traditional attributes of a governing party (the separation of powers, elected popular representation, the freedom from
political control of various areas of social and cultural life) apply to
the Communist system.

The ideological justification for the confiscation of politics is the
theory of substitution: the working class is the better self of the
nation; the Party is the vanguard of the working class; and the Party
leadership knows best which way the wind of history is blowing.
The Communists therefore are convinced that their rule is not only
necessary, but also irreversible.

This ideological claim (declared to be a 'scientific truth') is the origin of the extraordinary arrogance of Communist power in its determination to inflict a 'radiant future' on the most reluctant of societies.

It is inadequate to describe the lands of the Soviet bloc as one-party states. The Communist Party tolerates, at least formally, several satellite parties (admittedly without real power), but more than that, the expression is misleading because it may suggest that the institutions of these countries are similar to those of the Western democracies except that the ruling party has somehow managed to bar its opponents from access to power. In fact the nature of the political system is fundamentally different in that it is precisely the Party which controls all existing institutions, all social organizations and, most important, the state itself. The Czech-born sociologist Thomas Lowit even maintains that the state in the Soviet bloc has become a legal fiction, a mere extension of the 'polymorphous' Party.

So if the Party is not really a political party, the state is not actually a state. Since the distinguishing feature of the Communist Party is its merger with the state, a more accurate description would be that of Party-state. No major decision by a government ministry can be taken without prior consultation with the Shadow Cabinet in the Secretariat of the Communist Party, and all state organs at every level operate under the direct control of the corresponding Party organ. This is clearly explained in a textbook published in the 1970s for the Hungarian Party School, where future apparatchiks are trained:

> The central organs of the state (Parliament, Council of the Presidency of the People's Republic, the government, the ministries) are placed under the guidance and control of the central Party organs . . .: the Central Committee of the Party, the Political Committee, the Secretariat of the Central Committee. . . . At every level, it is the Party territorial organizations and their leading organs which direct and control the organs of the state. At every level, these [Party] bodies decide the most important questions of the work of the state.

Similar statements are to be found in Party guidelines in all the countries of the Other Europe. They explain in concrete terms what is meant in their respective constitutions by the 'leading role' of the Party. Any opposition to Party policy can be branded as 'illegal' and prosecuted as 'anti-state subversion'. The Party cells that operate within each institution serve to supervise the implementation of the Party's leading role.

The key to understanding the Party-state is the personnel selection system known as the nomenklatura. It is essentially a list of posts in the state bureaucracy which can be filled only by people properly vetted by the Party. The nomenklatura system, a Soviet invention exported to Eastern Europe, operates at different levels – central, district or local – of the Party. So the Premier of a Soviet bloc country is an appointee of the Party leadership, just as a town-hall clerk owes his job to the local Party committee. The wording of Party guidelines concerning the nomenklatura is remarkably similar from country to country. Here is a sample from Czechoslovakia:

> The Central Committee of the Communist Party of Czecho-slovakia and the organs of the higher echelons of the Party have full decision-making power in the field of cadres.... The implementation of the nomenklatura constitutes the manifestation of the leading role of the Party and of democratic centralism.... The nomenklatura must be observed by all leading personnel in all spheres of social life.... Nobody can be appointed to a nomenklatura post, nor be recalled from office, without the prior approval of the competent Party organ.

This implies that political loyalty, rather than merit or competence, is the guarantee of tenure in office. 'Negative selection' is the basic principle of co-option into the nomenklatura. Though vital for the understanding of how these countries are ruled, the nomenklatura document remains confidential. A Polish nomenklatura list from the 1970s (published in the West) reveals the astonishing degree to which the Party controls appointments not just in the state administration or, as might be expected, in the army and in the police, but also in the so-called social organizations. These include, in addition to the trade unions and the organized youth and women's movements, the lawyers' and journalists' associations, sports organizations and even the volunteer fire department.

The size of the nomenklatura varies, but the trend, especially in the Brezhnev era, has been one of expansion. As an East German Party journal put it, 'The greater the progress in the building of socialism, the greater the role and the responsibilities of the Party.' Generally speaking, the nomenklatura grows in periods of tightening Party control. The Polish nomenklatura was estimated at 160,000 posts at the end of the 1970s; after martial law it mushroomed to 250,000. In 'normalized' Czechoslovakia the figure is 115,000–130,000, double the figure of twenty years ago. However, the actual number of people involved is much higher, since certain posts are filled by more than one official. Conversely, the upper echelons of the state are filled with senior Party apparatchiks, who thus hold a dual position. The historian Bronislaw Geremek has written that in the past the Polish aristocracy represented about 10 per cent of the nation. Today, the power is in the hands of a party representing less than 5 per cent of the population. In turn, the nomenklatura, the 'inner party', represents less than 1 per cent of the population.

Being co-opted into the nomenklatura brings with it material privileges. Former Hungarian Premier Andros Hegedus recalls that in the 1950s 'we had practically no expenses. We could order cloth at the Party's tailor. We did not even have to pay for what they delivered from the department store. We did receive some sort of symbolic bill, but I guess it was only for administrative purposes.... We lived in a sort of consumer Communism.' The 'we' applies, of course, to the Party elite. Meanwhile, an ordinary housewife would have to queue for hours to buy a couple of pounds of potatoes.

Administrative corruption and nepotism in the Balkans is as widespread today as it ever was. But Central Europe used to be different. Today it is rampant there in economic life as well as in the state administration. In pre-1968 Czechoslovakia President Novotny used to give senior Party officials an envelope every month containing varying amounts of cash; how much depended on the degree of loyalty of the particular official or on the need to buy his quiescence or support. Under 'normalization' the phenomenon has only increased. Politically one of the most sensitive scandals in the two decades since the Soviet invasion erupted in 1986–7, when numerous officials, including Foreign Minister Chnoupek, were implicated in charges that lavish gifts to politicians had secured favourable treatment for an ambitious Slovak district.

If power corrupts, absolute power corrupts absolutely. The post-ideological ethos of the 1970s and 1980s has encouraged a highly acquisitive mood inside the Party establishments. The massive availability of hard currency thanks to foreign credits (a relatively new factor in Communist politics) did the rest.

The disclosures made during the Solidarity period revealed the extent of the corruption in Poland and the way it was directly derived from the total interpenetration of Party and state apparatus. Sixteen members of the Central Committee had to be sacked and several ministers arrested, half the Party first secretaries and provincial chiefs (*wojewodstwa*) were removed and the line of corruption went (like most things in the Party) all the way down the chain of command to local officials and the industrial managers they were supposed to supervise. Some 3400 Party cadres were sanctioned for corruption in 1981. During the hearings of the Grabski Commission set up that year to investigate the causes of the Polish crisis, one of its members, Wronski, spoke of the emergence of a 'large bourgeoisie' in the country that was living 'above acceptable standards; and this in a socialist country ruled by the Communist Party! And there was another bourgeoisie too, of those with Party cards, and they too were living beyond their means.'

It would be naive, of course, to assume that bribery, nepotism and embezzlement of public funds in the ruling caste have simply disappeared in the wake of Gorbachev's anti-corruption rhetoric or because a general is in charge. It will take the next political upheaval to give the public once again the privilege of looking into the opaque practices of the nomenklatura.

In the meantime the Polish nomenklaturists seem to have done rather well under Jaruzelski. In the words of J. Winiecki:

After martial law the number of posts covered by the nomenklatura increased sharply to 250,000. To increase the number of posts filled on the basis of Party loyalty rather than competence, of course, casts a shadow on the real intentions for reform of the authorities. This is one way of saying that things have got worse. Another indication is the allocation of scarce foods. For instance, 40 per cent of the cars destined for the domestic market went through their nomenklatura system for the faithful, rather than through the market. And this is only one example among many.

The nomenklatura is the nearest thing to Orwell's 'inner-party'. Its monopoly of power cannot be challenged from without – not even (except in crisis situations) from within the Party itself. There are in fact two parties in one: the apparat, or hard core, and the rank and file. The total membership of the ruling Communist Parties represents less than 10 per cent of the population, but all power rests in the hands of the apparat, representing roughly 10 per cent of the Party membership. The dual party is the result of an apparent contradiction in Marx's views. He held that the dominant ideology in society is that of the ruling bourgeoisie; but at the same time the liberation of the workers will be the task of the workers themselves. This left the future of the revolution highly uncertain. Lenin solved the problem with his concept of the 'professional revolutionary': the Party is the vanguard of the workers and the apparat is the vanguard of the vanguard.

This division materialized in the very early days of the new regimes in East-Central Europe. In 1948, for instance, the Hungarian Party issued 106,859 Party cards to the hard-core activists (total Party membership, after the merger with the Social Democrats, stood at 1.1 million members). So it is not just that society is divided between Party members and the rest of the population, who are treated like second-class citizens, but that the Party itself is divided between members of the apparat and the rest enjoying, so to speak, second-class membership.

Why does the apparat bother to surround itself with a relatively powerless Party membership? The answer is that it blurs the dividing line between those who have power and the have-nots. The power of the apparat is legitimized in its own eyes by the support of the members who, in their various walks of life, see to it that decisions are implemented, and thus perform a control function in the society. In this sense, the Party is the instrument of the apparat.

The membership also provides a permanent reservoir of prospective officials. These are not elected but rather co-opted into the Party elite, as Hungarian writer Gaspar Miklos Tamas points out: 'They are hand-picked by the top, but slightly different people are picked now than before; not the enthusiasts, not the fanatics, but those people generally in factories who are seen as upwardly mobile, people who want to make a career and who did show some signs of loyalty in their work, in a factory Party cell, in the workers' militia or in another such organization.'

What is in it for the rank and file? Why do people join the Party in these days of ordinary, routine socialism, now that the great ideological promise has fizzled out? There are a variety of motivations. For most – especially for white-collar workers and the intelligentsia – it is the necessary prerequisite for a promotion in their field. The Party card is in effect a work permit. Others become members simply because they do not dare turn down an insistent offer. In most cases one is indeed asked to join the Party at the workplace: the head of the local Party organization needs to fill a quota and to turn him down might have unpleasant professional consequences. Some genuinely seek to gain even a limited role in local affairs. In exchange for a tiny portion of power (and the accompanying prestige that might be attached to it) the rank-and-file member acknowledges the absolute authority of the apparat. Krzysztof Pomian describes this as a tacit 'deal' between the apparat and the members in which the latter become 'accomplices': 'it allows them to satisfy their legitimate aspirations for social recognition and allows the apparat to turn them into a part of its support system of power, using them to subject the whole society to a surveillance which would otherwise be impossible to achieve.'

No wonder the 'deal' breeds cynicism and apathy. The Czechoslovak Party paper *Rudé Pravo* (24 August 1983) bitterly deplored this state of affairs: 'It is a serious matter that our Party members live in near-anonymity. They cannot be formally rebuked for this, because they pay their membership dues, regularly attend Party meetings, and take part in agit-prop sessions. However, they have nothing to say on serious matters under discussion, they never raise their hands, and they never speak their mind. They never oppose others, but they never fight for their Party.'

Karel Kaplan joined the Czechoslovak Communist Party at the end of the war in the town of Zlin (now called Gottwaldor) where, like the current Party leader Milos Jakes, he worked in the well-known Bata shoe factory. After 1948, he became a Party functionary, so he knows both the rank and file and the apparat.

'Most members react to their powerlessness with apathy,' writes Kaplan.

> This is the way they express distaste for carrying out policies in which they do not believe. They also know that they can play no role in the formation of policy or even influence policy in their own situations. Yet they do not want to break with the Party or are afraid to. Most Communists thus live at odds with themselves.

Political participation, a favourite topic of Western political scientists, exists only on the surface; it resembles the Olympic ideal of Baron de Coubertin, namely that the important thing is not to win (the elections) but to take part. Political life has been turned into a ritual punctuated by major non-events such as May Day, the anniversary of the Bolshevik revolution or a Party conference. This is because real power, real politics are confined to the top of the Party hierarchy.

The chief characteristic of the Communist political system is its extreme form of concentration of power. Total power is in the hands of the Party Politburo and the secretaries of the Central Committee – in all about twenty people. According to the theory of 'democratic centralism' the Party Congress elects a central committee which in turn chooses a praesidium. In practice it is exactly the other way around: the twenty 'strong men' from the Praesidium and the Secretariat select the Central Committee members to be formally approved by the Congress. The Congress delegates themselves are similarly selected under the supervision of the apparat. The Party is a pyramid where communication is only vertical (horizontal links are formally prohibited) and where decisions tend to be handed down from the top. The apparat is subordinated to the Secretariat and to the Party leader. Zdenek Mlynar is a former member of the Czechoslovak Party Politburo, from which he resigned in the aftermath of the Soviet-led invasion of August 1968. This is how today he described the extent of the concentration of power, unparalleled by any other type of regime:

> The Party apparat controls the whole state, the economy, the army, the judiciary, etc., without actually being accountable to anyone. Because it does not actually manage anything, only controls and appoints, it does not need any qualifications. And this makes it an apparat of pure power, which makes it possible for a small group at the top, which forms the Party Politburo, twelve people in fact, to be able, when they want, to decide, whenever they want, about anything and everything, about laws, international agreements, the economic plan, about hiring or firing someone from his job.

Soviet-style socialism failed to create the 'new man' its ideology promised, unless one counts the apparatchik. Based on his twenty years' experience in the Party machine, Karel Kaplan offers interesting insights into the apparatchik's mental world and way of life:

> Joining the power group means entering a different world – the world of powerholders, with their narrow set of interests, desires and range of conversation. They create their own lifestyle, different not only from that of ordinary people but also from the lifestyle of lower-level functionaries. They have their own morals, their own manner of discussion and manner of speech. Their lives are free of the burdens of ordinary everyday life. Their thinking, intentionally, tends to be as close as possible to the thoughts and desires of the number-one man in the state.

The personal lives of the officials at the central headquarters are supposed to be above suspicion. Family problems, drunkenness, etc., are, says Kaplan, considered 'political' and dealt with by a Party committee. What in Stalin's days used to apply to the whole population and in particular to all Party members (the abolition of the separation between public and private life) is now sustained only in the Party bunker. The Central Committee Secretariat has become the ultimate depository of 'real socialism':

> Apparatchiks who work in the Secretariat look after their own interests and satisfy their appetites for power. This world is, however, completely different from its surroundings – the real world. It defies comparison with the everyday life of ordinary citizens. Here the voice of social reality sounds muffled and

distant. There is no interest in sounds that clash with the mentality of the majority of the apparatchiks in the Secretariat. They are repressed and silenced. Most significant, perhaps, is the fact that these apparatchiks think that their world mirrors society as a whole; that their opinions, interests, and wishes reflect those of the Party and citizenry.

The reluctance to leave the Party (especially in the more tightly run regimes in Czechoslovakia, East Germany or Romania) is often based on much the same reasons as the eagerness to join it in the first place: careerism and a certain protection from the political repression to which the rest of the population is subjected. The only category of the population that does not have to play this game for professional reasons are the workers, for you cannot be demoted from the working class. But there too, as even a brief visit to the Party cell at the salami factory in the Hungarian city of Szeged reveals, Party life gives an impression of apathy and excruciating boredom. Imre Bokray has just been invited to join the Party. 'No,' he says, 'you don't need any special characteristics to become a Party member; you must above all be a good worker, and know the Party's work well.' Was his joining likely to alter his relationship with fellow salami workers? 'There should be no difference in my relationship with my fellow workers because I have joined the Party. The most important role of a Party member within the factory is to do his best in his productive work, and to be able to influence his fellow workers in a suitable, positive direction.' While Imre Bokray is joining the Party, with what seem to be limited ideological interests beyond the idea of becoming a 'model worker', Istvan Tilinko has just left that same Party organization because of, among other things, what he describes as a too low boredom threshold:

> Party meetings cannot be described as interesting. The meetings are altogether monotonous, devoted just to one topic, the economic situation. When they hold Party conferences, then they bring it up, the same thing that was already adopted at a higher level of the Party or in the Ministry; they more or less repeat the same thing that people hear on TV or on the radio. They always go on about the state of the economy; that's all. Some people take a nap. . . .

Boring or not, the Party is particularly anxious, for ideological reasons, to keep a high proportion of workers among the rank and file (corresponding partly to their proportion in the population and partly to the political orthodoxy of the Party). In Czechoslovakia, the post-1968 purge of the Party was accompanied by a massive reproletarianization of the Party membership (nearly half of the members are allegedly workers). In Kadar's Hungary, where the emphasis was on winning the new white-collar class, the workers represent less than a third of the membership. One may, of course, question the meaning of such statistics. On the eve of the birth of Solidarity in 1980 the Polish Party proudly announced that 45 per cent of its three million members were workers. Within months of the announcement the Party faced a general strike in which the overwhelming majority of its working-class members joined the new Solidarity trade union. When the crunch came, formal membership brought less than formal support.

The ruling Parties of the Other Europe have always oscillated between the concept of 'Leninist' vanguard party and the mass party model. In the immediate aftermath of a crisis, they claim to be the misunderstood vanguard. This was the case after 1956 in Hungary, 1968 in Czechoslovakia and 1981 in Poland. Later, when the self-confidence (or simply confusion) has returned, a new recruitment drive is launched. In Poland, following the workers' riots of December 1970, the Party lost 110,000 members, leaving just over two million. By 1975 the figure was 2.3 million, after which the Party recruitment machine went wild: by January 1980 membership topped the 3-million mark to reach 3,160,000 in June, only weeks before the collapse. This works out to an impressive average of 13,000 new members a month over the last five years of the Gierek leadership. Clearly, the Gierek regime lived not just on inflation and borrowed money; it also lived on inflated membership figures and borrowed legitimacy.

The most striking feature of the membership boom of the Gierek years in Poland was its extremely high turnover. While a million and a half new members joined in the 1970s, half a million members (mainly workers) left the Party. This suggests that, at least in some of the Soviet bloc countries, to leave the Party (as opposed to being expelled) is no big deal any more. Poland, as always, merely magnified a more general trend. Between 1970 and 1975 the Hungarian Party recruited 200,000 new members, a quarter of the total membership. The idea behind the recruitment drive was a sort of 'salami tactic' in reverse: to win, 'slice by slice' (to use Rakosi's formula), different sections of society for the Kadarist compromise. It seemed to work in the 1970s but it no longer does. Between 1975 and 1985 41,000 members left the Party (another 15,000 were expelled and 35,000 removed for minor offences). The Party paper *Magyaroszag* announced in April 1988 that 46,000 people (5 per cent of the total) had not 'renewed their cards' that winter.

The acceleration of membership turnover has in a way trivialized the image of the Party and deflated the Communist mystique. It has become the common feature of the decay of ruling Communist Parties in East-Central Europe. The most dramatic cases are, of course, the major political crises. In 1956 the Hungarian Communist Party collapsed during the October revolution, with membership of the new post-revolutionary Party climbing back up to around 80,000, a mere 10 per cent of the old membership. In post-1968 Czechoslovakia the Party was purged of half a million members. In Poland, thanks to the combined effects of Solidarity and martial law, the Party lost one million members in 1981. If we add to this the scale of the Party purges of the Stalinist era we come to the conclusion that roughly every third adult in Central Europe has been, at one point or another, a member of the Communist Party. The Party is in fact a large 'sieve' through which considerable sections of society (and not just idealistic intellectuals or careerist technocrats) have at various stages passed. This, to be sure, lends a special nuance to the 'them and us' image that these societies have of their relationship with the state. The largest party in Central Europe today is the party of the former Communists; expelled or drop-outs, merely disillusioned or overtly hostile, they are the reminder of the failure of the socialist dream.

Variations on a Theme: Nationalism and Decay

After more than forty years the power of the nomenklatura is still the basis of Party rule in most of the Soviet bloc. Yet, over the years, it has become less effective and, at the same time, has undergone a process of diversification from country to country. The collapse of Communist ideology as a source of legitimacy leads most parties to seek nationalist substitutes, while the economic and social decay of the system provokes a variety of responses from the ruling Party: greater emphasis on total control in East Germany, Czechoslovakia and Romania, and a tendency to relinquish some control in Poland and Hungary. What is too often presented as a debate between reformers and conservatives in the Gorbachev era concerns essentially different assessments of the balance between viability and control, reflecting degrees of decay and retreat.

It is not easy to speak about a vanishing subject. How can one reconcile the apparent contradictions inherent in East-Central European Communism at the end of the 1980s? Ideology is all-pervasive yet, as a means of communication between the powers that be and society, completely bankrupt. One answer is to see Communist ideology no longer in terms of its intellectual merits or historical connections with the European socialist tradition, but essentially as an instrument of power.

Intellectual sterility does not mean that the ideology has become dispensable as the prime source of legitimacy of Communist rule. What, historically, distinguishes the Communist regimes from other, often more brutal, dictatorships is precisely their ideological claim. Not only did the Party tell you what to do, it told you what to think. And the Party paper was always there to make sure that everybody knew what the official version of truth was at a given point in time. This Stalinist concept of ideology as a secular religion began to crumble in 1956 when it became clear that Stalin and his faithful disciples in the Soviet bloc merely used ideology to justify the unjustifiable: sending alleged class enemies to labour camps and sometimes Party comrades to the gallows, or invading a neighbouring country simply because it had a different view of socialism.

Today, there are many practitioners but few real believers in the Communist Church, and the Communist Party has learned over the years that nobody really believes in its ideology any more. Yet it cannot afford to drop its ideological claim altogether, because ultimately that is the regime's only source of legitimacy. The Communists have some difficulty asserting their right to rule in the name of the nations' past and they certainly cannot claim a democratic mandate for the present. So they have to cling to ideological legitimacy as an imaginary mandate from the Communist future. Now this may not be very convincing for the peoples of Central Europe, but it remains vital for the internal cohesion of the Party, for its sense of purpose. To abandon ideology would be admitting bankruptcy and would demoralize the entire Party down to the last secret policeman.

Thus ideology remains in place as a ritual and as an instrument of social control. Instead of the 'end of ideology' it might be more appropriate to speak of the exhaustion of the utopian and mobilizing dimensions of Communist ideology. These had survived the Stalinist era: Khrushchev in 1961 still planned not only to 'catch up and overtake' the capitalist West, but to achieve the Communist paradise by 1980! In some ways Dubček's 'socialism with a human face' was the last attempt to rejuvenate Communism in Central Europe within that utopian ideological framework.

The post-1968 period was marked by the return from utopia to the realities of Communist power. Hence the concept of 'real' or 'developed' socialism emerged, and the Communist future fades away from the ideological horizon. Real socialism is not the projection of a new society, but merely a preparatory stage. As Czech philosopher Lubos Sochor put it: 'reality itself becomes the projection'.

This deflation of ideology has a double advantage over the utopianism of the past. It conveniently removes the possibility of questioning policies in the name of ideals. The lack of illusions also presumably spares the pain of disillusionment, which had been one of the main factors in the 'revisionist' pressure for change in the de-Stalinization era. The concept of 'real' or 'really existing' socialism, rehashed *ad nauseam* by Soviet bloc ideologists as a response to the Prague Spring and later to Eurocommunism, came to mean both the only existing and the only genuine kind of socialism.

Within the context of Marxist theory the concept of 'real' socialism is a dubious one; it is rather reminiscent of the well-known Hegelian formula: 'What is rational is real; what is real is rational.' The Soviet bloc ideologists of the 1970s and 1980s seem to be saying: 'What is socialist is real; and what is real is socialist.' From the exhaustion of utopia to the preservation of the status quo, 'real' socialism is the ideological monument to the deep-seated conservatism of the ruling nomenklatura.

Though necessary to sustain the cohesiveness of the Party, even revised and now, under Gorbachev, updated versions of the ideology are of little use in dealing with society as a whole. Hence the search in recent years to fill the ideological vacuum with substitute sources of legitimacy: economic modernization on the one hand, and nationalism on the other. The former means that the Party leaves aside the Communist utopia and claims to be the sole force capable of bringing these (with the exception of East Germany and Czechoslovakia) less developed countries into the age of industrial modernity. The most explicit proponents of this shift were Gierek in Poland and Kadar in Hungary, but most of the other parties followed in the same footsteps. Political discourse since the 1970s has been reduced to economic performance accompanied by (in the early stages) promises of improved living standards. Today's reformist *perestroika* is a variation on this theme.

However, with economic recession and the exhaustion of foreign credits, economic legitimacy too became a spent force. So the parties reached into the bottomless reservoir of East-Central European nationalism. After the 'radiant future' and the modernization of the present this was a leap into the past in search of what has been the dominant political ideology since the nineteenth century and, of course, the prime rival of socialist internationalism. In contrast to the staleness of the rhetoric of 'real' (sometimes 'surreal') socialism, nationalism seemed the most mobilizing of available ideologies.

This is not to be confused with the brief and, in most cases, not very convincing attempt by the Communist Parties at the end of the war to present themselves as the descendants of the progressive or revolutionary traditions of their nations. The current reappropriation of nationalism by the Communist apparat usually concerns the most authoritarian (right-wing) and ethnic brands of nationalism.

In this respect it goes beyond 'national Communism' as it emerged first in the Balkans. The Balkan model was essentially an attempt by a Communist apparat to gain a degree of autonomy from Moscow while maintaining – even strengthening – internal orthodoxy. This was initially the case in Yugoslavia after 1948 (liberalization started only much later). Enver Hoxha's Albania after the break with Moscow in 1961 was turned into ultra-Stalinist autarchy; since the mid-1960s a similar pattern has emerged in Ceausescu's Romania. Interestingly, these countries were economically the most backward in the socialist camp and, from Moscow's point of view, strategically less important than Central Europe.

The last decade has seen less emphasis on the alleged independence of a Communist apparat from the Soviet overlord (the limits of that are known to all in Central Europe), and a growing reliance on attempts to tap the brand of nationalism where the apparat hopes to find the most popular support. Here, authoritarian nationalism (often connected with pre-war traditions) and ethnic nationalism come into play. General Jaruzelski, after first trying to imitate Pilsudski, now courts the 'realist' nationalists by catering to the tradition of the pre-war National Democracy movement of Roman Dmowski. Ceausescu flirts on and off with the fascist ideology of the Iron Guard. The same tendency can be seen, in a more benign form, in the East German Party's reconciliation with Prussian authoritarianism.

The exploitation of ethnic nationalism within Communist Party-states has become even more explicit, whether it is turned inward (discrimination against national minorities, anti-Semitism) or directed outwards (against a neighbouring Communist state). Extreme anti-minority policies currently affect the Hungarians living in Romania and the Turks in Bulgaria. In Czechoslovakia Husak used the Slovak card to gain a modicum of support for his policy of normalization, or at least as a divide-and-rule tactic. In retrospect the anti-Semitic campaign launched by the Polish Party after the events of March 1968 was perhaps the first major and most blatant antecedent.

Poland: After the Party in Uniform

On 13 December 1981, General Jaruzelski went on Polish television to announce martial law and the crushing of Solidarity. He did not once mention the Polish Party of which he was the head. Claiming to speak as a military man, he put forward the idea that the army and the Church should replace the Party and Solidarity, which were locked in a suicidal confrontation as the representatives of state and society. What the subsequent months and years have shown is that Jaruzelski was merely the Party in uniform rescuing a fast-disintegrating Polish United Workers' Party which by then was not very united and certainly no spokesman for the workers.

The Polish military takeover had all the standard ingredients of a military coup (draconian martial law, mass internments, the seizure of the communication networks) except one: it was aimed not at overthrowing the existing civilian power (the Communist Party) but rather at liquidating the main force that had challenged the Party's political monopoly of power. In effect, the Polish Army stepped in to fill a political vacuum left by the vanishing authority of its own Party. That collapse was rooted in the deep and chronic social and political crisis which culminated in the summer of 1980 with the defiance of the Party by the entire working class in whose name it claimed to rule. The speed with which the Party's authority collapsed was proportional to the rapid emergence of Solidarity as an independent social movement and the genuine voice for popular aspirations. The 'withering away' not of the state (as Lenin predicted in 1917) but of the leading role of the Party within it has been a central feature – though obviously with varying degrees of intensity – in all the major post-war crises in Central Europe. In 1956, 1968, 1981, the dual nature of the ruling Party was brought out into the open: there was the mass Party which was disintegrating and the apparat, with its key security component, which did not collapse. Thus in Poland, while the rank-and-file members were, under the impact of Solidarity, leaving the Party or trying to democratize it from within, the hard core stayed put and waited. As we now know from Colonel Kuklinski (a close associate of Jaruzelski who defected to the West), on the very day Solidarity was born plans for martial law got under way. Everything was prepared long in advance for the moment when, in the words of hardliner Marian Orzechowski, 'the force of arguments would be replaced by the arguments of force'. The only problem was who would actually take the decision and when. And that depended on Moscow's limited patience and the internal struggle within the Polish leadership.

Several months before the coup, the Polish government organs had been undergoing a process of creeping militarization. Army generals assumed key government posts and military squads were despatched to some two thousand towns and villages to prop up faltering local administrations. These actions were clearly part of a dress rehearsal for the military takeover. After the coup, the Military Council announced that it would exercise power through 'departmental, provincial, municipal and parish military plenipotentiaries'. Other military plenipotentiaries had been despatched to government ministries, provinces, towns and even factories, to ensure what was described as the 'normalization of social and economic life'. They were mainly high-ranking officers (colonels or generals) who had the right to remove governors (*wojewodas*), plant managers or other officials. It seems that the military also played a significant part in the purge of the Party after 13 December.

The fact that the Party's military–security apparatus retained its cohesion and ability to act in a crisis marked by the collapse of most institutions has far-reaching significance. It is a precedent that points to the primarily domestic function of the armies of the Warsaw Pact allies of the Soviet Union. If the current decay of the system continues, the militarization of Communism might prove an attractive option for others as well. Tomorrow it might be used in Romania or in Yugoslavia.

The rise of the Party in uniform was significant in yet another way. In the face of the demise of Communist ideology as the source of its legitimacy, the Party tried to draw on nationalism as a surrogate rallying force. Though Jaruzelski paid lip-service to Party ideology, his main concern was to exploit traditional popular pride in the army as the embodiment of patriotic values and 'law and order'. The political expression of this was supposed to be PRON, the Patriotic Movement of National Revival. As the late Polish writer Konstanti (Kot) Jelenski remarked: 'There is a limit to how many times you can use the word "nation" in an acronym; but if they had thought it possible to use it five times, they would have tried to.'

A 1981 opinion poll asked which institutions the public had greatest confidence in. The Catholic Church came in first, followed by Solidarity. The army came in a good third, far ahead of the Party. Hence the idea of an ideological transfusion from the army to the Party. Hence also Jaruzelski's efforts to present himself as the new

Pilsudski. The good standing which the Polish Army enjoys in the eyes of Polish society predates Communism. For historical reasons the very concept of civil war was alien to the Poles and the army was always perceived as an integral part of the nation. Marshal Pilsudski's name remains associated with Polish independence from Germany and Russia but also with his political role in the pre-war republic. In 1926, Pilsudski staged a coup 'to put the house in order' after a period of unrest and parliamentary chaos. And this is indeed the 'Bonapartist' image that General Jaruzelski wanted to capture for himself and the Party in uniform. In what Marx might have called the '18th Brumaire of General Jaruzelski', the army presented itself as the arbiter between an incompetent (and corrupt) Party bureaucracy and the old demons of anarchy allegedly represented by Solidarity.

This argument could not really be sustained by the arrest of a few corrupt Party officials while five thousand Solidarity activists were being interned in what is suitably called 'Hell Peninsula'. Although Jaruzelski himself might have preferred his coup to be compared to the 1926 Pilsudski model, rather than to the suppression of the Hungarian revolt of 1956 or of the Prague Spring of 1968, the attempt failed as soon as the first workers were shot at Gdansk and at the Wujek mine. Thus, given the limited credibility of the 'civil war' argument, Jaruzelski used, more effectively, the 'lesser evil' argument, still repeated today by his assistant Major Gornicki to justify the rise of the Party in uniform:

> This is a necessity. When the stakes are so high, you have to choose the lesser evil. This is precisely the word the general used while proclaiming martial law, and I don't think there was another way out, except a much more harmful and dangerous one.

In other words, the Polish Army intervened only to preempt intervention by the Soviet Army. On this, opinions are divided between those, like the then West German Chancellor Helmut Schmidt, who believe that Jaruzelski is first of all a Pole and a military man and only then a Communist, and those who think he is first of all a Communist, then a military man who happens to be a Pole. The idea that Jaruzelski saved Poland from itself is dismissed by Solidarity as a pseudo-patriotic varnish on the destruction of a social movement which needed no lessons in patriotism. If anything, says Solidarity, this is a case of mistaken identity: the coup saved the Party from society rather than Poland from 'you know whom'.

However, although the Party in uniform (including Jaruzelski himself) now prefers to return to civilian clothes, it cannot restore the old ideology. It is now stuck with its nationalist prop. The Polish Party thus represents more clearly than any other the various stages of the erosion of official ideology: the transition, under Gierek, from the Marxist promises of the past towards economic legitimacy based on modernization and the improvement of living standards; and the transition, under Jaruzelski, towards realpolitik nationalism.

Ironically, the fact that Jaruzelski's leadership, installed by a military coup, is by definition authoritarian does not mean it is conservative. Indeed, the Party in uniform ignored the old hardliners (such as Olszowski or Grabski) in favour of a more pragmatic wing which claimed that the restoration of social stability was the pre-condition for the introduction of reform, and that the crushing of Solidarity could still lead to some form of Party-controlled dialogue with society. The scale of the economic disaster and pressure from the opposition and the Church have now led the Party to re-examine more realistically its concept of its leading role.

Mieczyslaw Rakowski is perhaps the best-known spokesman for this line. After twenty-five years as the editor of the weekly *Polityka*, Rakowski earned the reputation of a reformer. Though today, after his close association with General Jaruzelski during martial law, he is more popular with the Western media than with the Warsaw intelligentsia, his return to the Politburo in 1987 has been heralded as the true advent of Polish-style Gorbachevism.

The Party itself, according to Rakowski, should be at once stronger and more realistic in order to push through its package of economic and institutional reforms. Internal cohesion or 'unity' is, in the Leninist vocabulary, the prerequisite for a degree of self-limitation. 'There is no doubt', Rakowski says, 'that democracy was limited in our country, and in the whole socialist bloc, for forty years. But now at the end of the 1980s we are facing a new generation which grew up after the war. It has totally different experiences from my generation, which I call the war generation. And this is why we have to make the next step towards democratization now.' So should one conclude that forty years of one-party rule have made the country ripe for more democracy? Not quite; both sides have simply been forced to tone down their ambitions. The new generation, indeed society as a whole, is completely oblivious to official ideology: 'It is ready to accept socialism on one condition, that there are no more gaps between words and facts.' The basic assumption is that the Communists are here to stay because of the Soviet factor. Provided the proper conclusions are drawn from this, the message goes, the Party would be prepared to admit defeat in certain spheres (such as the management of the economy or ideological control) and give up its claim to be the sole representative of 'the moral and political unity of the Polish nation'.

In recent years, the authorities have tried to launch a series of consultative bodies (starting with the Patriotic Movement of National Revival and ending with the Consultative Council) intended to give some representation to society, but they had little credibility and produced few tangible results. The failure led to the implicit suggestion by Rakowski and others that the overtures, to become plausible, would have to go further. Initially, Rakowski thought he could get away with concessions to the Church and to the 'national realists' associated with the pre-war tradition of the National-Democracy movement. But the strikes of August 1988 brought Solidarity back to the centre of the Polish political scene. It marked an unexpected reversal of the situation even for the opposition which, while remaining attached to Solidarity as a symbol, was undergoing a process of decline and fragmentation. In order to defuse the strikes and mainly in order to buy an insurance policy for the future, the Jaruzelski regime was brought to accept the return of Walesa's Solidarity which they had tried to destroy. Imagine that: Generals Jaruzelski and Kiszczak in a dialogue with Kuron and Michnik, the very people they had put in jail after the military coup of 1981. However, such concessions to the pressures of society in a context of economic disaster should not be confused with Hungarian-style reformism. In November 1988 Rakowski still claimed that the re-legalization of Solidarity was out of the question. In January 1989 he admitted dialogue with Solidarity provided it parted with the leaders and the ideas which had kept it alive under martial law. In March he negotiated without conditions. This is not reform, but a debacle by any other name.

Even though Jaruzelski's motives are purely tactical ones (make Solidarity share responsibility for the necessary introduction of drastic economic policies), it is difficult to over-estimate the political significance of the concessions made: for the first time since the war the political monopoly of power by the Communist Party has been broken, thus opening a period of transition in which democratic forces can resurface as legitimate political actors. By the same token the simple dichotomies of the past (state versus society) are being altered: new divides appear in both camps. Jaruzelski has had to impose his compromise with Solidarity on the Party hardliners, while Walesa faces opposition by his grass-roots radicals who fear a 'sell-out'.

The Polish Party makes such concessions as a means of staying in power. Yet it remains unclear which way the new political system will evolve. Some, like Bronislaw Geremek, who led the round-table negotiations with the authorities, believe that the June elections are the first step in a gradual and peaceful transition to democracy. Others see the possibility of an evolution from totalitarianism towards a more benign form of 'ordinary authoritarianism' which could turn out to be a transitory phase towards democracy. Communist rule as we knew it has ended, but no one can predict with confidence what even the near future has in store. Poland, as often in the past, remains the laboratory for political change for the whole of the Other Europe.

Romania's Dynastic Communism

Why was 25 January 1988 'a most significant moment for the entire Romanian nation'? Because 'the great hero among the heroes of the nation, the architect of modern socialist Romania' had turned seventy. This was not the latest Romanian joke, but the birthday message of the Central Committee of the Romanian Communist Party to its leader. Actually, leader is too weak a word. The proper term is *Conducator* best translated as Guide, *Führer* in German or *Vozhd* in Russian. Perhaps the most accurate translation, one that best conveys the tragicomical character of the man and the grotesque pomposity of the occasion, would be *Duce*. 'The greatest son of the Romanian people' received (or rather awarded himself) several new honours, including, for the fourth time, Hero of the Socialist Republic of Romania. Only President Nicolae Ceausescu and his wife Elena are holders of that award, an illustration of their special place at the top of the Romanian Party; others have to content themselves with being more mundane Heroes of Socialist Labour or of the New Agricultural Revolution. In addition to the national commendations Ceausescu reaped on his birthday, the Order of Lenin arrived from Moscow, the Order of the White Lion from Prague and, appropriately, the Karl Marx Order sent by the East German Party. As if this were not enough, the Party journal *Lumea* published an imaginary birthday message from Queen Elizabeth II praising Ceausescu's 'widely recognized excellence, experience and influence'. As it turned out, the 'message' was taken from the Queen's toast at a state banquet in Buckingham Palace, during Ceausescu's visit to Britain in 1978. This little manoeuvre shows just how desperate Communist dictators can be for international recognition, as well as the extent to which Western enthusiasm for Romania's allegedly maverick caudillo has diminished over the last decade.

Romanian political life is now reduced to orchestrated celebrations of the merits and achievements of the 'helmsman of national destiny'. Party conferences and the anniversary of the National Liberation of 23 August are merely occasions for measuring the 'leading role' of the Party in terms of displays of devotion to a megalomaniac who personally selects the slogans to be chanted when he comes on stage. Five minutes before the opening of the gala performance for/by the presidential couple, the five thousand people who have been officially invited and duly screened at the entrance fall into total silence; they hold their breath as the atmosphere becomes oppressive, almost unbearable (at least to those not familiar with this kind of group therapy). Then, suddenly, they explode in a frenetic standing ovation as 'He' enters the presidential box. Once you recover from the shock of the thunderous applause and rhythmic chanting of 'Ceausescu– PCR' (which stands for both Romanian Communist Party and Partidul–Ceausescu–Romania), there is a moment of disappointment: you expected the *Duce*, or at least a tall, imposing figure *à la* de Gaulle; instead what appears is a midget of a man, undistinguished, grimacing unpleasantly to a crowd which takes it as an encouragement to step up its welcome.

The 'genius of the Carpathians' may have been a bit of a letdown, but the grandiose show that follows makes up for it. Even if you have seen all the documentaries from the 1950s, read learned articles about the totalitarian ritual, this is the nearest one comes nowadays to the 'real thing', the perfection of Stalinist kitsch. The speech to the *Conducator*'s glory is interrupted at regular (two-minute) intervals with a standing ovation not for the speaker (the audience actually turn their backs on him) but for 'Him'. Then a choir of young pioneers picks up from there:

> Vibrant is in us our ardent love
> and our hearts are filled with songs
> What we are, we owe it to the Party
> And the Party made us masters of all that is
> Under the banner of red truth
> The country is united
> Facing the future
> Let's march forward cheerfully
> Let's march forward with the Party of
> Our beloved *Conducator*

A mauve light introduces a leading actress who reads eulogies and poems inspired by you know whom:

We have to be grateful for the providential existence of this man, so deeply attached to our ancestral soil, we have to be grateful for his eternal youth, we have to be grateful for being his contemporaries and thank him for all this. It is only through his willingness that we are really masters in the house of our souls.

The phrase 'eternal youth' immediately acquires real meaning as you see 'Him' on a giant screen, looking twenty years younger, visiting a steel mill or lecturing the peasants on a collective farm on the merits of chemical fertilizers. Elena Ceausescu is never far behind, modestly described as 'the most eminent personality of everyday and international scientific life'. Meanwhile the stage is invaded by men in blue overalls and women in white doctor's coats (supposedly representing the workers and professional classes), who chant something to the effect that they make up the social base of the regime. At the climax of the three-hour show, they are joined on stage by folk dancers from the various provinces of Romania. The whole society, the whole nation, demonstrates loyalty and gratitude to the Party and to 'Him'.

Romanians always refer to 'Him'; even in private they avoid mentioning his name. Just in case 'They' overhear. 'They' stand for the omnipresent and much feared *Securitate*, the secret police. Ceausescu's wife is called simply Elena. So with 'Him', 'Them' and 'Elena' you have all you need to know about contemporary Romanian politics.

The Romanian Party has been confiscated *de facto* by the Ceausescu clan. Ceausescu became Party chief in 1965, Elena Ceausescu was promoted to the Party leadership in 1972. Long in charge of Ideology (a Romanian imitation of the Chinese Cultural Revolution), she is now directly in charge of personnel appointments in the Secretariat of the Romanian Party. Thus the Ceausescus were able to consolidate their power by eliminating all those who did not owe their position to their clan. Another technique is the quasi-permanent reshuffle of government and Party officials designed to prevent anybody from staying long enough in office to build a power base which could be used, one day, to challenge the presidential couple. Ceausescu's narcissistic and nepotistic rule means job insecurity for the nomenklatura. His son Nicu, thirty-eight, is a member of the leadership, and some fifty close or more distant relatives hold key posts in the Romanian nomenklatura. But that is not enough. To ensure that his personality cult continues after his death, the ageing leader has extended the cult to his family and appointed Nicu to the Party executive and, in October 1987, as head of the Party in the important province of Sibiu. This post is intended to provide an adequate power base and training ground for when succession time comes. In the name of the father...

The Ceausescu regime is without doubt the most repressive in the Soviet bloc today. Its appalling human-rights record has led to the loss of support even from the West, including United States suspension of Romania's Most Favoured Nation (MFN) trading status. Though enjoying a number of material privileges, Party officials themselves fear the whims of the presidential couple. A document written by an official from the Hungarian minority in Transylvania and recently published in Hungarian *samizdat* describes the situation as follows:

> The presidential couple decides personally in which apartment [senior officials] can live; when, for how long, where they will spend their holidays. It might seem unbelievable, but it is so. All the systems in the world are based on reward and punishment. Ceausescu works only with punishment. It is a reward that there is no punishment.

One of the perennial problems of Communist politics is that too much power is concentrated in too few hands. In Romania the hands happen to belong to the Ceausescu family. Since the deaths of Stalin and Mao no Communist leader has indulged in such an overriding personality cult as the *Conducator*, with the possible exception of North Korea's Kim Il Sung. His dictatorial regime too rests on a most curious mixture of Marxism–Leninism and virulent nationalism. On one level, 'Ceausescu' looks like a sequel to the Stalinist era. Vladimir Tismeanu speaks of a combination of Stalinism with the Byzantine tradition, the personality cult as 'the main institution which guarantees political and symbolic reproduction of the system'. But in many ways the extravagance and the ruthlessness of Romania's ruling family seems closer to the most extreme Third World dictatorships, such as that of Idi Amin or Emperor Bokassa. When he finally does go, there will be a sigh of relief, even – or especially – among those who, year after year, are brought in to cheer him.

'He is Romania. We are his sons.' This statement from the Party press provides a clue to the connection between the personality cult and the other key feature of Romanian Communism, its virulent nationalism. The origins go back to the 1960s, when the Romanian leadership resisted Soviet economic policies. But the real launch came in August 1968, at the time of the Soviet-led invasion of Czechoslovakia, when Ceausescu made his famous speech defying the Soviet Union. This was the first overt effort to channel popular nationalist feelings in support of the Romanian Party. But even then it was clear that Ceausescu was not defending Dubček's demo-cratization programme, but merely claiming the right to autonomy for each Party. As it turned out, he meant autonomy to extend the Party's absolute power as far as possible.

The historical irony is that of all the Soviet bloc parties the Romanian has the least indigenous roots. It counted less than a thousand members when it was brought to power by Russian tanks in 1944. Today its ideology is adamantly nationalistic. This naturally posed a few problems, but nothing that the properly guided rewriting of history could not handle, provided it assimilated the basic principle that nationalism is the love of the fatherland, and the Party is the modern embodiment of the nation. History thus became a centrepiece of Party propaganda.

First came the anti-Russian component in the form of various discussions (in those days still quoting Marx) regarding the province of Bessarabia, which was annexed by Russia in 1877, included in Romania in 1918, and retaken by the Soviets during the Second World War. The next step was to downplay the Russian role in securing Romanian independence as a result of the Russo-Turkish war of 1877. Finally there is the extraordinary claim that the liberation of the country and the anti-German coup of August 1944 was the work of the Romanian Party (under the influence of the then unknown Ceausescu), virtually without Soviet help. Romanian films even show how the Romanian Army (which incidentally fought bravely alongside the Germans on the Eastern Front) single-handedly liberated the country and then proceeded to liberate Hungary.

Relations with Hungary provide another focus for Romanian nationalism. The main bone of contention is Transylvania, where nearly two million Hungarians are deprived of basic minority rights, especially in cultural life. The region has been part of Romania since 1918. For most of its previous history it was part of Hungarian civilization (even though Hungarians have always been a minority there). This at least is the claim of the three-volume *History of Transylvania* published in Budapest in 1986 by the Hungarian Academy of Sciences under the editorship of the Minister of Culture, Béla Kopeczi. The study provoked merely the latest in a long series of polemics between the two countries in which Romanian historians are obliged to substantiate the Party's nationalist claims. Thus, in April 1987, *The Times* of London carried a full-page Romanian advertisement denouncing the Hungarian work as 'A Conscious Forgery under the Aegis of the Hungarian Academy of Sciences' –

the history of Transylvania presented as a history of Hungarian conquest.

The battle for Transylvania centres on the question of who was there first. The Hungarian *History* states baldly that 'before the beginning of the thirteenth century, there is no evidence – historical, archaeological, toponymic – for the existence of a Romanian population in Transylvania.' According to the Hungarians, the original population of Transylvania was Slavic (Russian, Bulgarian), not Latin as the Romanians maintain.

The official view from Bucharest is that the Romanian nation had already formed long before the Slavs reached this territory. The superiority of their civilization led naturally to the assimilation of other (Slavic or German) populations. The ultimate exercise in ethnogenesis is the theory of the Dacian origins of the Romanian nation put forward on the instructions of the Party in the 1980s. While in the 1970s the official version had been satisfied with the influence of the Latin legacy on the shaping of early Romanian history, in the 1980s the Party set out on an unending quest for Romania's mythical Dacian beginnings, long before the Roman conquest in the second century. Despite their defeat, the Daco-Romanians were revealed to have been the equals of – and in many ways superior to – the Romans. Much as the Albanians claim to descend from the Illyrians or the Bulgarians from the Thracians, the Romanians go back to the Dacians. Bombastic articles about the 'Dacian Empire' or the 'Dacian Imperial Millennium' started to appear, reaching new heights of absurdity. A Romanian singer who had lost her voice and turned to the study of Dacian culture discovered, among other things, that the Dacians must have been familiar with acupuncture.

In 1980 the Romanian Communist Party celebrated the 2050th anniversary of the 'first centralized independent Dacian state'. In case 'centralized' and 'independent' reminded the reader of something, 'it is not by chance,' as the Marxists say. After a brief liberalization at the end of the 1960s all the institutes of historical research were directly subordinated to the Academy, and directly to Elena Ceausescu. Thus, for the first time, history appeared in the Party programme at the Ninth Congress of the Romanian Communist Party in 1975. Who said that under Communism the future is known and that the most difficult thing to predict is the past?

At a meeting of its Political Executive Committee in May 1986, the Party decided to commemorate the 600th anniversary of Prince Mircea the Old's accession to the Wallachian throne. The Prince, no longer to be called 'the Old' but rather 'the Great', was 'among the great European rulers' of his time, whose political and diplomatic achievements supposedly lend themselves to parallels with today's Romania. At his presidential inauguration in 1974, Ceausescu was presented with a sceptre giving the first monarchic touch to his 'Communism in one family'. Articles then appeared comparing him to Julius Caesar or to Napoleon (quite a change from Lenin, the model of the past). Lately Party instructions are to go more native. So Ceausescu is now presented as the latest in a long, prestigious line of national heroes. This is sometimes easier to achieve through the agency of inspired poets than by historians. Victor Tulbure, in the weekly *Contemporaneul,* praised the spiritual affiliation of Ceausescu with (in order of appearance) Horea, the leader of a peasant uprising in Transylvania at the end of the eighteenth century, with the fifteenth-century Prince of Moldavia Stephen the Great, with Nicolae Balcescu, a prominent figure in the revolution of 1848, with Prince Cantemir, a political thinker of the early eighteenth century, with Mihail Eminescu, Romania's national poet in the second half of the nineteenth century, and with Prince Michael the Brave who, at the end of the sixteenth century, first unified the principalities of Wallachia, Moldavia and Transylvania:

> He [Ceausescu] descends from Horea's bones, from
> Stefan's breath
> From Balcescu's light, and from Cantemir's thought
> He is a dream out of Eminescu's dreams, and he descends
> from Michael who
> wanted a sole abode for his people under eternal stars.

Thus do Ceausescu and his Party claim to rule in the name of two thousand years of Romanian history. In a curious blend of Communist dogma and nationalism, they have gradually tried to reclaim or absorb everything nationalistic and authoritarian. The latest development is the rapprochement with the ideology of the pre-war Romanian extreme right, with General Antonescu (who also called himself *Conducator*) and the Iron Guard. They converge in their traditionalist nationalism (what the late Romanian philosopher Constantin Noica called in a famous essay 'The Romanian feeling of being') and in their radically anti-Western, anti-liberal stance. A novel by Constantin Toiu, published in Bucharest in 1987, entitled *The Fall in the World* is one of many illustrations of this trend. It is the story of the reconciliation of two men, one an ideologically motivated Communist, and the other, a no less idealistic follower of the Iron Guard who dies in 1939. The message is that there is little doubt where the latter's 'heart and mind' would be if he had had the luck to live in Ceausescu's Romania.

Ceausescu's attempt to co-opt in support of his dictatorial rule some of the more unpleasant traditions of Romanian nationalism is by far the most blatant in the Soviet bloc. Like most such attempts it is a surrogate and a fraud.

In true totalitarian fashion, at the same time as Romanian Communists reclaim the past they are destroying and falsifying it. While Party historians labour to try to establish the Dacian origins of Communist rule, scholarly historiography has been purged and virtually eliminated over the last decade, as becomes clear from even a brief visit to the Museum of National History in Bucharest. A whole floor of the Museum is devoted to iconography – portraits, tapestries, sculptures – of the presidential couple. A huge room presents Ceausescu as world statesman. A map of the world, showing Bucharest as its centre, indicates his two hundred visits to more than eighty countries. Next to it are displays of photographs of him with the numerous world leaders he has met. These serve as a depressing reminder of the West's long infatuation with a dictator who is considered in the whole of East-Central Europe to be a disgrace to European civilization.

While official historians and poets portray Ceausescu as the culmination of a long line of historical figures, his clan has systematically crushed or forced into emigration the nation's intellectual elite. Popular culture is hailed as the true art form of the socialist future, with endless folk dancing dominating the already brief (two hours daily) television programming. Yet the Romanian village, the last remnant of that traditional culture, now faces eradication under a continuing project called 'systematization', which has already been applied to towns and cities. Under current plans for 'rural consolidation', seven thousand villages (including, naturally, those of the ethnic minorities) with old individual houses are to be demolished by the year 2000 and the people rehoused in three-storey apartment blocks with communal kitchens.

Urbanization of the countryside might seem an odd step for a regime intent on appropriating national history, but Ceausescu is above all obsessed with leaving his stamp on the face of his country. He has already done irrevocable damage to the capital, where his urban-renewal scheme has resulted in overnight razing of villa districts in the old heart of Bucharest. Sixteenth- and seventeenth-century churches and monasteries were not spared; nor was the town's only Sephardic synagogue. As if one could imagine Paris without Le Marais or Prague without Mala Strana! The continuing obliteration of old Bucharest is also the ultimate onslaught on what is left of the old cultural elite. One case among many is that of the painter Nicolas Vermont and his daughter Zoe, also a painter. Ordered to leave their family home at one day's notice, Zoe jumped from the window of her apartment when the bulldozers moved into her garden. Forty thousand people have been expelled from their homes under similar conditions.

What then has replaced the jewels of Byzantine architecture, the highly individual villas, the gardens? A correspondent for the *Economist* vividly described the scene:

> During the day much of the city lies under choking dust clouds kicked up by the building work. The work continues through the night, illuminated only by occasional arc lights (normal street lighting is virtually non-existent, because of a shortage of electricity). The shadows of troglodyte figures scurrying home across devastated building sites are momentarily cast up high against the sides of buildings by the intense light of acetylene torches. The majestic horror conjures up images of Dante's inferno.

Ceausescu's inferno is exemplified by a vast square worthy of the vision of Albert Speer. Here the individual feels appropriately puny in the face of the all-white Mussolini-style 'civic centre', which house government bureaucracies and the palatial headquarters of the Communist Party. But then the Piata was not built for individuals but for the masses. It is intended to hold crowds of half a million people on national holidays and Ceausescu's birthday celebrations. From there the brand-new 150-yard-wide motorway called Boulevard of the Victory of Socialism leads straight to the presidential palace – a grandiose architectural extension of Ceausescu's ego.

After being manipulated, the country's past is now being destroyed. Ceausescu's refusal in 1968 to take part in the Warsaw Pact invasion of Czechoslovakia gave him a 'maverick' image in the West and helped him to use nationalism to win popular support. After twenty years of alleged independence, Ceausescu's nationalist balloon has been pricked. Bankrupt, economically dependent on Moscow, he now pitifully returns begging to the Soviet fold while an exasperated population watches Bulgarian television as a form of escapism and prays for Gorbachev to shorten its ordeal. Romania's Communist nationalism comes full circle: *Ex oriente lux*.

Hungary: Towards Constitutional Communism?

'To what extent is the Party prepared to share power? And who actually sets the limits?' These two simple yet fundamental questions were put by the editors of the Hungarian Communist Youth journal *Magyar Ifjusag* (in the January 1988 issue) to the Politburo member in charge of ideology, Janos Berecz. They are an indication (among many) of how far ahead of Gorbachev's *glasnost* the Hungarian debate is, and how rapidly the mood of the country and of the Party had changed at the end of the Kadar era.

The basic tenet of Kadar's policy for the last twenty years was that, given what happened in Czechoslovakia in 1968 (not to mention in Hungary in 1956), the prerequisite for the safe pursuit of gradual economic reform was the absence of all political reform. Hungarian 'goulash Communism' developed while the political strings remained firmly in the hands of the Party apparat.

This Kadarian model, which had some success in the 1970s and was still being praised (after the defeat of Solidarity in Poland) as the best of all possible Communist worlds, has now effectively collapsed. Kadar's replacement in May 1988, after more than thirty years as Party leader, marks the end of an era. The generational turnover in the leadership (Kadar's successor Karoly Grosz is fifty-seven) coincides with long-overdue political changes. Not that a complete reversal of policy is likely now that the Gorbachev generation ('youths who start their political careers at fifty and blossom at sixty,' remarks Hungarian writer György Dalos) can at last indulge their taste for power. In fact, in contrast to Poland where Party leaders are changed only after workers' strikes, the Hungarian transition was smooth. Brought to power by Soviet tanks, Kadar won a measure of tacit consent, then lost his way at the end, backtracking on reforms which (to outsiders) were associated with his name. He was pushed out but could have left just three or four years earlier without being hated. 'The man was in many ways better than his system,' says Dalos, and compared to Ceausescu, Zhivkov, Ulbricht or Husak his standing 'would not be so bad, if there had not been a certain Alexander Dubček...'

The Kadarist consensus with society was based on economic reforms, some real, some merely anticipated. Ironically, it was the reform economists who delivered the first devastating blow to Kadar's old concept of the 'leading role' of the Party. In a study completed at the end of 1986 entitled 'Turning Point and Reform' a team of Hungary's leading economists concluded that reform just does not work and that what is needed to put things right is not simply more free-market measures but democratization of decision-making as well. The Party should cease interfering with the management of the economy. The separation of Party and state – the extent of whose authority should be defined by law – would then provide an adequate framework for economic activity. This implies decentralization and the assigning of priority to professional competence over political reliability – an overt challenge to the nomenklatura. In other words, political reform has become the acknowledged precondition for the pursuit of economic reform.

The most comprehensive proposal from within the Party came from Mihaly Bihari, then an adviser to Imre Poszgay, the leading figure in the reform wing of the Party. Bihari's report, *Reform and Democracy*, submitted at the end of 1987, opened with a forceful indictment of the paralysis of the Party leadership under Kadar: it accused the ageing leadership of fearing the very idea of change, of refusing to face the facts about the crisis or to hear criticism from the rank and file, even those from its own apparat. In trying to preserve the bureaucratic stalemate the leadership had created a crisis of confidence in the Party, Bihari said. The implementation of even half of Bihari's proposals for political reform would amount to a *de facto* dismantling of the 'leading role' of the Party as we know it. One proposal is that the separation of Party and state, much like the separation of Church and state in nineteenth-century France, be written into the constitution. The separation of powers implies an independent judiciary, and the proposal advocates the establishment of a Constitutional Council (to check the constitutionality of laws) and a Supreme Court. The rule of law, the return to a *Rechtstaat*, which Hungary, like the rest of the Habsburg Empire, enjoyed back in the nineteenth century, is presented as a necessary modernization of a decaying Communist political system.

Budapest's Westminster-like Parliament is a reminder that a century ago Hungary aspired to become a Western-style democracy. For decades the largest parliamentary building in Europe was merely a façade. The real decisions were taken at the White House, the local nickname for the Party headquarters just a stone's throw away. But now, after the 'rule of law' and 'modernization', 'pluralism' has become part of the reformers' vocabulary. Party reformers, like Imre Poszgay, have moved further than in any other Party in the Soviet bloc to reconcile the Communist Party with pluralism in society, and have argued that Parliament should become a genuine forum for interest groups such as trade unions, farmers or environmentalists. For the optimists, this is a move in the right direction, from the recognition of pluralism to democratization at both the local and the national level. Most reform proposals wanted the government to be made answerable to a Parliament in which different groups would be allowed to present competing programmes or bills. In other words, a multiparty system by another name.

To the sceptics all this looks like an attempt to square the circle. At best, 'pluralism' in a one-party system could lead to a Communist version of corporatism. Instead of claiming to represent all interests in society, the Party would become the supreme arbitrator between them. This, a Budapest historian suggested, could lead to increased 'feudalization' of the Party. Senior Party barons, representing various industrial or regional branches, are already competing for centrally distributed resources – one of the legacies of the Kadar era. The extension of 'pluralism' to new corporations might help open up the system or it might simply accelerate its 'feudalization', its breakdown into fiefdoms and corresponding decline, much like (and this is the privilege of a historian's detachment) seventeenth-century Poland or Bohemia. This trend would certainly be the antithesis of the spirit of Gorbachev's reforms, which are aimed at restoring the power of the centre through a sort of enlightened despotism.

The decisive factor in judging the chances of the optimistic and sceptic scenarios will be the amount of autonomy granted to society in the form of freedom of association and expression, and the changes in internal Party life. In other words, the Communist Party should return to the way things were before Lenin issued his ban on factions in 1921. This proposal, coming twenty years after the crushing of the Czechoslovak reform movement, is tantamount to a rehabilitation of its programme.

Perhaps the most remarkable aspect of the current discussion on political reform in Hungary is the steady penetration of ideas, which until a few years ago were confined to the ranks of the democratic opposition, into the programme of the Party reformers. It could be argued that, in striking contrast to Poland, the ideas of the Hungarian opposition have had a growing influence on the more enlightened circles of the Party while so far having relatively little impact on society at large. The Party is flirting most conspicuously with the 'neo-populist' wing of the Hungarian opposition. Poszgay attended in September 1987 the founding meeting of the Democratic Forum, a grouping of reformers and populists whose attitude to the government is more conciliatory than that of the 'urbanist' intellectuals of the democratic opposition. One of the Forum's main concerns is calling attention to the suppressed Hungarian minority in Transylvania. In January 1988 the Hungarian Party leadership issued a statement declaring responsibility for the fate of Hungarians wherever they are (meaning, specifically, in Transylvania). Efforts to provide assistance to the flood of over 40,000 refugees from Romania could be considered as hints in the same direction. The different treatment by the authorities of two demonstrations in June 1988 is another indication: repression of a gathering of the democratic opposition on Batani Square commemorating the execution in 1958 of Imre Nagy; tacit approval of the mass demonstration on behalf of the Hungarians from Transylvania.

In June 1987 the *samizdat* journal *Beszelö* published a political programme entitled 'Social Contract', written by leading spokesmen for the democratic opposition Janos Kis, Ferenc Koszeg and Ottila Solt. The document proposes a compromise in which the Party would retain its authority over defence and foreign affairs (i.e. dealings with Moscow), while society would recover its autonomy and democratic institutions. Parliament would assume sovereignty with the Party holding only the power of veto. After constitutional monarchy this, for all practical purposes, is constitutional Communism ...

To be sure, there were important differences between Party reformers such as Poszgay and the programme of the democratic opposition. The former give priority to institutional changes and inner party structure, while the latter are more concerned with gaining autonomy for civil society. But they converge in their aim of dismantling the 'leading role' of the Party. In September 1987 a letter addressed to the authorities was signed by one hundred prominent Hungarian intellectuals including dissidents, economists, Party reformers and hitherto moderate members of the Establishment. The letter makes the connection between the economic crisis of the system and the 'urgent need for institutional reform': 'The refrain that a widely based socialist democracy and social consensus exist in Hungary must be abandoned. The construction of a system of balancing the interests of the different apparats leads neither to democracy nor to the securing of consensus, nor is it suitable for the strengthening of government power.' There follows a long list of demands which point the way from Party-controlled democratization to democracy: freedom of association, freedom of speech and of information, local self-government in villages and towns (an old Hungarian tradition), democratization of the electoral law, and the responsibility of the government to Parliament.

The pace of political reform in Hungary accelerated dramatically after Kadar's removal from office in May 1988. A mixture of boldness, confusion and outright demoralization in the Communist Party combines with the emergence of new political parties whose very existence marks the end of the post-war era. The signs of disarray in the Party are unmistakable. First, there is a mass exodus from the Party. Asked about his Party membership, a well-known academic quipped ironically: 'I am not leaving the Party because I don't want to be taken for an opportunist.' Although the size of the Party apparatus is shrinking rapidly, it has become extremely difficult to fill vacant Party positions. In a provincial town the job of Party Secretary (which until recently would have been considered by many a desirable springboard for a career) has been filled only by the twenty-eighth candidate invited to apply! A factory manager, asked on Hungarian television whether he would take the post as Party Secretary for the 13th District of Budapest, answered that he might consider it, but only on an unpaid part-time basis. Hungarian Communism has now invented the free-lance apparatchik!

Political divides are no less important. A senior official commented ironically on the state of the Party in the spring of 1989: 'There are now three parties in one: that of the social-democratic reformers (led by Poszgay), the moderate pragmatic socialists (led by Prime Minister Nemeth), and that of the "true" Communists (who put their hopes in Karoly Grosz). We'll have to resign ourselves to the likely departure of the "true" Communists . . .'

The scope of the new freedom of expression and associations granted to the opposition is virtually unprecedented in post-1918 Hungarian history. And to some extent the demoralization of the Party goes hand in hand with economic failure and the rise of democratic aspirations in society. Yet it would be misleading to attribute the spectacular political changes in Hungary merely to the deterioration of the economy or to the pressures of a dissatisfied society (as is the case in Poland). The floodgates were not broken through from below, but opened from above. The novelty of the policy of the Hungarian Communists in the Gorbachev era is their capacity to anticipate change; to accept it and even sometimes introduce it before the pressure builds up. They have discovered that the best way to absorb or defuse democratic change is to create space for it before the opposition can position itself as a credible alternative. It is the opposition parties, still in a formative stage, who are asking that the call for free elections not be rushed. The Party used to shoot on everything that moved. Today, in Hungary, they try to preempt the movement by joining it. Any new idea or proposal from the opposition is immediately trivialized by the Communists' acceptance. When you run out of things to say the idea is to pretend that nothing any longer matters. This is the Communist version of what Marcuse used to call 'repressive tolerance'.

7 The Economy: 'What is to be Done?'

There is no unemployment, but nobody works.
Nobody works, but the plan is fulfilled.
The plan is fulfilled, but there is nothing to buy.
There is nothing to buy, but you can find anything.
You can find anything, but everybody steals.
Everybody steals, but nothing has been stolen.
Nothing has been stolen, but it's impossible to work.
It's impossible to work, but there is no unemployment.
(Anon, 'The Eight Wonders of the Socialist Economy')

John Maynard Keynes noted sixty years ago that Leninism was a mixture of business and religion. Today, the religion is dead and the business nearly bankrupt. The mix did not gel; the religion (the ideological straitjacket) eventually brought the economy to a halt, while the economic collapse in turn accelerated the demise of the utopian vision.

Was it the wrong religion then? After all, we know from Max Weber that the Protestant ethic can blend with the spirit of capitalism. Paradoxically, a system based on faith in the primacy of economics had produced appalling economic results. The current crisis in East-Central Europe does not imply the imminent collapse of the regimes there; rather it is a sign that a gradual process of decay is undermining the foundations of the Communist system. In Marxist terms, this looks like a case of the collapse of the economic base threatening the stability of the superstructure.

The unmistakable omen of decline at the beginning of the 1980s was the fall in the growth rate. The average annual growth rate of the Soviet bloc countries dropped from 10 per cent in the 1950s to 7 per cent in the 1960s and to less than 5 per cent in the 1970s. Their performance in the crisis-ridden 1980s approaches zero growth, the target set twenty years ago by the Club of Rome, though not by socialist economic planners. East Germany – with West German help – is doing somewhat better, and Poland somewhat worse, than the average.

Some of the countries are really much nearer to economic collapse than Eastern officials are prepared to admit to their populace or Western bankers to themselves. The decline has to some extent been cushioned by Western loans, which have been rising to record levels since the mid-1980s, reaching $90 billion in 1987 according to the OECD (the net debt is over $70 billion). Top of the list are Poland and Hungary, whose debts stand respectively at $39 and $19 billion (for a population of 36 and 10 million). Export prospects look gloomy (exported goods are not up to Western quality standards). It is estimated that in 1989 Hungary's debt service will soak up 90 per cent of its foreign earnings. The delusion that Poland might one day repay its gigantic debt is sustained by the rescheduling of payment and the granting of further loans to help pay at least the interest on it. Overt default must be avoided in order to prevent a chain reaction among the indebted countries of the Third World. In the meantime, World Bank President Robert MacNamara declared his 'great faith in the financial morality of socialist countries'. So it is back to mixing business with religion.

The one country which is proudly paying back its foreign debt on time is Romania (it has dropped from $10 billion to $5 billion in the 1980s). This, however, is only possible at the cost of inflicting unprecedented hardship on the population. Even staples like milk, bread and cooking oil are rationed. Cheese, butter, flour and sausages are sold in hard-currency shops along with souvenirs and leather jackets. Romania, once the 'breadbasket' of the Balkans, has now been reduced to semi-starvation. With its oil and mining reserves the country used to be virtually self-sufficient in terms of energy, but Ceausescu's pharaonic projects, the development of huge petro-chemical complexes and other energy-hungry industries have provoked a self-generated energy crisis. As a result there is virtually no public lighting in the streets of Bucharest and only one low-wattage light-bulb per room is allowed in private apartments. The near-blackout is accompanied by switched-off radiators (except for two hours in the evening). The same applies to refrigerators, presumably because the apartments themselves are turned into ice-boxes. 'It's just like during the war,' say the Romanians, 'except that then we had some meat.'

Is Poland turning into another Romania? The collapse of the

Polish economy is certainly the most dramatic in the bloc; it even led the economists to invent the concept of 'negative growth'. Between 1980 and 1986 national income declined, according to official data, by 4.3 per cent while real wages dropped by 17 per cent. In 1987 inflation ran officially at 26 per cent, and by 1989 at 100 per cent. Marx's theory of the pauperization of the workers, which has never been relevant to the capitalist economy, is now a fitting description of the situation under Communism.

In March 1988, the official Polish press for the first time gave vivid accounts of homelessness in the capital. *Express Wieczorny* put the number of homeless Warsawians at 15,000 in a town of 1.5 million. 'They live in railway stations, in staircases, in garbage dumps and even in [sewage] canals,' said the paper, which also mentioned the Church's active role in trying to arrange shelters. The rapidly deteriorating economy has created a new category in Polish society: the 'new poor'. An article in the January 1988 issue of the unofficial journal *Samorzadna Rzeczpospolita* offered the following description:

> Several decades ago they were one of those rarely encountered elements of city folklore. They were usually from the margins of society: alcoholics, aged prostitutes, the mentally subnormal, or people without families. Today there are many of them, more and more each month. They are the 'divers': people who search the city garbage cans for things to eat, wear or sell. 'Divers' of the old category are hardly ever seen today. The garbage cans today are frequented by people who look as though they could be members of the intelligentsia. . . . When their coat and their last pair of shoes are finally worn out and they do not have enough money to replace them, people who until recently would never have dreamt of it, overcome their feelings of disgust and shame and will set off for the garbage cans.

The author of the article derides the government's claim to have raised minimum pensions and allowances to 10,000 zloty as 'simply laughable' given the sharp price increases at the beginning of 1988: 40 per cent for food, 50 per cent for housing, 100 per cent for heating and electricity.

A worker whose yearly salary is 30,000 zloty (a researcher at an institute of the Academy of Sciences earns 20,000) spends at least half of his income on rent; he pays 500 zloty for a kilo of apples. How is he to find the year's salary needed to jump the five-year waiting list for a telephone line or to grease his child's admission into a kindergarten? The price hikes which provoked a tide of strikes from Gdansk to Nowa Huta in the spring of 1988 amount to the most sweeping assault on the population's standard of living since the crushing of Solidarity in December 1981. Officially, the price rises are called the first stage of economic reform; no wonder there is little enthusiasm for the second, which was inaugurated with a referendum that asked people whether they wanted more of the same (and worse) for three years as a prerequisite for a 'radical cure' of the ailing economy. If you ask a silly question you should not be surprised to get the answer you deserve. (A third of the electorate failed to take part in the referendum, in which the government failed to get a majority for its programme. But it is still pressing on with a revised version of 'reform'.)

Trying to convey to a Western audience the real meaning of his cost-of-living data, a Polish economist calculated how much a New York municipal worker (earning $15 an hour) would have to pay in dollars for some basic consumer items were he to change places with a Polish worker. The result was the following: $23 for a movie ticket, $26 for a gallon of petrol, $77 for a pound of steak, $1154 for imported jeans, $19,673 for a colour television set, $95,625 for a small car – all depending, of course, on the availability of the goods. A hint of how basic the shortages can be: one banner carried by demonstrators in the spring of 1988 in Wroclaw read: 'Socialism has raised toilet paper to the rank of a first-rate economic problem.'

It used to be said that in socialist economies shortages are the hidden inflation. Now they have both shortages *and* inflation. The only way to beat them is to have dollars, the second (in practice the first) currency throughout East-Central Europe. The dollar rules not only on the indispensable black market, but also in the special hard-currency shops which were once reserved for foreigners and Party officials. The authorities opened them to the public to drain the remittances to Poles and Czechoslovaks coming from relatives in the West. The turnover of the Pewex chain in Poland was $440 million in 1987, up 19 per cent over the previous year. The worse the economic situation gets, the greater the reliance on foreign currency. The population becomes divided between those who have dollars (through relatives or bought on the black market) and those who don't. This is not just a matter of access to luxuries in duty-free shops. The longest (and most shocking) queues in Poland are for certain medicines, including antibiotics that are available only in exchange for dollars.

Thus has the deteriorating economy undermined the welfare state, once the main claim to fame of the regime: you might not have

Western freedoms, it told a mostly hostile populace, but instead you enjoy the benefits of job security and social services, cheap housing and free health care. Today, half of the young couples do not have an apartment of their own and the waiting list is up to fifteen years. Polish hospitals are in a shocking state, overcrowded, ill-equipped and short not just of medicine but of basic supplies (even bandages are washed for re-use). Of the 2314 varieties of medicine that should be available according to an official list, about half are completely unavailable. Speaking on Warsaw Radio, Marek Okulski, an expert with the United Nations Population Department, said that the standard of sanitation in Poland was on the nineteenth-century level. It was impossible to find a clean lavatory in Warsaw; there was no toilet paper, no soap in schools and other public buildings. It is not a question of starting hygiene courses, he added, but of ensuring the necessary supply of material and personnel. A survey conducted by the Warsaw daily *Zycie Warszawy* concluded that 29 per cent of the food in general, 17 per cent of the meat and 42 per cent of products such as shoes, furniture, textiles and cosmetics were of such poor quality that they were not worth buying. 'We eat inedible food, we drink unpotable water, we walk in shoes unfit for walking, we make ourselves up with old cosmetics,' said the article.

What is happening in Poland cannot be adequately described in economic terms alone. Economic collapse is destroying the basic infrastructure and with it the fabric of everyday life. It has plunged the majority of the country on to or below what the statistics call the minimum living standard. In contrast to the rising expectations of the 1970s, the 1980s saw the nation subjected to humiliation by poverty.

Hungary's most likely future is either one of 'Polonization' or of 'Yugoslavization', says writer Janos Kenedi only half-jokingly. 'But Grosz probably thinks he can avoid the unpleasant side-effects of both: the free speech of the Poles and the autonomy of society and independence of the Yugoslavs.'

Since the 1970s goulash Communism has been praised in the West and envied in the East as the model of Soviet bloc consumerism. And it is true that the shops on Vaci Street in Budapest, with their videos and Western sportswear, do provide a sharp contrast with the somewhat puritanical and egalitarian streak of the Communist idealism of the early days. This, to some extent, was a case of making a virtue out of necessity: the economy of scarcity used to be presented as a transition stage to the Communism of abundance. People were treated as producers rather than consumers. Kadar changed all that and, just like Husak in Czechoslovakia or Poland's Gierek in the early 1970s, he catered to consumerism as a means of buying quiescence after a period of unrest. The trouble with socialist consumerism is that it tends to be an imitation (and not always a very good one). More important, it might be a difficult road to follow if you raise expectations that you cannot fulfil. And this is now happening.

Kadar's conciliatory slogan of the 1960s was, 'He who is not against us is with us.' The follow-up motto of the 1970s (like that of Guizot in nineteenth-century France) was 'Enrichissez vous!' The tolerant attitude toward the development of a 'parallel' or black economy was part and parcel of that search for consensus. Today, taking only a second (legal) or even a third (illegal) job has become the only way to maintain one's living standard in Hungary's consumer-rat-race society. It has become a necessity, as real incomes have been falling while inflation has risen to nearly 20 per cent. As Communist Europe's first income tax was being introduced in 1988 real incomes dropped by as much as 15 per cent. 'Now we have Swedish taxes on our Ethiopian wages,' say Hungarian critics. A quarter of the population – pensioners, teachers, employees unable to join the second economy – live below the poverty line. Others have done quite well, as shown by the luxurious villas built by the private entrepreneurs on the hills of Buda.

But the social cost is a heavy one. Sociologist Elemer Hankiss points to the extreme degree of tension and confusion in contemporary Hungary:

> A normal Hungarian gets up in the morning and goes to the factory, where he works according to the rules of the game of the bureaucratic technocratic principle of organization; in the afternoon, when he works on his own private plot in his own 'second economy', he works according to the rules of the market mechanisms. If he goes to the town hall for a permit, then there he is the client of the bureaucracy and he has to behave in a subservient way to the bureaucracy. If he wants to put his son in a good university, then he has to find a patron somewhere, and has to conform to the rules of the client networks in this country. So he has to switch discourse, style of speech, modes of behaviour, several times a day, which is not an easy way to live.

Hungary is probably first in Europe in per-capita work hours. But overwork and alcoholism have contributed to the near-doubling of the death rate among men aged thirty-five to forty-nine in the last twenty years; it is almost twice the European average. Suicide has long been a Central European speciality, as shown by Tomáš

Masaryk's doctoral dissertation on the subject a century ago. But Hungary, with a sharp increase over the last decade, is now number one in Europe (48 per 10,000), well ahead of neighbouring Slovenia or the Czech lands. This is in a country once described as 'the merriest barrack in the socialist camp' . . .

While other socialist economies, including those most involved with reform, are on the verge of collapse, two countries, East Germany and Czechoslovakia, following fairly conservative economic policies, seem to be doing better. Politically they are more tightly run regimes than Hungary or Poland, but they are also better off in terms of living standards. Though Hungary is associated, in the Western media, with unbridled consumerism, the statistics draw a somewhat different picture. For instance, in 1982 there were 110 private cars (mainly Czech or East German) per 1000 inhabitants in Hungary, compared to 153 in Czechoslovakia and 158 in East Germany. The respective figures for television sets were 265 in Hungary, 384 in Czechoslovakia and 434 in East Germany. Roughly the same proportions apply to the distribution of other consumer durables. Even more surprisingly, however, a Hungarian study showed that the consumption of meat, dairy products and vegetables is also lower in Hungary than in Czechoslovakia or East Germany.

The best jokes about central planning come from Poland, but the best results come from East Germany, which in the 1970s even made it briefly into the top ten industrial countries in the world. It is certainly the leading economy in Comecon, just as West Germany boasts the best economic performance in the Common Market. Why then have the East Germans succeeded where others have failed? Because they are Germans, is part of the answer; and Germans can make anything work, even Communism. The legacy of traditional patterns of social organization or of the work ethic of an established working class may account for the relatively good performance of the command economy in East Germany and to a lesser extent in Czechoslovakia. East Germany also benefits from being the unofficial thirteenth member of the Common Market, receiving heavy subsidies and technology transfers from West Germany. But the main reason lies elsewhere: both Germany and Czechoslovakia were advanced industrial nations long before the Communist takeovers. The Czech lands were already the most industrialized part of the Austrian Empire by the turn of the century. Even at the end of the Second World War Czechoslovakia belonged to the six or seven most advanced industrial countries in the world. In other words, both countries are better off than their socialist neighbours because of their capitalist past.

For a Czech, however, to be told that he is better off than a Romanian or a Bulgarian is meagre consolation. Forty years ago he was either better off than, or at least on a par with, his Austrian or German neighbour. Similarly, the East German citizen tends to compare his living standard not with the Pole's, but rather with that of his West German brother. And compared to him, he still has a long way to go.

Ota Šik, the 'father' of the Czechoslovak economic reform of the 1960s, elaborates the point that for East Germany and Czechoslovakia it is the relative decline compared to the West that matters:

> The fact is that in comparison with Western countries they are terribly backward despite being ahead in the Eastern bloc. Before the war the Czechoslovak economy was, in terms of per-capita production and standard of living, approximately on the same level as Germany's. After forty years of socialist development, it is so far behind Germany that it is profoundly shocking. Today per-capita production in West Germany is nearly three times higher than in Czechoslovakia, which means that real wages are three times higher as well. And the same applies to other areas such as housing, social welfare or hospitals. In every sector, the standard of living is several times higher in West Germany and this is a terrible indictment of the socialist economy. The gap between the Eastern and Western half of Europe does not diminish but increases every year.

A similar point can be made about the two Germanies. According to Polish economist Jan Winiecki, 'the economy of the territories now making up East Germany was before the war at 98% of the economy of the territories now part of West Germany. By the late 1940s it was already 83% and, according to a study done in West Berlin, in 1967 it was about three-quarters of the West German level. At the end of the 1980s the East German level is about half that of its Western neighbour. So they are clearly falling behind.'

The alleged East German *Wirtschaftswunder* looks even more deceptive when one takes into account the fact that the East Germans are, along with the Bulgarians, considered experts at forging their economic statistics. A study of growth rates by the United Nations Economic Commission for Europe shows that, in line with what Alec Nove calls the 'law of equal cheating', the average overstatement of growth rates among the Comecon countries since the 1950s was at least 2 per cent. But in East Germany the overstatement was by far the highest, sometimes as much as 8 per cent. According to an American study, the real East German growth rate for the period

1975–82 was only about half the official figures. Why is East Germany even more prone to the manipulation of economic statistics than other socialist countries? There are the obvious propaganda requirements of a regime that has tried to pretend that its economic miracle was more than a match for that of post-war West Germany. But, as Jan Winiecki suggests, there is a political aim as well: 'To show that the GDR, the stalwart of central planning orthodoxy, is immune to the marked economic decline visible elsewhere in Eastern Europe. The change from the need to prove supremacy over the Federal Republic to the need to prove merely the ability to avoid decline in itself says a lot about the lowered expectations in Eastern Europe.'

Many observers predicted the collapse of the Czechoslovak economy due to the ban on reform imposed there after 1968. This did not happen and the rise of the standard of living was undoubtedly the mainstay of the unpopular Husak regime. Consumption has been privileged at the expense of investment. 'They had to give something to a population incensed by the military intervention and the removal of reforms,' says Ota Šik. 'But it is a disastrous policy for the future. Our whole modernization programme has fallen terribly behind.'

At the top of the socialist league East Germany and Czechoslovakia both have an old industrial base inherited from the nineteenth century and expanded under Stalinism. Today, just as in Belgium or the English Midlands, they are witnessing the inevitable decline of large-scale traditional industries, experiencing a process of 'de-modernization' and over-delayed restructuring. Both countries also represent the most rigid and 'stable' brand of state socialism, characterized by its over-controlled socialist company towns combining economic and political integration of the labour force.

An obsolete heavy industrial base accounts for yet another common feature: they are the two most polluted countries in Europe. In both cases the scale of industrial pollution borders on ecological disaster. Entire forest ranges on the border between East Germany and Czechoslovakia look like a landscape of nuclear devastation. In 1982, Eastern Europe (excluding the Soviet Union) emitted over 40 million tons of sulphur dioxide, well over double that produced by the EEC countries. Pollution is sometimes associated with the level of industrial development, but in this case it is the other way round. East Germany's per-capita sulphur-dioxide pollution, the highest in Europe, is four times higher than that of West Germany, though its industrial development is much lower.

According to a secret study prepared in 1983 by the Czechoslovak Academy of Sciences, a third of the forests in the western half of the country are dead or dying and another third are at risk if nothing is done soon. Thirty per cent of all animal life and 50 per cent of all plant life is threatened. A third of all rivers are biologically dead. The water is contaminated with a high level of nitrates, and is therefore unsuitable for babies and expectant mothers. Nearly half of the country's population lives in ecologically devastated areas. Prague is one of them. According to an official report, 'the situation in the badly ventilated Prague basin has now reached a state of emergency'. But the same report also warned that if the current trend continues pollution levels in the city centre will rise by the early 1990s by about 20 per cent over those of the early 1980s: 'The average amount of fly-ash fallout in greater Prague is between 220 and 240 tonnes per square km. The top values sometimes exceed 1000 tonnes per square km. Moreover, fly-ash contains high concentrations of heavy metals and other poisonous elements.' Recently a two-stage warning system has been introduced in the Czechoslovak capital. It goes into effect when pollution reaches dangerous levels. During such periods people are advised to keep children indoors.

These official documents have been made public by the Charter 77 movement, which in 1987 released a lengthy survey of the problem entitled *Let the People Breathe*. According to the Charter, whose documents are not known for excessive dramatization, the situation has reached a point where 'national survival' is at stake. The environmental report opens with the following description by Eduard Vacek, an electrical engineer, of one morning in the life of a citizen in the town of Teplice in Northern Bohemia.

> It was one of those nasty autumn days when you wake up with a dull headache. A quick glance through the window tells you that the dark blanket suspended over the town for more than a week has not lifted. Out again into that muck, you think, locking the door behind you. God, what a stench! What have they been releasing into the air now! I don't believe it! They're waging chemical war against their own people!

Nowhere is concern for the environment so acute, so desperately felt as a matter of survival, as in Central Europe. The idea that, having failed to destroy the spirit of resistance, 'they' are now destroying the physical conditions of life is a remark any visitor to Cracow must have heard. Beyond the damage done to the splendid architecture of that city, the stories from everyday life are simply harrowing. A professor at the Jagiellonian University, not yet forty, is told by his doctor that his bone disease is 'normal', considering he is a Cracow native, but also incurable. To be sure, adds the doctor, a drug which might help exists, but there is no point in prescribing it to you since it is not available in the country. So, unless you have contacts abroad. . . . His wife has just given birth to a daughter and is considering moving for a year to stay with the grandparents in the country so that the baby can escape the pollution of the Cracow area. But the parents are firmly rebuked by the paediatrician: if the child spent its first year in the country and then returned to town, for the rest of its life it would be even more prone to respiratory diseases. The only way to survive in highly polluted areas is to adapt the organism to poison from birth.

Pollution in Poland has reached the stage where even health resorts can do you more harm than good. Jan Winiecki says that 'some health resorts, such as Krynica, are so polluted that the water people drink to cure themselves in fact contains such a high level of lead that it is actually dangerous to their health.'

The prime cause of air pollution is heavy industry, particularly the lignite-burning power plants and chemical industries. Sulphur dioxide returns to the earth as acid rain or fog all over Central Europe. The emphasis on energy-inefficient heavy industries is such that the GDR and Czechoslovakia rank respectively second and third in the world in per-capita consumption of primary energy. Southern Poland's coal and steel complexes (Nowa Huta, Huta Katowice) belong to the same category. According to 1977 figures Czechoslovakia annually produces a tonne of steel per capita, double the United States production. Czechoslovakia also produces annually 649 kilograms of cement per capita, again twice as much as the United States. This Stalinist bias in favour of coal and steel is the prime cause of the country's economic decline and of environmental damage in Czechoslovakia, East Germany and Poland. Today the world market is saturated with cheap steel from Asia, and the Comecon countries simply refuse to make the painful adjustments that Western Europe undertook in the last decade. As the Charter 77 document put it: 'what we should be selling abroad are not tonnes of steel, but our skill and know-how.' Under state socialism there is no incentive for factories to purchase expensive anti-pollution equipment. Nor are existing pollution-control regulations properly enforced. Given that environmental groups cannot operate as a counterweight to the heavy-industry lobby, there is little chance that the present trend of devastation will be reversed. The only officially proposed alternative to lignite-burning power plants is nuclear energy. Czechoslovakia has even announced that by the year 2000 half of its electricity needs should be generated by nuclear power. But this is hardly reassuring as the existing nuclear plants, such as the one at Jaslovske Bohunice near Bratislava, are already breaking down. In an unusual display of *glasnost* the Slovak Party paper *Pravda* (8 May 1987) admitted 350 faults and manufacturing deficiencies at several nuclear reactors in Czechoslovakia. In the wake of the Chernobyl catastrophe the Soviet-style 'all-nuke' alternative is almost as terrifying as the prospect of a slow and steady destruction of the environment. The Communist political system could perhaps be replaced by a democratic one on fairly short notice; but the environmental damage it would leave behind may be irreversible.

So, the decay of the command economies undermines not just the wealth of nations but also the health of nations. Pollution has increased the number of cases of cancer and respiratory diseases. The stress of living under difficult conditions now combines with the erosion of the welfare state to account for astonishing health reversals: the increase of mortality, especially among men, and a general decline of life expectancy. In the old days the Soviet bloc regimes used to pride themselves on increased life-expectancy rates, which they ascribed to the merits of socialist medical care. The gap between the two halves of Europe seemed to be narrowing. Since the 1970s, however, it has widened again and by the 1980s life expectancy in Western Europe was nearly five years longer. Between 1960 and 1980 (the figures are likely to be even worse for the following decade) mortality among men aged thirty-five to sixty-five increased by over a quarter in Hungary, by a fifth in Czechoslovakia and by some 15 per cent in Poland, while it declined in all West European countries.

Such reversals of health improvements in advanced industrialized societies are without precedent. At the beginning of the 1980s Nicholas Eberstadt, of the Harvard University Centre for Population Studies, drew attention to developments in the Soviet Union where life expectancy among men may have dropped by as much as five years since the 1960s. His latest analysis of official data shows that, even in this domain, the countries of East-Central Europe seem to follow the Soviet pattern.

The situation is not helped by a rapid increase in smoking and alcoholism. Between 1965 and 1985, cigarette consumption per adult rose by nearly a third in Poland and by more than half in East Germany. Similarly, the consumption of hard liquor, already considered slightly higher than in Western Europe in 1960, was more than 70 per cent higher by 1980. The greater vulnerability of the peoples of East-Central Europe to health threats – whether inflicted by the crisis-hit economic system or by their own lifestyle – is, according to Eberstadt's study, attributable to the failure of the Soviet-type public health system. Like the rest of the economy, the labour-intensive health system is inadequate in meeting current health needs because:

> priority is on the quantity of doctors fielded rather than on the quality of training or equipment for those people designated to be medical professionals. . . . However social policies may be designed in Eastern Europe, mortality rates suggest that the vulnerable and the exposed have not acquired the additional protection needed simply to keep death rates stable during a period of economic turbulence. The business cycle may no longer affect the health of the general populace in Western countries, but adult Eastern European populations, as a whole, do not appear to enjoy the same good fortune.

Crisis has definitely arrived and the prognosis for recovery is most uncertain. East Germany and Czechoslovakia face a steady process of decline and demodernization. In Hungary there is talk of Polonization, in Poland of Romanization, in Romania of Albanization. In short, economic collapse, decaying infrastructures and the inefficacy of the welfare state now presents the Other Europe with the depressing prospect of being reduced to Third World status. Not only is the area falling behind the advanced industrial countries of the West, but it is also trailing newly developing countries such as South Korea and Taiwan. The East European obsession with 'catching up', economically, with Western Europe, dates back to the nineteenth century. Even among those who disapproved of Communist methods, many believed that, in some way, state socialism might help these countries to come to terms with their 'neurosis of backwardness'. After four decades that hope has failed and the gulf between the two Europes, in terms of technological innovation and living standards, is widening. As one Polish economist observed ruefully: 'We used to think of ourselves as the east of the West; now we've become the west of the East.'

The Origins of the Crisis: The Soviet Model

Now that the crisis has reached all the countries in the Soviet bloc, it can no longer be dismissed as local mismanagement. Its origins, as leading Hungarian, Czech and Polish economists point out, must be sought in the nature of the Soviet-imposed command economy.

The Soviet model introduced after the war put the Party-state in charge of the economy. The state, it was believed even by many non-Communists, was able to concentrate resources to carry out the post-war reconstruction. In reality, however, it was designed to help the Soviet Union cream off the resources of the most advanced countries on the western periphery of its empire. The reconstruction was, if anything, slowed by Soviet transfers of machinery and sometimes whole industries to the USSR. Economist Paul Marer estimated 'the value of the unrequited flow of resources from Eastern Europe to the Soviet Union during the first post-war decade to be roughly $14 billion, or of the same order of magnitude as the aid the United States gave to Western Europe under the Marshall Plan'.

The main features of the system were state ownership of the economy, extreme centralization of decision making, and the authoritarian mobilization of human and material resources for the fulfilment of the plan. State control over the economy is the centrepiece of the system from which everything else follows. It was achieved in several stages. At first, in 1945, there was the nationalization of property belonging to Germans or to collaborators. Then, between 1945 and 1948, came the nationalization of all key sectors of industry and banking. East Germany tolerated small businesses and artisans for somewhat longer than the others. State ownership of the economy became the rule (special concessions were the exception); it was accompanied by a ban on setting up new enterprises. The state monopoly on enterprise creation represented, as Peter Kende observed, the real foundation of a Soviet-type economy.

For the Communists, nationalization always meant étatization. Their doctrine does not distinguish between étatization and socialization; the state is completely merged with society. The final stage of the nationalizations occurred after 1948, culminating in the forcible collectivization of agriculture. This was imposed by Stalin on sometimes reluctant Parties. The Poles, for example, shrank from the daunting task. Stefan Staszewski, Poland's former Agriculture Minister, recalls how, in 1948, he received a visit from a Soviet journalist who asked him how many private peasant farms there were in Poland. When told the number was four million, the visitor casually remarked that in that case some 400,000 kulak families (two million people) would have to be resettled after collectivization. The basic motivation for the collective farms, says economist Wlodzimierz Brus, was that 'it offered the best system of control; their economic performance was secondary. If you have millions of peasants and farmers it is difficult to ensure grain procurements. But if you have a series of large units dependent on the state for machinery, control is much easier. Control was Stalin's most fundamental political objective.'

The direct consequence of complete étatization of the economy is its extreme centralization of management. Planning is not, strictly speaking, derived from socialist ideas, but from the state monopoly of ownership and therefore of management. The rejection of horizontal market relations led to a vertical planning system. The allegedly irrational forces of the market were replaced by the great wisdom of the central planner which was to decide how many tonnes of steel and how many brown shoes size ten were needed by society. Agnes Heller and Ferenc Feher call this 'the dictatorship over needs'.

The Soviet model of planning had to be copied faithfully in the most minute detail. Czech economist Jiři Slama was employed in the early 1950s in the Workers' Planning School in Prague where Communist Party officials were trained as planners. Knowledge of Russian and some imagination seem to have been among the requirements for the job:

> I remember that in 1950 we received the first guidelines for drafting the plan for Czechoslovakia according to Soviet methods. Actually it was nothing but a translation of Soviet guidelines. The people in charge either had no time or could not be bothered to change things which had no validity whatsoever for Czechoslovakia. For instance, I can remember that among the headings in the plan there was one stating 'The number of reindeer herdsmen', although there are no reindeer in Czechoslovakia. Or it was also concerned with 'fishing at sea', again something else that did not apply to Czechoslovakia. Such things could, of course, be very easily removed and they did not appear in the guidelines the following year. But the more essential replicas of Soviet methods were there to stay for a very long time.

The 'rationality' of the planner's decisions was later to be enhanced by the introduction of scientific or computerized planning. The latter, however, depends on the quality of the available information. The command economy is a pyramid of lies in which each factory, each bureaucracy, lies to the levels above and below in the hierarchy about its performance and optimum plan targets. So, in line with the 'garbage in – garbage out' theory, computerized central planning is a flop.

'Economic statistics are like a bikini,' says a Hungarian economist. 'They can reveal a lot but, on the other hand, they must cover the essentials; otherwise a scandal might occur.' Hungary has some of the best statistics in the Soviet bloc. Poland is not so lucky. Like the others, this problem too goes back to the 1950s, as Professor Brus recalls:

The pre-war statistics in Poland were good and even during the Nazi occupation amazingly good statistics had been kept by the underground. But the publication of statistical yearbooks was stopped in 1949. I naively assumed that they were being collected and circulated only at the highest Party levels, to protect the economy from sabotage or Western propaganda. But in 1954 I was made a member of a Party commission dealing with statistics. Only then did I discover that no proper statistical collection or research had been carried out since 1948. There were output figures produced by factory managers but no attempt had been made to establish production costs. The planning system was indeed industrializing Poland. But at what cost? We didn't know. When this Iron Curtain of ignorance was lifted, we were horrified.

Such disregard for accurate statistics might seem astonishing in command economies geared for extensive growth and emphasizing quantitative targets over quality of produced goods. Western economic history saw the development of small light industries eventually leading to the development of heavy industry. The Soviet-imposed model of extensive growth was the opposite: it gave absolute priority to heavy industry at the expense of consumer needs. There were, naturally, ideological motives involved, such as the transformation of a conservative peasantry into a socialist proletariat. But the prime aim to which all the economic strategies were subordinated was to maximize the Soviet bloc's military potential. Stalinism was above all a war economy.

Massive steel mills were built as showpieces of socialist industrialization. 'Think big' was the Stalinist order of the day and every ruling Communist Party was eager to build gigantic coal and steel complexes, such as Nowa Huta near Cracow, as a shortcut to industrial modernity and a do-it-yourself proletariat. Whatever the initial merits of this Soviet-imposed crash-course in industrialization (in terms of rapid growth rates), its limits were soon reached. It proved unable to adapt to a new 'intensive' stage of economic growth and became an impediment to the development of consumer industries and to technological innovation. The East-Central European model of industrialization blended features of nineteenth-century Germany and 1930s Stalinist Russia. In other words, the model of the future failed because it was in fact a model of the past.

Today, these showpieces of socialist heavy industry – be it the

Schwarze Pumpe complex at Hoyerswerda in East Germany, Huta Katowice in Poland or Ostrava-Karvina in Czechoslovakia – look like museums of the early industrial age.

Why then is this completely obsolete sector maintained? A major factor is that heavy industry represents the most powerful political lobby throughout the Soviet bloc. So far, no leadership has managed to curb its influence or reduce the share of GNP it consumes. Polish economist Andrzej Wroblewski describes the circular nature of this economic system: 'They work in a way for themselves: coal mines produce coal which is used in steel mills. Steel mills produce steel which is used to build more steel mills. And we, society, feel like we are standing on the sidelines and think that maybe, if there is something that they don't need, we might be able to use it. I exaggerate a little, but basically that's the way it is.' Capitalism has been described as conspicuous consumption. Communism then must surely be conspicuous production.

But the ultimate responsibility for preserving an economic order that so obviously does not work lies with the Party and its nomenklatura system. So long as the economy is run by people who are nominated on the basis of their political loyalty, there is no reason to expect that they will follow the most profitable option for their enterprise rather than the suggestions of those who appointed them. This 'dictatorship of ignoramuses' explains why it is difficult to do away with what economists call the 'soft budget constraint' on the enterprises, meaning that in the end the state will always cover their losses. After all, the manager was only following Party instructions. The system has over the years been strengthened by rotation within the nomenklatura: apparatchiks become managers and managers can become apparatchiks. The nomenklatura is one big family.

For Hungarian economist Janos Kornai, author of *Economics of Shortage*, paternalism and shortages are the main features of the socialist economy: 'The state is a universal insurance company which compensates the damaged sooner or later for every loss. The paternalistic state guarantees automatically the survival of the firm.' Just as the over-protected child will become passive and helpless, the enterprise tends to cling to its dependency on the state.

This system has killed economic incentive and produced both slack and shortages. Labour productivity is three times lower than in the West because the workers know that raising their output would lead to an increase of their production norms. That is to say, they would have to work harder for the same money. The other, more important reason is the chronic shortage of supplies. Workers can work hard for half a day and then wait out the rest of the shift for supplies to arrive. Andrzej Wroblewski provides a classic illustration:

> Most Polish assembly factories stand idle for an hour or two a day because of supply shortages. The most dramatic example is a car factory in Warsaw which has suppliers all over the country. One of them, which makes steering mechanisms in Szczecin, is usually so late that the factory in Warsaw has to charter a helicopter to transport the parts so as not to keep the assembly line idle. Such a flight costs 700,000 zloty, which is roughly the price of one car. But they prefer that to losing a couple of million because the assembly line is at a standstill.

In a planned economy, according to a Polish joke, you end up attempting to assemble ten bicycles with nine screws. The bicycles do not work; nor do the enterprises dependent on monopoly suppliers. Systematic misinformation and state monopolies eventually lead to widespread shortages and extreme inefficiency. This is the situation today, but the diagnosis has been known to Soviet bloc economists for more than thirty years. On three occasions, usually coinciding with a period of political change, they have proposed market-orientated reforms which so far have either failed or not been properly implemented.

The Politics of Economic Reform

The first comprehensive reform was launched in Poland during the popular unrest of 1956. It was the handiwork of the Economic Council under Oskar Lange and Wlodzimierz Brus. Lange was certainly a leading influence on the entire post-war generation of economists in Central Europe. They remembered how Lange, still at the University of Chicago before his return to Poland, had forcefully argued the socialist case against Ludwig von Mises' championing of the free market. In 1956, against the background of the Poznan workers' riots, Lange proposed a 'socialist market', a system in which central planning would be carried out through market mechanisms and decentralization. The second proposal was to introduce Yugoslav-style workers' councils; direct industrial democracy was to be the counterweight to the Party's economic bureaucracy. But Gomulka's post-1957 retreat from reform emasculated the first far-reaching economic reform in Central Europe.

The second round of economic reformism came ten years later when, under Kosygin's sponsorship, Moscow seemed to give the green light to what was meant initially as a decentralizing, 'technocratic' reform. In Czechoslovakia it was taken further by a team of experts under Ota Šik, an economist and influential Central Committee member. They were responding to the recession that slowed down the Czechoslovak economy in the early 1960s and eventually they put forward the most comprehensive reform proposal to date. Although it was formally approved in 1966, its genuine implementation had to wait for the Prague Spring of 1968. The aim was a 'socialist market' system in which there would still be collective ownership of the means of production, but enterprises would be competing in the market place rather than simply fulfilling the plan targets. Today, twenty years after the military defeat of the Czechoslovak experiment, Ota Šik remains faithful to his idea of a 'third way' between capitalism and Soviet-style socialism:

> The old directive plan must disappear and in its place should be introduced a macro-plan which would provide the framework for the long-term goals of the economy. These goals can be achieved with the help of an incomes policy, a policy of public spending, a monetary policy, all of which can be combined with the market mechanisms without actually limiting them. These are policy instruments which the state can use in the best interests of the workers. And it would be more socialist and more democratic if such plans existed in two or three variants so that the population could participate in drawing them up and choose the plan considered best suited for its development. That is the basis of socialism as I see it.

The radical novelty of the Czechoslovak Spring was the realization that economic decentralization is impossible without political decentralization and that there must be a simultaneous introduction of economic and political reform. In short: the autonomy given to the enterprises constitutes a direct threat to the Party bureaucracy. Ota Šik, who played a decisive role in the downfall of Antonin Novotny and the election of Alexander Dubček, says that confrontation with the Party apparat is the prerequisite for change: 'Power corrupts. A Party secretary can decide who will do what and where; he can also decide who will belong to the management of an enterprise and what the enterprise will produce. But it can go much further when, with the help of those enterprises, he can receive certain services or scarce goods. So when the reform gives independence to the enterprises, the whole Party apparatus, inflated in size by the central planning system, suddenly loses power.' With the loss of power comes the loss of privilege. Since apparatchiks have no qualifications to do anything else but control, they have resisted fiercely any effort to render them superfluous. The only way to introduce reforms, the Czechs and Slovaks argued in 1968, was to dismantle the power of the apparat and democratize political life. And it is precisely for that reason that Moscow decided to put an end to what was denounced as a dangerous attempt to 'restore capitalism'.

Under the Brezhnev regime, now denounced by Gorbachev as an 'era of stagnation', the emphasis was on seeking alternatives to reform without completely reverting to the Stalinist pattern. One option was the streamlined centralized system based on the East German *Kombinat* (cartel) model: the centre's task is rendered less onerous by reducing the number of enterprises subjected to planning by merger. The 'cartels' subdivide tasks among their subordinate management, but the basic concept is still essentially a vertical one in that the *Kombinat* is in charge of production from the raw materials to the end-product. It is an attempt to make what remains a centrally administered economy more efficient.

The other substitute for reform was the policy of massive importation of Western technology and consumer goods. Gierek's Poland in the 1970s was the leading exponent of this modernizing yet fundamentally conservative approach. Its limits were rapidly reached. Observing the situation in their country at the end of the 1970s a group of critical Polish intellectuals and experts close to the Party, and calling itself 'Experience and Future', returned to the theme of reform:

> Any plan for the resolution of the crisis which is based strictly on the use of economic means is now unrealistic, since the underlying causes of the crisis are not economic. Unless the system of management is reformed and unless the general climate of social life is altered, it is inconceivable that any way will be found to harness any untapped resources in the economic realm.

The economic collapse and the advent of Solidarity in 1980 vindicated this analysis. It also marked the end of certain assumptions of the post-1968 period: the Polish case proved, for example, that the grafting of Western technology on to a fundamentally unreconstructed command economy cannot work unless the whole economic system is overhauled; imports merely delay the day of reckoning. The massive debt accumulated in that period by Poland among others was basically used to prop up inefficient bureaucracies pursuing conservative policies. Another lesson of the Polish crisis of 1980 concerned the connection between economic reform and political and social change. Under Gierek, the workers had confined themselves to an essentially negative, anti-reformist posture. Their successful strikes against price increases in 1970, 1976 and 1980 gave them a *de facto* veto power over government economic policies without any positive input. As reform became merely a code word for price increases, the strikes looked like the defence of vested interests and a block to economic reform. The rise of Solidarity helped to change that pattern. Unable to defuse the movement by mere economic concessions, the regime had to make political ones, thus creating a new context for posing the problem of reform. As a result, a radical reform proposal was drawn up in 1980–1 and seemed to win approval from both the Party leadership and Solidarity. The introduction of market mechanisms and the granting of autonomy to individual enterprises was to be combined with self-management principles, the rationale being that a move towards marketization would be acceptable to the workers only if they recovered genuine union power and workers' councils. Independent trade unions would ensure the defence of their economic interests, while the factory workers' councils were intended to provide a counterweight to the Party bureaucracy in the management of some 6500 state enterprises. Clearly, this model was not devoid of contradictions. Would the new unions be prepared to accept the necessary period of economic hardship that any transition towards market reform implies? Would workers' councils be able to recognize the long-term interests of their firms? The Yugoslav experience invites scepticism in this respect. The natural tendency of self-management organs (assuming they really become independent from the Party) is to seek instant gratification. They tend to prefer wage increases now to investment strategies which might yield results only some time down the line. This is why a number of Yugoslav, as well as Hungarian and Polish economists, have come to speak of the need to rehabilitate the 'entrepreneurial function' as a means of correcting the abuses of state-run planning, and also to promote the application of rational economic strategies in the emerging market.

General Jaruzelski made sure that we will never know the answer to some of these questions. The imposition of 'martial law' meant the suspension of the workers' councils, while factory managers were placed under the supervision of military commissars. However, Jaruzelski did not simply restore the old command economy. In the following years, he proposed his own, admittedly trimmed-down, version of reform. The General's message to Western *Finanz Kapital* was that Solidarity-led strikes and strong union power do not really create the proper environment for introducing reform. Only the military could impose it simultaneously on the conservative Party apparat and an unruly working class; the method was political restraint for the former and wage restraint for the latter.

The 1980s' Polish recipe for rescuing the economy was known as the 'Three S' policy: self-autonomy, self-financing, self-management. Enterprises were to enjoy more autonomy from the central planner and their wage policies were to be made dependent on their financial results. Factory councils were to be restored, albeit with more limited powers. After several years of would-be reform none of the three principles has actually been implemented. The state organs still interfere with the running of the enterprises: 90 per cent of managers, as was the case under Gierek, are still Party members; the enterprises' goals are not specified in monetary terms, so that the notion of profitability remains a rather theoretical one; and the employees' councils – with merely consultative powers – are too weak compared to the economic authorities. The 'Three S' reform is so far only a cosmetic, and it looks as if the General will not enter the history books as the first to reconcile Communism with self-financing and self-management.

So what do you do when the first round of pseudo-reforms fails to get off the ground? You launch the 'second stage' of reform. The November 1987 referendum, in which the Polish authorities failed to gain a clear majority of support for their austerity package combined with a promise of economic reform, appeared at first to be a setback for the reformers inside the Establishment. In fact, it widened the General's options. At least he could claim the backing of 46 per cent of the voters; that, in Polish terms, might be considered a paradoxical success. It could also provide an excuse to ditch fundamental reform while asking Western bankers for greater patience and understanding in the face of double adversity: a conservative bureaucracy on the one hand, a conservative society on the other.

The evidence suggests that Jaruzelski's attempt to introduce economic reform while staving off political change has failed. Whatever the intentions of the modernizing wing of the Polish Party (and there is little reason to doubt the competence or the reformist convictions of men such as Economic Minister Sadowski) their policy was unworkable because Jaruzelski lacked political credibility in the eyes of society. Lack of public confidence in the government led to a lack of confidence over economic prospects. In a country like Poland you could not, as you could in Hungary under Kadar, start with measured economic reform in the hope of winning a degree of acceptance in the long run. In Poland, the emergence of a social consensus in favour of a programme of economic restructuring necessarily presupposes a political dialogue between rulers and ruled.

In the meantime, ten years were lost with severe economic consequences. Today the disintegration of the economy is forcing the Party to retreat. The chances of an evolution towards a more market-orientated economy in the 1990s will depend less on yet another blueprint of Jaruzelski's for a Polish-style *perestroika* than simply on his ability to get the Party to loosen its stranglehold on the economy and allow private enterprise to have a try.

Whereas in the rest of Central Europe the story is one of aborted reform attempts, Hungary is the only country where reform has actually been implemented, with ups and downs, for two decades. Although Kadar's departure from the political scene was not a glorious one, whatever the limitations of his narrow-minded pragmatism he can be given credit for the fact that he, alone in the Soviet bloc, kept the idea of reformism alive during the conservative Brezhnev era. In practice it was another matter; there were in retrospect very damaging setbacks for the Hungarian reform after 1972 and again in the mid-1980s. But at no point were the ideas of a market-orientated reform rejected as illegitimate. This is a lasting legacy of Kadarism and, judging by the experience of neighbouring countries, by no means a negligible achievement.

Kadar's great wisdom, as most Western experts saw it, was that, unlike the Czechs and Slovaks in 1968, he realized that the only way to push through an economic reform successfully was to avoid political reform. Kadar could afford to do so in that the Hungarian Party seemed cured of reformist delusions after 1956 and, unlike the Polish Party, it could count on a society politically under anaesthesia. Depoliticization of economics and gradualism seemed the prime assets of the Kadarist strategy. In retrospect, these also proved to be its limits.

In the 1970s, Hungary's limited reform seemed to work; greater leeway was given to private initiative on the periphery of the economy (agriculture and services) while subsidies and central appointment of managers were still pervasive practices at its core. Privatized agriculture and the so-called parallel economy were instrumental in ensuring consumer satisfaction and compensation for the deficiencies of the state sector. Other factors also helped to introduce sometimes real, sometimes superficial improvements: among them were realistic exchange rates and an old tradition of keeping competent economists not too far from the corridors of power, rather than cleaning windows as they do in Prague. But structural change was avoided, while pragmatism and consensus politics on borrowed money eventually exploded the myth of goulash Communism.

'Why has Kadar delayed leaving the Party leadership? Because he wanted to return the country to the state he found it in.' The popular jokes in Budapest are only slightly off the mark. A report on the economy by leading experts headed by Antal Laszlo was endorsed by the authorities in the spring of 1987. It presented a devastating picture. After twenty years of reform the economy is in a shambles. Reform has failed, because it was either ill-conceived or insufficiently implemented. The report concludes that nothing short of full marketization will in the long run stand a chance of putting the Hungarian economy on the right track.

In examining the failure of the reform Hungarian economists suggest several causes. The most important, says Antal Laszlo, is that 'the state-owned companies are not geared to be managed profitably because they need not be afraid of failure'. The state support of so-called 'lame ducks' as well as price subsidies contradicted official endorsement of market principles. The second wave of reform in the early 1980s did reduce the role of the central planner, but often merely replaced direct with indirect means of influence. The 'second economy' was gradually legalized and praised as a model of coexistence between a state-controlled economy and a growing private sector. But here, too, closer examination reveals that the theory looks far better than the practice.

There are three main categories of private enterprise in Hungary, employing some 400,000 people. In the first category are shop-keepers and tradesmen, who are usually thought to be thriving. However, a report in the Budapest daily *Magyar Hirlap* noted that in the year 1984 alone some 4000 private shopkeepers (or one in five) went out of business. The second category concerns state-owned enterprises operated on a franchise basis by their managers. The operators pay a rental fee and keep the profit. This has apparently become the most successful form of private business, especially in catering.

The third category are the so-called 'economic work collectives' within state enterprises, which operate outside regular working hours. Their productivity then allegedly increases by up to 50 per cent and this is hailed as a great achievement. But it is merely a glorified (if well-paid) form of overtime. What actually happens is that workers tend to be semi-idle in the first economy to save their energy for their second or third shifts in the parallel economy.

The main obstacle to the development of private enterprise is constant state interference. One example among many is that of the Hotel Victoria in Budapest, the first privately built hotel in the Soviet bloc which opened at the end of 1984. The owner, Zoltan

Palmai, waited three years to obtain a building permit and had to raise 32 million forints without the help of the State Bank. He did it by teaming up with a dozen other investors. It was only after the hotel opened that the owner was informed that private hotels were allowed to accommodate a maximum of thirty guests. The top two floors of the building had therefore to remain vacant and within a year the hotel closed down.

A similar point could be made about the bankruptcy law which came into effect in September 1986. Antal Laszlo argues that only a massive reduction of subsidies and the consistent implementation of the law or, as he says, 'policies similar to those implemented by Western governments in recent years', could help Hungary overcome its crisis. But here again it is not easy to reconcile the Western inspiration with the 'Eastern' reality. Hungarian economists believe that seven or eight out of the ten largest enterprises in the country are technically bankrupt. So it is impossible to start applying market principles overnight.

What you have in the meantime is a hybrid which is no longer central planning but is not yet the market, and often combines the worst of both worlds. Sandor Demjan is the founder of Skala, Budapest's showpiece privately-owned department store. He also launched Hungary's first independent bank, in which the state does not hold a majority of voting shares. He has a bust of Lenin on his desk, but talks with confidence about his bank's decision not to bail out the VAEV construction firm in the town of Veszprem, thus precipitating in 1987, yet another first, the first Hungarian bankruptcy. Demjan insists: 'It is just as necessary to liquidate unprofitable firms under socialism as it is in England or in Germany. If we keep such firms going artificially, there will be no funds left to finance those that develop dynamically. The firm in Veszprem managed to take several thousand forints out of the pocket of every Hungarian citizen. Unfortunately some 2600 people will have to look for a job elsewhere but that is a normal concomitant of economic life.'

Such dilemmas have existed for years. Now the scale of the economic crisis puts pressure on the authorities to take the market reform further. The problem is that, at least in the short run, extending the reform is likely to accelerate the deterioration of the situation. In other words, things will get much worse before they get better. Until recently, such an approach would have been met in Moscow with utmost suspicion, but now, with Gorbachev, it seems that the Soviet veto has been lifted so that, particularly in Hungary and Poland, economists and some managers advocate free-market reforms sometimes with the zeal of newcomers to the liberal club: the 'invisible hand' of the market is supposed to replace the all too visible (and clumsy) hand of the Party.

Yet major obstacles block the implementation of a market-orientated system. There is, of course, political resistance. The Party and the state bureaucracy, the nomenklatura, are always reluctant to give up power. But marketization brings with it social consequences as well. Bankruptcies and unemployment, as in Hungary, threaten to disrupt the old-established tacit social contract summed up in the adage: 'You pretend to pay us and we pretend to work.' So there is a conservative reaction on both sides: from Party bureaucrats who fear loss of political control and from social groups, such as workers in highly subsidized industries, who feel threatened by the promises of Communist free-marketeers.

The economic crisis has created divisions both within the Party and within society. It is no longer simply a 'them and us' situation. The Kadar succession struggle revealed deep splits between the followers of the Old Man and those who want to extend reform from the economic to the political sphere. Hungarian society too is less homogeneous in its response to the crisis: the 'new rich' are discovering taxation and the 'new poor' seek unemployment benefits. The democratic opposition has been converted, since the end of the 1970s, to market principles, while campaigning for the right to create independent associations. As the crisis deepens, such independent trade unions are beginning to emerge. They are likely to fight redundancies and the consequences of the market, thus creating new relations between society and the opposition, and, naturally, new divisions within the opposition. This is the end of the Kadar consensus. It also heralds the end of unanimity (if there ever was any) within the opposition. In other words, from the crisis and decay of Communism comes the return of politics.

The deterioration of the economy has been accompanied by several important shifts in thinking in Central Europe in the Gorbachev era. One of them is the conversion to the market principle among economists, Establishment reformers and dissidents alike. The second is the recognition that economic and political reform are inseparable. Both phenomena point to the Party's retreat from the economic sphere.

Both Kadar (since the 1970s) and Jaruzelski (in the 1980s) put forward programmes of moderate economic reforms without political change. The 1968 Czechoslovak Spring and the Solidarity experience were seen as a warning against mixing the two. Now that Kadar is gone and Jaruzelski has so obviously failed to introduce genuine reform, the old question is back with a vengeance. New Hungarian Politburo members Rezso Nyers, the father of the economic reform in 1968, and government minister Imre Poszgay both claim that only a fundamental revision of political institutions and of the Party's role in them can create the appropriate framework for economic changes. The introduction of market mechanisms, the reformers argue, leads naturally to the emergence of conflicting interests. These must no longer be suppressed; on the contrary, they should be articulated within the political system. Different economic interest groups (entrepreneurs and workers, farmers and environmentalists) should be represented in Parliament and allowed to put forward competing economic programmes or legislation. Only the separation of the Party and the state can lead to their withdrawal from economic management. Freer economics, Hungarian reformers are the first to admit, requires freer politics.

Another by-product of the economic crisis of the 1980s is the triumph of liberalism. The conversion to the market has been irresistible not just among economists but also among dissidents; even Party reformers (at least in Poland and Hungary) have dropped the adjective 'socialist' when they talk about the market. In the above-mentioned debate between Oskar Lange and Ludwig von Mises, Central Europeans voted with their feet for the free-marketeer. Of course the miraculous healing powers of the market are all the more idealized for being out of reach. Nowhere can you find in Europe more orthodox disciples of Milton Friedman's free-market theories than in Poland which combines a dramatic economic collapse of the state-controlled industries with a backward private agriculture.

The appeal of economic liberalism in Central Europe is manifold. The Party reformers are aware that their championing of it is an admission of failure, but it is neither the first nor the last, and they can always reassure themselves by remembering the lessons of the Soviet New Economic Policy (NEP) in the 1920s: economic concessions need not imply the loss of political power. On the other hand, while the economic results of market reforms are far from certain, an ideological muddle is definitely taking place. You can quote Marx, like the Bible, to justify just about anything. But there is a limit to how long Lenin busts on the desks of Hungarian stockbrokers will sustain the pretence. The essence of Leninism is control and guidance and as such it is fundamentally incompatible with the market. Trying to inject a measure of market into the Communist system is like being just a little pregnant.

Economic neo-liberalism provides the most radical alternative to socialist planning. The attraction of the integral market varies from country to country, proportional to the degree of collapse of the economy. The ungenerous view of this phenomenon is that, at least for some new converts, it gives the impression that you can overcome the crisis without actually doing much of anything; just let the market forces do their work. The more serious point is that the crisis is such that piecemeal improvements no longer work and the very foundations of economic life have to be rethought. From Tibor Liska, Professor at the Karl Marx University in Budapest and disciple of Milton Friedman, to Miroslaw Dzielski, the leader of the neo-liberal Association for Free Enterprise in Cracow, one finds a common reference to the Viennese school (Friedrich von Hayek, von Mises) and its extension, the Chicago school. It is part of a rediscovery of an indigenous Central European liberal tradition which recognized the connection between the triumph of étatism and what Hayek called the 'roads to serfdom'. Conversely the introduction of the market and of privatization is a way of taking power away from the state, forcing the Party to retreat and helping society stand on its own feet.

Miroslaw Dzielski believes that the Polish government reform proposals are a move in the right direction in that they create more space for private initiative from below. The aim of his Association is to help fill that space. At the moment it is still an elitist club with annual membership fees at twice the average monthly salary and lectures on 'how to start a business'. The aim is to win the 'struggle for free enterprise' not just against the apparat but in the realm of public opinion as well: 'Decentralization and democratization,' says Dzielski, 'could give more power to people on the local level whose mentality is even more hostile to genuine entrepreneurship than that of the generals in Warsaw.'

Since the imposition of martial law in 1981 Miroslaw Dzielski and his friends have published *13*, a *samizdat* journal described as 'Christian–liberal'. This is not an easy combination in a country where Catholicism has traditionally been associated with corporatism and a critique of both Communism and capitalism. Dzielski's free-market convictions are at least as fervent as his religious faith. A follower of Milton Friedman, Dzielski advocates an unrestricted market and is full of praise for Adenauer's Germany and Mrs Thatcher's Britain. But when asked about the Christian component of his liberalism, this member of the Polish Primate's Advisory Council is quick to revert to the social doctrine of the Church: Communist collectivism from the East is economically and morally unjustifiable and bound to disintegrate. But Western capitalism has succumbed to the frenzy of consumerism. What is needed is a market economy reconciled with Christian ethics, with the counterweight of a redistribution of wealth generated by the market not through the state but through society itself. Of course only a society with a very high sense of Christian values would be capable of that. Neither Communism nor consumerism will do; Poland must show a 'third way'.

Is this brand of 'constructive anti-Communism' plausible? Only provided that Russia is not left out in this economic roll-back of the Communist state. Gorbachev, says Dzielski, provides a unique opportunity to 'civilize' and 'Europeanize' Russia through the introduction there too of a market economy. 'Gorbachev must understand that a Poland (and more generally, a Central Europe) with a disintegrating economy is a liability, always prone to working-class unrest and perpetuating the myth of a coming anti-Russian insurrection. A market-orientated Polish economy would be more prosperous, thus more stable and thus a more reliable neighbour.'

To be sure, Gorbachev's Russia and Jaruzelski's Poland will remain tightly run regimes, but a market economy will help the transition from totalitarian to ordinary authoritarian rule, Dzielski predicts. 'It is not the military, not even the police, but the Party bureaucrats, the nomenklatura, who are the main opponents of the market.' The economic scenario is thus also meant as a lesson in realpolitik. Whether or not one is prepared to follow the logic, one cannot help thinking that only in Poland can 'neo-liberalism' claim to reconcile Milton Friedman, Pope Wojtyla and Gorbachev!

The emergence of the doctrine of economic liberalism in Central Europe is a sign of the failure of the command economies. But the limits to its realization will depend on the balance between decay and Party retreat from economic management. But what is supposed to be the social base of this liberal revival? The new individualism and *embourgeoisement* have their limits. You cannot rebuild a liberal economy just with taxi drivers and shoe-repairmen. To paraphrase Henri Michaux's famous aphorism: the liberals of a nation of hairdressers will always be more hairdressers than liberals.

As Montesquieu knew in the eighteenth century, there is no power without ownership, and an economic market is unlikely without a political market. The challenge of the 1990s for East-Central Europe is whether the crumbling of the economy can bring the Party to accept the idea of the 'minimal state' and thus create space for the emancipation of society. In the 1970s it was assumed that a more prosperous socialist economy would give civil society more room for manoeuvre. Today it is economic collapse that is forcing change. Can a more open economy lead to a more open society?

8 The Politics of Culture

One of the implications of history today, and still more
of history tomorrow, is the struggle between the artists
and the new conquerors, between the witnesses to the
creative revolution and the founders of the nihilist
revolution. As to the outcome of the struggle, it is only
possible to make inspired guesses. At least we know that
it must henceforth be carried on to the bitter end.

(Albert Camus)

When the Polish writer Czeslaw Milosz wrote his famous essay *The
Captive Mind* in 1952, he saw the triumph of Communist ideology
as irreversible. A writer, Milosz thought, had only three options: he
could collaborate, emigrate or remain silent. Fortunately, the history
of Central Europe since 1956 has disproved that pessimistic verdict
from the Stalinist era. Whereas in the 1950s the Communist regimes
could count on substantial (genuine or merely enforced) support
among intellectuals, today the bulk of cultural life worth speaking
of takes place largely outside the realm of official ideology, either
because the boundaries of official tolerance have been stretched or
because culture has been driven underground. From legitimizers of
the powers-that-be the intellectuals have become a moral counterweight. For intellectuals, both the self-emancipation from censorship and the parting with political power have played a key role
in the emergence of dissent.

Socialist Realism

It is difficult today, when the official ideology has been turned into a mere ritual, to appreciate fully the extent of ideological control imposed on the Soviet bloc countries under Stalin. Marxist–Leninist dogma and the faithful imitation of Soviet norms affected all aspects of cultural life. Philosophy was reduced to the struggle of dialectical materialism (Diamat) against idealism. Even research in the fields of physics, biology (Lysenko) or physiology (Pavlov) was supposed to demonstrate the superiority of 'proletarian science'. The history of each nation was rewritten to give the appearance of legitimacy to regimes that had none, and to stress historical bonds with Russia. This proved a particularly difficult task in Poland, where even Communist leaders sometimes felt that excess zeal could be counter-productive. In 1951 the Poles translated a two-volume *History of Poland* which had been produced by the Institute of Slavic Studies in Moscow. Its first reader, Party leader Boleslaw Bierut, wisely decided not to publish a book that systematically presented Russian military expansion as stages in Poland's national liberation.

In the arts, the period was marked by the imposition of what Zhdanov, the chief Soviet ideologist of the day, called 'socialist realism': art had little to do with reality as it was but rather depicted reality as it ought to be. Here again ideological control went hand in hand with slavish adoption of the Soviet model. Jozsef Revai, known as the Hungarian Zhdanov, described in 1951 what Sovietization of culture meant:

> Soviet culture is the model, the schoolmaster of our new socialist culture. We can absorb and use the rich experience of the Communist Party [Bolshevik] of the Soviet Union not only in state-building and in the economy, not only in the techniques of class struggle, but also in the creation of a new socialist culture.

This meant in fact systematically rupturing the historical ties of the lands of Central Europe to Western culture and embarking on cultural Russification.

Art, literature, music – everything had to have a political purpose. In 1952 a leading Hungarian writer Tibor Déry published a novel, *The Reply*, dealing with pre-war Hungary and the role of the Communist Party. Himself a lifelong member of the Party, Déry claimed the right to write in terms that did not always fit the political clichés of the day. Revai, the chief inquisitor, promptly replied:

> In our country, the writer does not have such a 'right'. . . We don't give the writer a free pass, we don't give him the 'freedom' to distort the living truth. We don't accept the thesis that the 'taste and judgement' of the writer are superior criteria for what

he should write and the way he should do it. The taste and judgement of the writer can be contrary to the interests of the people or of the Party. It is not the state and the people who ought to conform to his taste and judgement; it is the writer who, through work and study, should express solidarity with the construction of socialism.

Needless to say, the literature produced under such guidance tended to be highly unreadable or, at the very least, required a special sense of humour. In *Life is Elsewhere*, Milan Kundera makes a distinction between lyrical poetry, which he equates with a quest for the absolute and as such highly compatible with revolution, which often turns into dictatorship, and the novel, which for him is the art of reason, maturity and truth where you cannot cheat. This is why there are no great Stalinist novels. But Stalinist poetry, from Nezval in Czechoslovakia to Aragon in France (or Kundera himself in his youth), left us beautiful verse because, says Kundera, 'through the magic of poetry, all statements become the truth, provided they are backed by the real power of real experience. And the poet certainly experiences deeply, so deeply his emotions smoulder and blaze. The smoke of their fiery feelings spread like a rainbow over the sky, a beautiful rainbow spanning prison walls....'

This 'lyrical' dimension of the Stalinism of the early days, however, does not mean socialist-realist poetry was always more readable than the fiction. Usually, it was just as conventional, just as subservient to politics or just as embarrassingly grotesque:

> I have a thousand smells in my nostrils:
> Perfumes, roses, chloroform
> But what is it compared to the smell of life
> When a turner beats his work-norm!

Czech poet Ivan Skala wrote those lines in a 'Letter to Poets' in 1950. 'No, one cannot be dead, quiet, without feeling/Today also grows, for us and in us, the sunny side of the world'. Skala composed verse of similar quality and enthusiasm for the 'sunny side of the world' to praise the hangings of 'traitors' to the Party and is, to this day, highly thought of in official Prague. But there were dozens of would-be official poets like him: 'He came into the world/as one bursts into a hurricane.' 'He' was Klement Gottwald and the author the most promising of the surrealists in the 1930s, Vitezslav Nezval. (Meanwhile Louis Aragon, Nezval's alter ego in Paris, was writing 'Ode à la GPU'.) An endless stream of poems about five-year plans, steel workers and, of course, tractor drivers issued forth: 'Today a young woman boldly sits/on a stormy tractor . . .' (Jan Pilar, 1950). The tone occasionally became menacing: 'He who does not keep in step with us/lash him with a belt!' (Jiri Sotola), or supremely self-confident: 'Wipe out the filth of sexuality! Let your verse/be charged like a machine gun/with truth and love where need be./And a thousand Sartres, Kierkegaards, Freuds will not be consoled' (Josef Kainar, 1950). A touching motif juxtaposed Lenin or Stalin with little girls: 'In front of Stalin of white marble, stands a girl with a necklace' (Vlastimil Skolaudy).

> For the eyes of a little girl, prematurely wide,
> he ordered to shoot and spare no one
> who hid grain and exchanged bread for jewels only.
> This is how much he loved children, comrade Lenin.
>   (V. Merhautova, 1952)

Even music was to be in tune with the Party's political needs. Following an international (mainly from the Soviet bloc) congress of composers held in Prague in 1948, where the composers pledged to rid themselves of 'subjectivist' and 'cosmopolitan' tendencies, the Union of Czech and Slovak Composers launched a musical five-year plan to match (and complement) the economic one. The text provides a unique insight into the new role of art under socialism. 'Music is to effect the plan of reconstruction and the heightened class struggle. We want to help fulfil the plan,' the musicians proclaimed. The distinction between so-called 'serious' and 'popular' music was to be abolished. 'Music for the people' was the motto of the day. But the people's needs had no longer to be ascertained from dubious surveys or commercial interests, but from the 'conscious Communist workers', 'a Marxist forecast of the development trend'. Each and every artist and musician 'must be an ambassador of the people's democratic regime, the herald of the new order, a fighter for socialism'. The five-year plan for music noted that, in order to convince others, the artist himself must first of all be convinced. 'Hence the need for Marxist training for all composers and musicologists.' In particular, vocal art should 'reflect the class struggle'. 'We must, therefore, put an end to any attempts at an apolitical approach and at ideological emasculation of vocal creation' (*sic*). This meant the eradication of 'instrumental formalism' and the emphasis on 'popular songs of Slavic nations, particularly the USSR'. The Communists in East-Central Europe were especially keen on folklore, which provided an art that was by definition 'popular' (i.e. as opposed to bourgeois art) and national. The aim was to 'teach the people their own songs and to this end learn to play light, portable popular instruments, such as the harmonica or the guitar'. The emphasis on collective singing and dancing ('especially for agitational purposes') required new lyrics. 'In the creation of new mass songs the composers will take into account the new hero of labour and the new working collective. This will be the basis of a new singing epic.' Socialist art, says the document, is no longer interested in 'sentimental stories' or 'individualistic tragedies'; it requires a 'new collective hero'. The individual is only relevant as an 'expression of the whole'. These guidelines were to apply to radio programming and film scores.

Unfortunately, one cannot in Czechoslovakia dismiss such a concept of culture as merely belonging to the Stalinist past. In fact it has been reimposed in post-1968 Czechoslovakia, often in almost identical terms, in the new, duly purged, artists' unions. Thus, to use only one example, a survey of post-war Czech music by Jaroslav Sedivy published in Prague in the 1980s again stresses the 'mobilizing and educational element in the civic, political sphere of art'. After the ideologically dubious 1960s with their emphasis on 'alienation', 'the Christian idea of love without a class perspective', Sedivy describes the 1970s as having witnessed the 'consolidation of the musical front', in which composers are again allegedly in tune with the Party. Radio, television, record companies need committed music. How do the Party cultural watchdogs assess the output? Compared to other art forms, like literature or paintings, 'postwar music devoted to the themes of the Victorious February 1948, Labour Day, the great works of Czechoslovak socialism, the socialist transformation of the countryside, cosmic flights (with reference to Soviet cooperation with socialist countries), V. I. Lenin, etc., has not yet produced truly exceptional works'. The author considers his criticism all the more justified in view of the allegedly high quality of music composed on other subjects such as the liberation of the country by the Red Army, peace, 'the struggle for social progress all over the world', or the sixtieth anniversary of the Communist Party.

This is one example among many from the Czechoslovakia of the 1980s. History repeats itself, Marx wrote, tragedy returns as farce. In contrast to the famous quip, Stalinist art of the 1950s was the farce; post-1968 cultural 'normalization' is the tragedy.

The iconography of socialist realism was everywhere the same: it hailed the advent of the new man. East-Central Europe of the 1940s and 1950s inherited it from the Soviet Union of the 1930s. In the 1980s it can still be found in Romania and Bulgaria as well as in Cuba or Ethiopia. Socialist realism derived from the Stalinist view that man was merely the product of society and that a radical change of society and culture was the surest way to change man's consciousness. So while social-realist painters portrayed workers and peasants cheerfully marching towards the radiant future, the 'new man' theory could also justify experiments in social engineering, even re-education in the gulag. The vision had a utopian, lyrical dimension (which accounts, at least in part, for its initial appeal among creative people); but the reality has chilling, totalitarian overtones.

The personality cult became, of course, a major inspiration for the arts. On the occasion of Stalin's seventieth birthday in December 1949, a competition was launched in Hungary for the design of a statue of Stalin to be erected in the centre of Budapest (an episode vividly described by Janos Poto in the Hungarian journal *Historia*). Some twenty-five sculptors presented their work to a selection committee chaired by the chief ideologue and Minister of Culture, Revai. He described the purpose of the exercise as follows: 'This statue is born of the soul of the Hungarian nation. It is a Hungarian statue. The political thought of the old ruling classes was symbolized by dwarfs such as Werboczy [who wrote the first Hungarian legal code]. We shall correct this. We shall symbolize our political will with real giants, with heroes of the nation, fighters for freedom and national independence.'

Some of the competitors apparently got a bit carried away, their version of Stalin sometimes resembling Napoleon or the Hungarian poet Petöfi. The head of the Budapest City Council complained about the bad taste of some of the statues: 'Some of the faces are so distorted that one should immediately start proceedings against the authors.' The happy winner of the contest, Sandort Mikus, tried to convey his deep involvement with the subject: 'Often at night Stalin's face appears to me; I turn on the light and draw the traits of his face, the way he stands, his gestures are engraved in my mind.'

The statue was inaugurated in Budapest on 16 December 1951, in front of 80,000 people. A writer in a literary weekly commented: 'How immense he is! that is our first thought. How good he is. This morning I read a poem by Lebedev which hails Stalin as the gardener of the earth. I still think of that poem: "The black earth breathes, the grass and the trees are full of dew. We know this well, our dear gardener's smile under his moustache".'

Less than five years later the 'gardener of the earth' was denounced by Khrushchev as one of the greatest criminals in the history of mankind. On 23 October 1956, on the first day of the Hungarian revolution, the statue of the hated dictator was pulled down and his head rolled in the streets of Budapest.

At the beginning of *Man of Marble* (1976) the Polish film director Andrzej Wajda makes an autobiographical allusion to his own film about a 'hero of socialist labour' from the Stalinist era. Today he recalls what socialist realism meant for the artists of his generation:

> There was a great deal of passion and misunderstanding at the beginning when all the implications were not clear yet. We thought that socialist realism was a kind of continuation of the Soviet artistic avant-garde of the 1920s. We thought that behind it was some idea, some urge to create a new art which would be different from Western art. We were young and searching in that direction. But it soon became clear that what the authorities had in mind was simply to imitate Soviet art. You had to paint the way the Soviets did, you had to compose the way they did and writers had to write like the writers in the Soviet Union. Of course, one has to ask, what was it all for? The reason was that the arts were a fragment of a larger whole with an aim to create a new, socialist man. He should have different feelings, a different morality and a different view of the world; so that he could, almost independently of those who lead him, know his place: to be a little screw in a huge machine.

Socialist realism attracted believers but also opportunists who used politics as a literary springboard. The Polish poet Zbigniew Herbert gave a merciless account of a young careerist's (he calls him Tadzio) imaginary, yet only too realistic 'confession': 'I went to a meeting with older writers who were supposed to instruct us,' says Tadzio. 'They were wonderful poets and novelists from before the war, but from the very beginning they did not like us because we were young. Therefore we launched a frontal attack. We told one of them that he was a symbolist – which was a terrible insult. We told another that he was a passéist – which was also an insult – and we left slamming the door. After we had left, we got together and decided to form a group.' But even the group, which initially enjoyed the sponsorship of the Minister of the Interior himself, eventually fell out of favour and dispersed: 'Miecek went to *Poglad* and started to praise socialist realism in art – all those peasant women with cows and happy miners. I continued to write. I was getting tired of poetry. The time is not suitable for poetry, I said, and I had better write a novel. It had to be a factory novel. But my colleagues were faster. Silesia and the miners were taken care of. Witold got the shipyards, somebody else – sugar plants. I got the furniture industry. A bit marginal, but I took it anyway.' The account is a bit 'rough', as Herbert admits, but probably close to the truth.

This all-encompassing Party control of cultural life gradually started to break down in the post-Stalin era. Adam Wazyk's famous 'Poem for Adults', published in Warsaw in 1955, marked the beginning of the end of the utopian age:

> I will never believe, my dear, in a magic spell;
> I will never believe in minds kept under glass;
> but I believe that a table has four legs,
> but I believe that a fifth leg is a chimera,
> and when the chimeras rally, my dear,
> then one dies slowly of a worn-out heart.

Wazyk spoke for a whole generation of 'believers', not just in Poland, when speaking of the grief entailed in his loss of faith: 'Have I lost the gift of seeing, or the gift of convenient blindness? I am left with a short note, with these verses of a new grief.'

But more than grief there was revolt among writers in Warsaw and Budapest at their parting with the ideological camouflage of terror. Within weeks of Khrushchev's denunciation of Stalin's crimes at the Twentieth Congress of the Soviet Party in Moscow in 1956, Polish, Hungarian and (more cautiously) Czech writers demanded greater creative freedom. At a session of the Polish Council of Culture and Art the poet Antoni Slonimski denounced socialist realism as 'a precision tool for destroying art'. The persecution of critical thought in past centuries, he added, appears to have been 'almost idyllic' compared to the Stalinist era. Jan Kot, Poland's leading expert on Shakespeare, said on the same occasion:

> We have been trying to explain reality and not to learn the truth; to explain and justify at any price, even at the price of truth.
> Thus modern history became a great mythology before our eyes. Whenever the facts stood in the way, the facts were changed. If genuine heroes were obstacles, they evaporated. Literature which was not allowed to speak about crimes, literature which had to keep silent about trials which shocked men's minds and which were the daily reality for years, literature which had a sealed lip and wandered even further and deeper into lies, created a more and more fictitious vision of reality.

Almost word for word similar voices were heard at the meetings of the Petofi circle in Budapest in 1956 or in Prague at the Writers' Congress in 1956 and again, more forcefully, in 1967.

But while Stalinist ideology crumbled, the institution of censorship it left behind was there to stay. Indeed the history of cultural life in Central Europe can be told as the artists' double emancipation:

from the regime's ideology and the straitjacket of censorship. Paradoxically, it is the regime's extreme politicization of culture which is the prime constraint on the artist, the writer and the film-maker, and makes him long for art that would escape political control, that would not be judged solely in terms of its political audacity. Yet the same constraints often give literature and the arts in the Other Europe that extra sharp edge and the writer a unique status in society. Stefan Heym, a leading East German writer who was expelled from the Writers' Union in 1979 after the publication in the West of his novel *Collin*, compares his situation to that of the writer in the West:

> As a writer in the West you can write practically anything you like, it doesn't make any difference, nobody gives a damn. Of course, your work is being read, people may be entertained by it, but it has very little political effect. In this part of the world it's entirely different. The writer has more weight; that is why you have censorship, because his word counts and because politicians must take what he writes seriously. Therefore it is much more fun to work in this so-called socialist part of the world.

Is it because the writer's word has more weight that you have censorship, or is it censorship that gives the writer's word more weight? At any rate, battles with the censor have not always been 'fun'. In a system where the news media are not free, where the average citizen tends to believe exactly the opposite of what he has heard on television, where people read only the sports page in newspapers because 'it's the place where they don't lie', literature and the arts is where people know they can find a more genuine insight into the world they live in. It is fiction that is often closest to the reality, to a basic human truth. Of course, under censorship, that truth is often conveyed indirectly; people learn to read between the lines. 'In Poland,' says Ryszard Kapuscinski, 'we read every text as allusive; every situation described – even the most remote in time and space – is immediately applied to Poland. Every text is a double text. Between the lines we look for the message written in invisible ink, and the hidden message we find is treated as the only true one.'

Kapuscinski's own book about Iran under the Shah is an illustration of what he describes, as is Stefan Heym's *King David Report*, which uses a biblical setting for a brilliant analysis of the historian's relationship with truth and power in a totalitarian state.

Art and especially literature becomes the mirror of a society, the only place where its contemporary problems or the 'white spots' in its history can be discussed. It is in this sense that literature gives the society its identity.

In East Germany in the early 1970s several young authors described in their books the alienation of youth in an authoritarian state. Ulrich Plenzdorf's *The New Sufferings of Young W*, which became a cult book in 1972, is the story of a teenager dropping out of the system after a row at work; his attempt to live freely on the margins of society ends tragically, with the suicide of the dropout, a hitherto unknown hero in East German literature. Wolker Braun's *Incomplete Story* and Reiner Kunze's *Wonderful Years* (1976) were moving depictions of the petty but relentless harassment of young people by officialdom. Clearly, the authorities were no longer prepared to tolerate any longer such exposés of their failure in the eyes of the young generation. Kunze was forced to emigrate after being told by a senior official, 'You won't survive what we have in store for you.' The rift between the writers and the regime became complete when the singer Wolf Biermann was forced into exile. Others followed: Jürgen Fuchs, Sarah Kirsch, Günter Künert, Thomas Brasch. It has been said that the best German literature is in the East. It should be added that some of the best East German literature is now in the West.

For a few years the authorities seemed to have bought some respite. But the alienation of the young generation, its resentment against militarism and ideological control, is stronger than ever. And there are new young writers to express its frustrations and aspirations. One of them is Lütz Rathenaw, born in 1952, first arrested in 1980 after the publication in the West of his short stories *Prepared for the Worst*. In one of the stories a ruler, declining to enforce his personality cult, demands that worship be accorded to his dog. In another, two men fight a duel over a disagreement as to how many times humanity could be annihilated in the next war. His view of German history is no more to the liking of the authorities than his humour:

> The finger I left at Verdun,
> an ear at Stalingrad –
> I give my head:
> to our new state.

The subject of censorship, the confrontation of the individual with the impersonal machine of the state, is also a theme in Monika Maron's writing. In *The Female Defector* she describes some of her own dilemmas through the thoughts of Josefa Nadler, a journalist and the main character of the novel: 'Whatever is not printable isn't thought through. It's only a short path from unprintable to unthinkable as soon as you agree to measure reality by this standard.'

The 'I' of the writer clashes with comrade 'We'. 'I will say this once and for all: whoever speaks of himself in the plural has to allow me to address him in the plural. Anyone who is a "we" also has to be a "you" and a "they". And if they make their opinions into mine without asking permission, I'll say "me" to me and "them" to them.'

Monika Maron's work is banned and her only contact with the public is through readings in Father Eppelmann's church in East Berlin. What she resents most about the current situation is less the degree of control *per se* than the constant 'patronizing guidance' of the state which affects people's everyday life: 'The GDR functions like an authoritarian kindergarten.'

The new realism and the art of the metaphor as counterweight to official dogma occur as well in the cinema, be it Polish films after 1956 (Polanski, Wajda, etc.), the Czech films of the 1960s or Hungarian films since the late 1970s.

The favourite themes of the Czech 'new wave' ranged from an indictment of impersonal bureaucratic rule to the exploration of sexual freedom. But all these films were, after all, produced by the state bureaucracy. One explanation is that, when ideology begins to crumble, the Party ideological watchdogs lose their touch and the empty space is filled by a new generation of film-makers, keen to break the official taboos. Not with politics, but with irony, with imagination, with a new language that society can identify with. The Czech 'new wave' was the product of a close interaction between film directors, writers and critics. There was a rich and free-spirited cultural life in the Prague of the 1960s which helped to bring about some of the masterpieces of European cinema.

For the first time Czechoslovak cinema became free from the constraints of the market, but also from the dictates of ideology. Antonin Liehm, a leading Czech literary and film critic at the time, explains this transformation:

In the 1950s it became increasingly clear that the liberation of film from the dictates of the market meant its subjugation to the dictates of the state. But when the system started to break down and the people in charge of film at all levels became unsure, less strict, the system regained some of its positive qualities: the creators of film were getting more control over the industry. The nationalized system could be the worst when it's tightly run but, as Czech director Ivan Passer [now living in the United States] said, when this system falls apart it is the best system you can have. Film-makers were never so free as in the 1960s in Czechoslovakia. The same is true, at different times, of the other film industries in East-Central Europe. And, who knows, something like that could now also happen in the Soviet Union.

Jiři Menzel, director of the Oscar-winning *Closely Observed Trains*, recalls the emergence of the 'new wave':

I remember that not just us at the FAMU Film School, but everybody felt some scorn for what they saw on the screens or read in newspapers. People would say 'it is like in a film' when they meant that something was not quite true. This created a craving for something truthful. I remember what a discovery at the end of the 1950s and early 1960s American documentary films were for us. They taught us how to use the camera. Cassavetes' *Shadows*, that was a great discovery for us, compared to those elaborate films made in studios with actors covered with make-up. A whole generation suddenly knew not how to make films, but what kind of films they did not want to make.

Milan Kundera, who was one of the teachers at the Prague Film School, calls that generation the 'children of Kafka'. This is because they shared with the author of *The Trial* a tragicomic vision of the world:

In contrast with the classical mind which divides the world between the sphere of tragedy and comedy, Prague (or Central European) humour ignores such boundaries. It is not therefore so much a different humour as a different view of the world which considers the comical side as an indivisible part of every human situation. Nothing, nobody is spared the comical which is part of our condition, our shadow, our relief and our condemnation. Forman leaves us in no doubt: *Firemen's Ball*, his last film shot in Czechoslovakia (1967), starts with a funny dialogue about the cancer of the firemen's chief, and his humour becomes unbearable and masterful when at the end another old man watches his house in flames.

In *The Castle*, Kundera notes, Kafka had also dealt with a firemen's feast which turns into a tragedy. 'Neither Forman nor Kafka meant to show disregard for the glory of fire extinguishing. But both like to show the behaviour of the institutionalized man (the representative, *par excellence*, of modern mankind) precisely in the most ordinary and absurd situations, precisely in its most subordinate and innocent incarnations.'

Firemen's Ball takes place in a provincial township in Bohemia. The ball is organized by a group of totally inept firemen who are unable even to prevent people from stealing the prizes for the lottery, let alone put out a fire. At the end of the film they discuss what they should tell people about the situation. But by the time they decide to go out and tell people the truth there is nobody there; nobody is interested any more because everybody knows. The film ends with the man whose house has burned and the fireman sleeping in the same bed in a snowstorm; the victim and his 'protector' find themselves in the same situation: they have both lost everything.

After the Soviet-led invasion *Firemen's Ball* featured prominently on the list of forbidden films. Next to it was another masterpiece of the late 1960s, Jan Nemec's *Report on the Party and the Guests*. The novelist Josef Škvorecký, closely associated with the Czech film-makers of the 1960s, explains why a film about an unusual birthday party provoked the 'normalized' censor to attach to Nemec's film the label 'banned forever':

> One of the ideas about Communism, never, of course, expressed in so many words, is that revolution, in spite of the feelings or wishes of the people, will force them into happiness. And that's what the film is about. A host invites guests to a party; many are uneasy, clearly not as happy as they should be and one of them decides to leave the party. So the host sends dogs after him. The film ends with the whole screen darkening and those hounds of Baskerville obviously hunting the man who decided not to be happy.

The party as a metaphor for the Party. Breaking the tacit loyalty to the Communist Party, and the will to act as an individual, was something subversive for both the purveyors of collective happiness and the silent majority. And this is why what might seem an elitist film for intellectuals had such an impact: 'It is a demanding film,' says Škvorecký. 'You have to have some experience of modern literature. But even not very educated people in Czechoslovakia understand Kafka better than most in the West. Take *The Trial*: a man is being arrested and does not know why; in the end he perishes without ever learning why. This is something that in Kafka's time was just a nightmare. But then it became a reality for many people in our country. So people understood such a film very well.'

Nothing could be further removed from Soviet-style film-making (where war movies were what Westerns are for American cinema) than the anti-heroic neo-realism of the Czech 'new wave'. What provided the discreet charm of the Czech films of the 1960s was the simplicity of their almost microscopic observation of reality (Ivan Passer's *Intimate Lighting* or Forman's *Loves of a Blonde*): in the microcosm of human action they found a portrait of society as a whole. This accounts for the political dimension of films with apparently non-political subjects such as *Firemen's Ball*: art as demystifier of ideology.

When censorship collapses the artist finds himself in a new situation, free to be concerned only with his art rather than with the fate of the nation. This is what Jan Nemec, director of *The Party and the Guests*, said to A. J. Liehm during the Prague Spring of 1968:

> The difference between today and yesterday is primarily that we all find ourselves in a situation that we were not ready for. The cards have been redealt, the game is open and, for a moment, everyone can play what he wants. The moving force of all our activity has been 'the struggle against the dark forces of reaction', to borrow a phrase from Stalin's *History of the Bolshevik Party*. The driving force has fallen by the wayside, at least for the present. When one lives in a society which is essentially unfree, it is the obligation of every thinking person to attack obstacles to freedom in every way at his disposal; which is what happened. Now, of course, everyone is faced with a choice: what does he really want? What does he feel must be done and said in the new situation, in which people are no longer behind barbed wire, but rather within a normal society so that, in our case, a different sort of activity will be called for?

We shall never know what Hungarian or Czech artists would have done with their newly conquered freedom in 1956 or 1968. One can note, however, that the great works of post-war Central European literature were not written and the great films were not conceived during the brief periods of freedom (when censorship collapsed) in 1956, 1968 or 1980, though many could then be published or shown to the public. This is even more striking in the Soviet Union today. No new names have appeared. There is a distinctly 'necrophiliac' feel about Moscow's bestseller list under *glasnost*. From Akhmatova's 'Requiem' to Tvardovski's 'Right to a Memory', from Pasternak's *Doctor Zhivago* to Grossman's *Life and Destiny*, from Platonov and Bek to the émigrés Nabokov and Bunin, all the missing pieces of Russian literature (and, through them, all the taboo subjects of post-revolutionary history) are now revealed to an insatiable public – posthumously. When censorship relaxes, it is time to empty the drawers.

Instead of a return to a 'normal society', as Jan Nemec hoped for, Czechoslovakia was promptly bullied into being a 'normalized' one. The intellectuals who played such a prominent part in preparing the cultural background to the Prague Spring naturally became the prime targets of the post-invasion 'restoration of order'. What followed was the most ruthless and uncompromising suppression of a culture in the Communist world, except perhaps for the Chinese Cultural Revolution. What the French poet Louis Aragon called the 'Biafra of the spirit' meant that hundreds of authors were banned and their works removed from libraries; more than two-thirds of journalists were purged; university professors (including 145 historians) became window cleaners, nightwatchmen or stokers. (Maybe this is what the Party ideologues meant by 'raising the cultural level of the working class'?) Their students were subjected to a very strict system of political vetting. To mention only one example of what 'normalization' of culture and education means, the 'loyalty oath' for high-school teachers states: 'In line with the principles of Communist education I will strive to develop my pupils' love for their socialist fatherland, to inspire respect for the working class and the Party and raise them in the spirit of Marxism–Leninism.' As Milan Kundera put it: 'In its duration, extent and consistency, the massacre of Czech culture after 1968 has had no analogue in the history of the country since the Thirty Years War.'

Josef Škvorecký, who, like Milan Kundera, now lives in exile, is best known in the West for his novel fittingly entitled *The Engineer of Human Souls*. But he is also a publisher of authors now banned in Czechoslovakia: 'We publish, among other things, a dictionary of banned Czech writers which now has some five hundred entries. I am not saying that all these people are geniuses. Many of them are, of course, average or worse than average. But they are writers and they have the right to express themselves. So imagine that in a country of ten million Czechs there are five hundred names on the blacklist. You would have to multiply this by twenty to get the number of American writers that would be banned under such a regime.'

Words such as 'counter-culture' or 'underground' culture have been used, sometimes too loosely, in the West since the 1960s. In Central Europe they have acquired a real meaning. Czech culture was literally driven underground by the Husak regime. Hence the extraordinary variety of unofficial cultural life: from *samizdat* publishing to the 'living-room theatre', from unofficial philosophy seminars to rock concerts by banned groups such as the Plastic People of the Universe. The poet and translator Jan Vladislav has been deeply involved with independent publishing in Czechoslovakia, not just since 1968 but since 1948:

Czechoslovakia's parallel culture is not merely the legacy of the
Prague Spring of 1968; it is the continuation of the spiritual
resistance of the 1950s. Interestingly, because it involved after
1968 a number of people who had worked for many years in the
official structures, it gave the independent activities a more
effective, more 'organized' character than before. The
'normalization' of the 1970s also engendered a change of outlook.
In the 1950s, Czech and Slovak spiritual resistance was geared,
quite naturally, to an eventual relaxation of regime pressure, and
events were to vindicate such an approach. During the 1970s the
resistance quickly came to realize that the prospects for change
from within the regime were far from favourable and it was
therefore vital, without delay, to work either on the fringes of the
official structures or entirely outside them.

For the writers this was a completely new situation. Writing
directly for *samizdat* was a liberation from censorship, and, perhaps
more importantly, from self-censorship. Although it can be a liberating experience, writing for the unofficial network also implies a
risk of being cut off from one's audience. Unlike in Poland where
samizdat publications are sold in thousands or tens of thousands, in
Czechoslovakia typewritten copies are distributed in hundreds. Even
though each copy reaches dozens of readers some writers are concerned about the danger of creating a closed, elitist culture which
remains divorced from the society at large. The situation is particularly difficult for a playwright like Vaclav Havel. For whom does
he write?

Drama is an art which is created in a concrete place, it has to
have a home. It is written for a certain cultural and spiritual
situation without which it cannot live. It is not something that
can be transferred at will and it was very difficult for me to get
used to writing plays which are then performed only abroad, in
England or in Yugoslavia. I write as if my plays were to be
performed here and now. My plays are circulated in *samizdat*,
on tape or even video cassettes. Actors from the Prague theatres
all know my plays and generally know more about my work than
I do about theirs. But a play is destined for the stage and I find,
time and time again, that people do not know how to read plays;
and why should they? Plays aren't meant to be read, but to be
seen on stage. So I find myself releasing into circulation some
kind of semi-finished product. It's tough but I've grown
accustomed to it.

Although the development of *samizdat* has since the 1970s become a common feature of cultural life in Central Europe, only 'normalized' Czechoslovakia displayed such a clear-cut divide between officially controlled and independent culture. The trial of the leaders of the Jazz Section of the Musicians' Union at the end of 1986 was the ultimate paranoid gesture in the authorities' attempt to suppress what Škvorecký aptly called the 'grey zone' between the two cultures.

Elsewhere in Central Europe the limits between them have recently become increasingly blurred – that is, in countries where there is an independent culture to speak of. In Romania there is no literary *samizdat* and the obsession with control even led Ceausescu to introduce a new law which requires all typewriters to be registered. Asked about the effects of the law a member of the Writers' Union answered, 'I would not know. I write in longhand . . .' In Poland and Hungary the combination of the vigour of independent culture with the relative tolerance of the authorities is creating a new situation in which the divides of yesterday no longer seem to be a sure guide.

In some countries such a 'grey zone' can develop thanks to the role of the Church, which is by definition an institution on the borderlines of dissent and officialdom, challenging the official ideology while enjoying a legal if constricted existence. In Poland, especially since martial law, the Catholic Church has provided protection for artists banned from the official media. Concerts, exhibitions, theatre performances, poetry readings take place in parish halls, the only place where people can gather freely.

A similar role, though on a smaller scale, is played by the East German Protestant Church. The Kirchentag, the annual festival of the Church, is the largest and certainly the freest cultural manifestation in East Germany. And because it is free it has its own 'dissidents'. This is a curious gathering, the socks-and-sandals brigade of the Christian–Marxist dialogue, hippies, egalitarian socialists, Christian ecolo-pacifists and punk groups. It is in East Germany that you will find the last sincere Marxists in the Soviet bloc. The ideology of East German counter-culture is a mixture of critical Marxism, Protestant moralism and 'Green' anti-authoritarianism. It has preserved a somewhat dated 1960s mixture of socialism and post-industrial utopia – and earnestness. . . . While in West Berlin angry punks and squatters fight all night with the police, a mere stone's throw from the Wall, expressing their bitter hatred for the capitalist society, in East Berlin even the punks have an innocent look in their eyes especially when, also a mere stone's throw from the Wall, they chant, 'Gorbachev! Gorbachev!'

In Poland, the Church is the official counter-culture, the repository of an alternative ideology. It has its Catholic University at Lublin, its Cracow-based publishing house (Znak) and its weekly *Tygodnik Powszechny*, the only truly independent legally published paper in the Communist world. Founded in 1945 the paper was shut down in 1953 when it courageously refused to print an obituary for Stalin. But since its revival in 1956 during a period of liberalization, it has managed to sustain its independence and a prestigious list of contributors, which includes the former Archbishop of Cracow, Pope Wojtyla. The quality and the moral stature of the paper has, according to its editor for forty years Jerzy Turowicz, been even more firmly established since its relationship with the censor has been made explicit:

> With the relatively more liberal law on censorship passed in 1981 we have the right to indicate the places where censorship interfered, so that the reader is aware of what is going on. Although we are reasonable and prudent people, with a lot of experience, we have every week two or three articles taken out, not to mention smaller cuts on virtually every page. They concern a variety of issues, especially politics, of course, and Church–state relations.

Despite the initial crackdown on the cultural milieu in the immediate aftermath of martial law, Poland has (once again) become the freest country in the Soviet bloc in terms of the regime's tolerance of unofficial views. This, despite official rhetoric, owes little to Gorbachev-inspired *glasnost*; it is the result of the formidable expansion of unofficial publishing over the last decade. Poland has moved from a situation where most of the leading intellectuals wrote directly for the *samizdat* to a situation where the same article can appear in both the official and the unofficial circuit. The *samizdat* is almost the victim of its own success.

The most telling illustration of the change was the legal publication in 1987 of a hitherto leading *samizdat* journal *Respublica*. There was a heated discussion in opposition circles about the political implications of breaking a boycott imposed on official media since the military coup of December 1981. Marcin Krol, a well-known historian, is the editor of the journal. What happens when a dissident meets a censor?

> It was a difficult dilemma, of course. But we thought that we could not spend the next twenty or thirty years waiting. Today we are the first journal which is totally independent of the state and of the Church. It is a strange feeling for me going to see the

censor, but hardly a totally new one in this country since the war. He says, 'I understand what you mean, but we have to do that'; and I say, 'I know you have to do that, but . . . ' I don't always understand their approach because they are interested in words, not in thoughts. For instance, you can describe all kinds of horrors so long as 'totalitarianism' or 'Communism' is replaced by 'Stalinism'. Or instead of 'the Soviet Union' you are asked to put 'a neighbouring country'. Most confiscated things actually concern the Soviet Union, but then everybody in Poland knows what the Soviet Union is; so it's hardly the most intellectually stimulating subject.

Most appropriately for a journal of liberal orientation *Respublica* is privately owned. Indeed, financial independence is, for Marcin Krol, a precondition of editorial independence: 'To promote independent culture you need a space. To have a space you also need money and in Poland there are only two sources of support: the state and the Church. I am a Catholic but we try to be independent of both.' Is he worried that his change of status from dissident to legal might, in the long run, jeopardize his integrity? 'You must know where you stand. If you are unsure of yourself, it is risky to try to reach a compromise. To make a compromise you have to have a very strong commitment to a set of values you wish to promote.'

Poland used to be the country where things were simple, the battle lines were clearly drawn. No longer so. Now it has been admitted, the ideological bankruptcy of the Party is being put to good use – to the confusion of everybody else. In this respect Poland's cultural life might come to resemble that of Hungary, the country *par excellence* of 'repressive tolerance'.

Hungarian intellectuals have become the most prolific writers on the subject of censorship, ever since censorship itself started withering away. That was fifteen years ago when leading philosophers of the Budapest school (A. Heller, F. Feher, G. Markus) were advised to exert their critical powers in Australia rather than in Budapest, when György Konrad became Hungary's best-known non-person, and Miklosz Haraszti went on trial for disseminating a manuscript rejected by an official publisher. The year was 1974, the title *Piecework*; Hungarian *samizdat* was born. The Party suffered a defeat and has since given up hope of restoring the ideological foundations of censorship. That was its original sin. By losing the ideological compass and becoming increasingly vague and permissive about norms and taboos that had been the spice of cultural life in Central Europe for more than four decades, the retreating

Party managed to spread utter confusion in the ranks of the Hungarian intelligentsia. Besides the 'happy few' such as Konrad, Kis or Haraszti who are published in *samizdat* (thanks to the diligence of their publisher, Gabor Demszky), the others suffer at the hands of a vanishing censor. Each step in the liberalization has only contributed to the brewing discontent. Now that there are almost no taboos left (except, of course, the Soviet Union) the revolt has been brought into the open. At the conference of the Writers' Union in 1987 the dissidents took over and the Party loyalists became the 'dissidents', forced to set up a rival confidential grouping. And the rallying cry of the triumphant yet increasingly angry mob of emancipated writers? 'Bring back censorship!'

This is a typically Hungarian paradox, but it is not meant to be funny. The writer Istvan Eorsi has been the first to launch the campaign for the restoration of censorship. The abolition of the office of the censor, the argument goes, has merely shifted the responsibility for censorship on to the editors and ultimately on to the writers themselves. Sandor Csoori, the best known of the 'populist' writers, denounced the unbearable lightness of self-censorship as something 'insidious as a fog or smoke: it does not suffocate you but makes you cough. You catch mental bronchitis.'

From the safe distance of the 'velvet prison' of *samizdat* Miklos Haraszti provided a compassionate verdict:

> The old censorship is increasingly being superseded by something altogether new, less visible and more dangerous.... Traditional censorship presupposes the inherent opposition of creators and censor; the new censorship strives to eliminate this antagonism. The artist and the censor – the two faces of official culture – diligently and cheerfully cultivate the gardens together. This new culture is the result not of raging censorship, but of its steady disappearance. Censorship professes itself to be freedom because it acts, like morality, as the common spirit of both rulers and ruled.

Intellectuals in Opposition

'None of this would have happened if a couple of writers had been shot in time.' Thus spoke with characteristic frankness Nikita Khrushchev, nine months after the Red Army had suppressed the Hungarian revolution of 1956. It reveals the (exaggerated) power Communist regimes then attributed to intellectuals. Intellectuals in the Other Europe have traditionally been seen as an alternative elite: spokesmen for nations without a state in the nineteenth century; for nations without a voice after the Second World War. From the poets of the revolution of 1848 to the dissidents of 1988, culture in Central Europe has often been the substitute for politics, and the intellectuals have been the 'conscience of their nation'.

But they were a 'false conscience' at the time of the Communist takeovers. Paradoxically, the advent of Communism, which destroyed the independence of cultural life, has been welcomed by a majority of intellectuals in Central Europe. They had identified with the ideological promise of the Party, which in turn rewarded them with the illusion of power and the realities of privilege. But soon they found their golden cage constricting, and the crimes committed in the name of lofty ideals too nauseating. Critics from within at first, they became critics from without; from advocates of the independence of culture they became advocates of the independence of society. As such the story of Central European intellectuals since the war is an integral part of the European intellectuals' love affair with Marxism – the story of the 'God that failed'.

'By the time the Communist Party openly took power,' notes Hungarian writer Miklos Haraszti, 'the majority of artists were already committed to loyal service.' This was particularly true of Czechoslovakia. A brochure entitled *My Attitude Towards the Communist Party* was published before the Communist takeover in 1948. It read like a 'Who's Who' of the Czechoslovak intellectual elite of the time. Communists did not rely only on force. In fact they followed a Gramscian model: achieving 'cultural hegemony' even before they won a complete monopoly of political power. The emergence of the 'organic intellectual', loyal to the Party, confusing truth with political expediency, was the result not just of fear, but of conviction. In Czeslaw Milosz's words: 'The pressure of the state machine is nothing compared with the pressure of a convincing argument.' Why did so many intellectuals succumb? Was it just a case of the intellectuals briefly going astray, or was it compromise with far-reaching consequences, what Julien Benda in the 1930s called the 'betrayal of the clerks'?

Milosz himself gave us memorable portraits of leading Polish intellectuals seduced by the 'New Faith' that came from the East: former Catholic nationalists (like Andrzejewski, author of *Ashes and Diamonds*) or survivors of the death camps; pre-war fellow travellers and post-war converts returning from exile to take part in the building of socialism (Galinski, Slonimski). There was a mixture of fascination and the feeling of impotence, opportunism and the urge to belong to an irresistible and irreversible force of history.

'Why did I become a Communist?' asks the main character in Kundera's novel *The Joke*, and explains the excitement of belonging to a movement that was at the 'steering wheel of history': 'At the time we could really decide the fate of the people' – not just 'dizziness with power', but also dizziness with mastering history. Marx, after all, claimed that the task of the intellectuals was no longer to interpret the world but to change it.

But there was also, Milosz suggested, an element of deceit, the 'art of the Ketman', of outward conformism, transposed from the Islamic to the Communist world – to the point where it became unclear who was deceiving whom. Might not the adapting conformist writer be in the end deceiving only himself?

Milan Kundera echoed this theme in his short story 'Edward and God': 'If you obstinately tell a man the truth to his face, it would mean that you are taking him seriously. And to take something so unimportant seriously means to become less than serious oneself. I, you see, *must* lie, if I don't want to take madmen seriously and become one of them myself.'

Beyond the paradoxes of fascination and deceit perhaps the main reason for the appeal of Communism at the end of the war was the collapse of the old world and its values. If you have seen and experienced hell you do not want to 'improve' it but radically to change it. As Jan Patočka observed, Masarykian liberal rationalism was not enough in the age of Hitler and Stalin. Widespread contempt for liberal values and politics accounts, at least in part, for the weak resistance to Communism. Antonin Liehm was part of that generation: 'At the end of the war the Soviet solution seemed to many of us to be the only one, because the Western solution had crashed so badly at Munich in 1938 and after. So, under the wings of our "progressive" tradition of a culture committed to social change and our young men's experience, we eventually ran directly, blindfolded, into the trap of Stalinism.'

The historical setting is no doubt essential, though perhaps not a sufficient explanation for understanding the post-war itinerary of Central European intellectuals. Professor Vaclav Černý (with Jan Patočka possibly the most important, yet marginal, intellectual figure in post-war Czechoslovakia) gives a less generous interpretation. In his memoirs (1984) he paints a devastating picture of the Communist generation, the 'class of 1948': zealots and opportunists, careerists quick to lead the purge and grab vacant jobs while the going was good. There is bitterness, sometimes unfairness, in his uncompromising account, but only a scholar of his stature and of his generation (born in 1905 like Sartre, whose existentialism was his philosophical inspiration, and like Raymond Aron, with whom he shared the privilege of being for four decades the lonely *spectateur-engagé*-proved-right-in-the-end) could write so freely about the glory and demise of the Czech intellectual.

Černý's alter ego in Poland is the poet Zbigniew Herbert. He challenges the view that there was no other way than to give in to the 'enslavement of the elite':

> The Great Linguist, Stalin, once said that one does not need to buy a nation. One simply has to have engineers of human souls. The government needed legitimacy which was provided by the intellectuals, the so-called 'creative' intelligentsia, and especially the writers. So I left the business. I did not want to be part of it.

Herbert, with false modesty, denies that saying 'no' to the Great Linguist required courage. For him it was ... 'a matter of taste'.

The years 1956 to 1968: reason versus conscience. De-Stalinization called off the period of 'gardening in a cemetery' and opened a period of soul-searching. What was the relationship between socialist theory and terrorist practice? Was Stalinism a mere 'deformation' on the otherwise healthy foundations of socialism? And if so one should be careful not to throw out the socialist baby with the dirty bathwater (the dirty bathwater being the millions who died in the gulag). Such questions dominated intellectual debate from Khrushchev's Twentieth Congress speech to the Prague Spring of 1968. Between 1956 and 1968 Central European intellectuals denounced Stalinist crimes in the name of socialist values and ideals. After the crushing of the Prague Spring they renounced socialist ideas in the name of the crimes committed after 1948 and again after 1968. Such a dialectic of 'crimes and ideals' is not unique to the Stalinist period. French intellectuals initially denounced slavery in the name of the ideas of the Enlightenment. Many of their twentieth-century successors denounced Western liberal values in the name of the crimes or injustices attributed to colonialism.

The intellectual foundations of 'revisionism', a critique of Stalinism from within the Marxist ideology, were remarkably similar in Poland, Hungary and Czechoslovakia. Its leading philosophers were Leszek Kolakowski, György Lukacs and Karel Kosík. It entailed a critique of Stalinism in the name of a return to an increasingly elastic interpretation of the thought of the 'young' Marx and of the 'old' Engels. Above all it rejected 'ends justify the means' theory and asserted the primacy of ethics over politics, of the Kantian 'categorical imperative' over Marx's laws of history.

Khrushchev's vehement denunciation of Stalinist crimes without offering a plausible explanation left the Marxist intellectuals in disarray. Many, as Norberto Bobbio wrote, were concerned that the famous secret speech was not a 'Marxist analysis'. But then, 'neither is *Macbeth* a Marxist text. A cry of horror is neither Marxist nor anti-Marxist: it is a cry.'

The itinerary of the leading philosophers of 'revisionism' in a way highlights the ambiguity of the phenomenon, its power to erode the system and its limitations. György Lukacs exemplified the contradictions of the Party intellectual. He was, as is well known, Thomas Mann's model for the character of Naphtha in *The Magic Mountain*. Like Naphtha, the Jesuit, Lukacs was torn between the rigours of an order with a universalistic ideology and the independence of a man of culture. Often on the margins of heresy, he eventually always gave in to the Party, accepting humiliating self-criticism in 1949 and again after 1956. He provided his numerous disciples (Agnes Heller, Ferenc Feher and Mihaly Vajda among others) with intellectual ammunition against the sterility of Communist dogma. Yet when it came to the crunch his motto remained: 'My Party right or wrong' – even when tanks were called in to settle philosophical arguments. In Istvan Eorsi's play appropriately called *His Master's Voice*, Lukacs is the main character. As Stalinist crimes come to be discussed the character of Lukacs answers: 'I too had many problems with Stalin. For example, I could never decide whether he had read Hegel.' One of the very few Marxist philosophers of stature will also go down in history paying tribute to political idiocy: 'Even the worst of socialism will always be preferable to the best capitalism.'

Kolakowski and Kosík represent a different itinerary: from 'revisionism' to a complete break with Communism. The former was forced into exile after his expulsion from Warsaw University and has published in the West a most devastating critical study of Marxist thought. He has remained a major intellectual influence on contemporary Polish dissent. Karel Kosík, author of *The Dialectic of the Concrete*, has been reduced to silence for twenty years. The last time he broke that silence was in 1975 when the police confiscated from him a thousand-page manuscript. Its title was: *On Truth*.

The Prague Spring of 1968 was the high point of 'revisionism', the culmination of the conflict between critical intellectuals and political power. Because the Czechoslovak de-Stalinization had been delayed, it eventually came with a vengeance. In the forefront was the Communist generation of 1948, recovering from its Stalinist hangover and compensating (sometimes over-compensating) for its past failures. A 'revolution within the revolution', 1968 marked the apotheosis of the political influence of the intellectuals acting as a bridge between the Party and the people, 'enlightening' the ruler while expressing the democratic aspirations of the society.

The tanks of August crushed the hopes of a reformed 'socialism with a human face' and defeated the intellectuals' attempt to salvage the ideals of their youth. Yet many experienced defeat as a liberation, a belated reconciliation with their nation. Pavel Kohout, the Communist poet, wrote in his *Diary of a Counter-Revolutionary*: 'For the first time, after twenty years, I have the sensation of belonging to the nation.' Milan Kundera wrote of the traumatic days of August 1968: 'It was the most beautiful week in our lives.' Eva Kánturková, the novelist and former Charter 77 spokesperson, recently described it as the 'expulsion from paradise', the prime virtue of which is that 'the one-time critical loyalists finally found themselves in the same position as the rest of the nation'.

The divorce was by no means confined to Czechoslovakia. In Poland it was completed with the pogrom against critical intellectuals following student unrest in March 1968. In Hungary it started with the petition against the invasion of Czechoslovakia (signed by Heller and Feher) – the first open protest against the Kadar leadership since the days of the Hungarian revolution – and culminated with the purge of the Budapest school (of Lukacs disciples) in the early 1970s.

The intellectuals' revolt against the bureaucratic machine could be effective only so long as ideology was taken seriously. In the era of routinized Marxism, the Party cared less and less for the support of the intellectuals. No need for 'engineers of human souls' any more. As Zbigniew Herbert put it, 'They loved us, they pampered us, and suddenly they dumped us.'

This marked the end of the utopian mentality and the advent of a new, more humble role for the intellectual. In Kolakowski's words, 'when intellectuals tried to become spiritual leaders or professional politicians, the results were not usually encouraging. The marketplace, with all its dangers, is in the end a more appropriate place for them than the royal court.'

The outcome of the failure of 'revisionism' and the divorce between the Party and the intellectuals was the collapse of Marxism in Central Europe. Except in East Germany, nobody takes it seriously any more. These developments, all associated with the emergence of dissent, have reshaped the intellectual landscape in Central Europe. First, there has been the return of genuine pluralism in a restored, independent intellectual community. The 'demotion' of the Communist intellectuals created a new equality of 'status' and access to *samizdat* publishing. For the first time since the war former Communists and conservative Catholics, liberals and social democrats engaged in genuine dialogue, united above all by a common concern for the defence of human rights and for the autonomy of society from the totalitarian state. The Polish Workers' Defence Committee (KOR) set up in 1976, the Charter 77 movement in Czechoslovakia or similar initiatives among the Hungarian democratic opposition testified to the changing role of dissent. Adam Michnik's 'new evolutionism' and Vaclav Havel's 'power of the powerless' provided the intellectual framework of this new approach: from the (pseudo) politics of reform from within the Party-state to the 'anti-politics' of the self-emancipation of civil society.

Yet that very process, which the intellectuals so ardently desired, may also help bring about their demise or at least leave them with a more marginal role in society. Different aspects of this trend are revealed in Poland, Hungary and Czechoslovakia.

In Poland, where civil society is strongest, the role of the dissident intellectual has been challenged in the 1980s from two sources: Solidarity and the Church. Aleksander Smolar has fittingly described the mixed feelings of the intellectuals during what Michnik called 'sixteen months of carnival':

> Paradoxically, for the intellectuals, the rise of Solidarity – this great achievement also of intellectuals – signified a sort of second fall. This time it was not a moral fall; it did not mean betrayal of their vocation or of national obligations. But after being demoted by Communist power at the beginning of its rule, they were now dethroned by the new worker elite. The names of the new national heroes and leaders were unknown only a day before: Lech Walesa, Zbigniew Bujak, Wladyslaw Frasyniuk, Anna Walentynowicz. They became moral, social and political authorities for millions of Poles.

Paradoxically, Smolar adds with a touch of irony, it was General Jaruzelski's crackdown on Solidarity in December 1981 which also marked the opposing intellectuals' 'comeback on the historical stage'.

Yet by that time the 'stage' was already occupied by another 'organic intellectual', the Catholic Church. In the aftermath of the defeat of Solidarity, as often in the past, the Church appeared to many as the ultimate rampart against totalitarianism. And the Church indeed provided consolation and a home for retreat. The defeat of society coincided with the spiritual triumph of the Catholic Church. The Church so effectively provided a shelter for alternative cultural activities that there is virtually no space left now between Church and State. As Marcin Krol put it: 'To be independent of the state is in a sense easier than to be independent of the Church.' Is there not a danger, as some already suggest, of a tacit duopoly in Poland between a totalitarian Party-state and the Church's hegemony in society? And if so, what does that imply for the Polish intellectual? He strove for forty years to make Polish culture independent from the state, but how independent is he now of the Catholic Church? Is there not a danger of a second 'betrayal of the clerks' as they abandon, once again, the intellectual's independence and identity?

Such provocative questions were asked by Adam Michnik, as if to dispel the very anxieties they reveal, in front of a packed audience in a Dominican church in Cracow. Michnik, after all, is perhaps the best qualified to discuss them. His essay 'The Church, The Left and Dialogue' in the mid-1970s had considerable influence in bringing about the convergence between the hitherto hostile traditions of the lay left and the Catholic Church. Such a convergence around the values of truth, human dignity and the defence of human rights is possible, Michnik argued, because under Communism it is precisely the Church that helped to preserve them in society. The Church in a way had to remain traditionalist, even obscurantist, to insulate the Polish people from spiritual Sovietization. But today Communist ideology is bankrupt and can hardly be presented as a major challenge. Rather, the triumph of the Church is such that questions can be asked about its likely effects on the pluralism of Polish culture, particularly the place of its lay, independent, free-thinking component. Michnik identified these two traditions with the names of Cardinal Wyszynski and Witold Gombrowicz:

> That which is valuable in contemporary Polish culture arose at the crossing of its great historical paths. At the meeting of the Christian spirit with the free-thinking spirit, competing with each other and mutually enriching each other.... We, unhumble Polish intellectuals, live between the prayer of Cardinal Wyszynski and the raillery of Gombrowicz, between the truth of the chaplain and the truth of the jester. Both are necessary to us because each of them in its own way teaches us efficiency and humility.

It is not easy to plead for pluralism and independence when the logic of a totalitarian system has stressed the primacy of the unity of the nation's spiritual resistance, its need to be identified with one institution. Yet this is what Adam Michnik, the most committed and independent of Polish intellectuals, calls for:

Be then devout, unhumble intellectual, but don't renounce
scepticism in a world of political commitments; member of an
anti-totalitarian community, protect your homelessness; while
preserving faithfulness to your national roots, nurse your
permanent uprootedness; into a world of shattered moral norms,
carry the simplicity of evangelical injunctions, and fill the smooth
world of officially codified values with the laughter of a jester
and the doubting of a libertine. For your destiny is neither to
celebrate political victory nor to flatter your own nation.

Hungary's equivalent of a civil society is the 'second economy'.
Whereas in Poland the social movements of the past, and the Church,
are powerful promoters of cohesion in society, the Hungarian
'second society' is atomized. The economic crisis has given it greater
autonomy, but it has also revealed its inner divisions and tensions.
This puts the opposing intellectual in a difficult position. It is not
easy to be a spokesman for an atomized society. Only nationalism
could provide such a possibility, as the populists are well aware. But
for the 'urbanist' of the democratic opposition, the spectre of anti-
Semitism prevents this from being an option.

In October 1987 a gathering of Hungarian intellectuals (writers,
economists, historians, philosophers) hired a boat for a trip down
the Danube. The topic was 'The Present Crisis: Prospects for the
Future'. Khrushchev's advice, to ensure the future of Communism
in Hungary, would probably have been to sink that boat. As it turned
out, the 'boat of the future' was a symbolic goodbye to the Kadar
era and to the 'prophetic' role of the dissident intellectual.

For how many years have we been afraid [asked György Konrad],
for how many years have we been speaking quietly among
ourselves? I am sorry, friends, but I was getting tired of this
extended state of being underage. We've created the aesthetics
of the 'how to remain a little boy, even with grey hair, even bald'.
There is a crisis? Great! The town is becoming interesting. There
is something in the air. The midwives are busy. A condition
wants to be over. A time of Chroniclers. What is it that wants
to be born? A new paradigm. The 'homo étaticus' opens like a
wardrobe, and out steps the citizen. The normal citizen, come
of age, who considers what he says and says what he thinks. He
doesn't ask permission for free-thinking. Here we are, socialist
citizens, Central Europeans. Marginal society on the margins of
East and West. And for that reason drawing from both
experiences.

After years of *embourgeoisement* the current economic and political crisis reveals a society in a state of flux. What sociologists describe as its atomization has also brought about a new individualism. Making money can be despised by intellectuals as an unhealthy obsession with consumerism, but the new 'burgher' (bourgeois/citizen) will now demand rights. Maybe the intellectual opposition as a community will become less important in an age of rampant individualism, but both the old intellectual and the new bourgeois will help recreate a civil society of citizens, emancipated from the paternalistic state.

Such an optimistic view of the crisis is challenged by Janos Kis, a philosopher and a leading figure of the democratic opposition. Whatever its initial merits, he argued, Konrad's 'anti-politics', or the moral superiority of 'anti-politics' over the 'filthy business' of politics, is hardly relevant in times of crisis. The idea of a convergence – the writer free from censorship and the entrepreneur free from bureaucracy, a mixture of economic individualism and ethical elitism – can hardly help a society to define what to think or how to act. The scale of the present crisis heralds the return of 'real' politics, of competing forces and answers to overcome it.

The return of the individualistic citizen and the return of 'real' politics may not be mutually exclusive. But both will challenge the role of the intellectual as a surrogate spokesman for society.

Czechoslovakia is a third case where the role of the intellectual has been altered, this time through isolation. After 1968 the intellectuals who had been the moving force behind the Prague Spring became the prime target of the repression that followed. For the Czech intellectual (the situation was somewhat different in Slovakia) this marked a shift from power to society, from politics to 'anti-politics'. The dissident intellectuals became a moral counter-power, partaking of Havel's 'power of the powerless'. In the words of Jan Vladislav:

Even if they do not strive directly for power in the community, in a sense they have it regardless. It is a power of a particular kind. In general it operates outside the established power structures, which is probably one of the main reasons why the powerful consider this kind of power so dangerous though its resources consist exclusively of words and ideas.

The politics of counter-culture and the ethics of spiritual resistance have created in Czechoslovakia a strong sense of a dissident community. They also account, at least in part, for its relative isolation.

The emergence in January 1977 of the Charter 77 human rights movement has created a new situation for the Czech intellectual: he has moved from autonomy to defiance of power. Vaclav Černý described the Charter as 'a milestone in the cultural development of the nation, a moment in the history of Czech spirit, restoring the moral backbone, reviving the feeling for law, justice, human dignity and the will for truth. It was a warning and a reminder to power-holders, all of them, everywhere.'

It was undoubtedly the philosopher Jan Patočka who became the *spiritus movens* in the shift from politics to the ethics of resistance. In attempting to define the nature of Charter 77 he stated:

> No society, no matter how good its technological foundations, can function without a moral foundation, without conviction that has nothing to do with opportunism, circumstances and expected advantage. Morality, however, does not just allow society to function, it simply allows human beings to be human. Man does not define morality according to the caprice of his needs, wishes, tendencies and cravings; it is morality that defines man.... The aforementioned relationship between the realms of morality and the state power indicate that Charter 77 is not a political act in the narrow sense, that it is not a matter of competing with or interfering in the sphere of any function of political power. Nor is Charter 77 an association or an organization. It is based on personal morality. It is aimed exclusively at cleansing and reinforcing the awareness that a higher authority does exist.

Jan Patočka, the first spokesman of the Charter, died after eight hours of police interrogation. The Husak regime's hysterical campaign against the Charter if anything reinforced the notion that the totalitarian challenge was above all a moral one. This accounted for the strength and the appeal of the intellectuals' ethics of resistance, but it also accounted for some of its limitations. As historian Petr Pithart observed, in the face of power, which is obsessed only with self-preservation, the opposing intellectual obtains, almost by default, a monopoly on truth. By the same token he must be aware of the dangers of confinement in a virtuous ghetto existence. Are the dissidents an isolated elite or the tip of the iceberg?

The Catholic philosopher Vaclav Benda was in 1978 the first to suggest the extension of ethical resistance to the creation of parallel structures: the assertion of the responsibility of each individual for the fate of society became rather the command to create an alternative society, a 'parallel polis'. The thinking was close to Michnik's 'new evolutionism', but the process of self-organization in civil society did not follow the Polish pattern, remaining confined to the cultural sphere. The passivity of an atomized society, the absence of independent institutions playing the part of the Polish Church, the intellectuals' preoccupation with a threatened European cultural identity rather than with the more mobilizing powers of nationalism, mark important differences between the Czech and Polish intellectuals' attempts to establish ties with their society over the last decade. The Czech intellectual did not manage to reach out to society the way his Polish counterpart did. But then, nor did he have to 'compete' for moral authority with the Church or with Solidarity.

The independent intellectual feels left out of the tacit social contract between a totalitarian power and a consumer oriented society on which 'normalization' rests. Respected, even admired by the society for his courage to 'live in truth' (which it does not have), feared by the powers-that-be for relentlessly exposing their illegitimacy, the Czech intellectual's cultural and moral substitutes for politics place him in a difficult yet in many ways gratifying position: he holds the symbolic power of the written word and of moral defiance. Virtuous and isolated, he sometimes wishes to be relieved of his role as the 'conscience of the nation' and to be, once again, 'just a writer'. Vaclav Havel's play *Largo Desolato* is a moving depiction of the intellectual over-burdened with demands from society, tired of his role as the professional supplier of hope.

Yet he cannot escape that role because it is, after all, his destiny as an intellectual. Havel, who after the death of Jan Patočka became the pivotal figure of Czech spiritual resistance, speaks of 'the tragedy of fate stemming from responsibility; the futility of all human endeavours to break out of the role that responsibility has imposed; responsibility as destiny'.

9 Beyond Failed Totalitarianism

Wherever there is tyranny
Tyranny there is
Not just in the muzzles of rifles
Not just in the prisons

Wherever there is tyranny
Everyone is a link in the chain
You are enmeshed in corruption
You too are tyranny

(Gyula Illyes, *A Sentence on Tyranny*, 1952)

The concept of totalitarianism has been fraught with paradox and misunderstandings in East–West communication. At a time when the countries of East-Central Europe were being incorporated in the Soviet bloc and were experiencing the 'pure' totalitarianism of the Stalinist era, they were, for obvious reasons, absent from the debate on the concept taking place in the West. Conversely, twenty years later, when the concept had been virtually banished from Western Sovietology as an unscientific product of the Cold War, it was reappropriated by all the independent thinkers in East-Central Europe. The watershed year 1968 marked a political parting of the ways and was the catalyst which set the concept of totalitarianism on a separate course, East and West. In the West, 1968 marked the dawning of détente, which profoundly affected the way in which politicians, academics and journalists assessed the nature of the Communist system. For the intellectuals of the Other Europe the Soviet tanks in Prague were seen as final evidence of the failure of reform from within and of the existence of a permanent 'totalitarian' core at the heart of the Communist system. Consequently, in examining the journey followed by the concept of totalitarianism, one must take into account the various attempts of the Central European intellectuals to make sense of the experience of their societies over the last forty years and the extent to which they affected, or were influenced by, West European perceptions of their predicament.

In the early days of Stalinism when a large number of leading intellectuals were engaged in providing the new Sovietized political system with legitimacy, while many others were silenced in the gulag or completely marginalized, independent ideas about the new regime of the 'radiant future' were confined to private diaries. Jiri Kolar's 1949 diary, now published under the title of *Eyewitness*, is a powerful testimony to an individual's spiritual resistance in the midst of surrounding 'total mobilization'. In the circumstances, East European involvement in the debate on totalitarianism could only be indirect, via such émigré authors as Czeslaw Milosz. In his *Captive Mind*, Milosz provided one of the most original insights into the subjugation of intellectuals by a totalitarian ideology, by what he called the 'new faith' from the East.

The poems of Gyula Illyes in Budapest, of Jiri Kolar in Prague or Zbigniew Herbert in Warsaw show that not all the intellectuals in the Other Europe swallowed the 'murtibing' pill Milosz spoke about, the pill that converts one to 'the new faith from the East'. They provided – with a lucidity never since equalled – remarkable insights into the nature of totalitarianism. Their writings point to another feature of attempts to define the totalitarian phenomenon: originally they tended to be literary and philosophical rather than political. In the West the concept had first assumed literary form through Orwell's *Nineteen Eighty-Four*, whose publication was followed by Hannah Arendt's classic work of political philosophy. Only after Orwell and Arendt was it systematized by political science.

Although the same sequence of literature–philosophy–politics can be discerned in both West and East, in the former it was condensed into the span of a few short years, while in the latter it has extended over three decades. There are a number of reasons for this. First, as soon as it appeared, and in spite of its limited circulation behind the Iron Curtain, Orwell's novel had a real impact in the intellectual circles there, whereas Western political science had a much delayed effect. East European intellectuals were not to come across Western political writings on the subject until the period of de-Stalinization, which naturally meant that they were more preoccupied with change from within the system rather than with totalitarian obstacles to change. In other words, between 1956 and 1968 they were keener to disprove the concept, reject it as outdated. Only after the crushing of the Prague Spring of 1968 did the word 'totalitarianism' make a fresh appearance among what became known as dissident circles.

This reappropriation of the concept by unofficial political thought in Central Europe has taken place on different levels. In the first place the word 'totalitarianism' or the adjective 'totalitarian' have become common parlance. A sociological survey of corruption conducted in post-Solidarity Poland (carried out by Kicinski in 1983) revealed that a majority of those polled considered the political system as its main cause. The most frequent responses encountered were 'the concentration of power in the hands of a few' and 'the lack of democracy, making control by society impossible', but there was also 'the system of totalitarian rule' and 'the nomenklatura'.

Secondly, the term has become the common denominator of dissident political writing. A recent instance of that – one which reveals how much the concept has taken different paths in Eastern and Western Europe – is the difference in the role played by references to totalitarianism in discussions about disarmament between Western peace movements and a major section of East European dissident opinion. Their disagreement can be summed up by saying that, in the eyes of many dissidents, Western pacifists tend to focus their attention on the manifestations of military threat, i.e. upon the stockpiling of nuclear weapons; for their part the 'dissidents' prefer to stress the roots of conflict, which they perceive as stemming from the logic of a totalitarian system which risks transforming the internal 'state of war' into an external one.

In the wake of 1968, political scientists in their approach to the Communist system took into account not only the concept of totalitarianism, but also the new realities of the Brezhnev era. The failed or interrupted revolutions of Budapest in 1956, of the 1968 Prague Spring, or of Solidarity in Poland in 1980–1 forced a double conclusion: that totalitarianism is no longer what it used to be, and that the Party-state hold over society has changed since the Stalin era. Those three great struggles (not to mention other minor ones) are proof that the system is far from static, and that its stability is extremely precarious. On the other hand, those three very different attempts to confront, dissolve and then neutralize the 'totalitarian core' of the system all came to grief, which has prompted dissident political writers to reconsider the concept of totalitarianism in the light of the constants as well as the realities of the Communist system.

The way the concept of totalitarianism is employed in the Other Europe also depends very much on circumstances, and on what might be described as 'the possible future', as it is perceived at a given point in time. Although it is an oversimplification, one is tempted to say that the concept of totalitarianism does not feature prominently in political vocabulary when there is a hope of change on the horizon. Conversely, the expression makes a comeback when the prospect of overcoming the Yalta legacy seems to have been postponed until doomsday. But here one should be careful not to over-generalize: Polish political discourse of the 1970s and 1980s referred to totalitarianism at the same time as it was preoccupied with the idea of transforming the relationship between state and society.

It is this interaction between the realities of Soviet-style Communism and their analysis by independent thinkers drawing on the different experiences of their countries that lies at the centre of the following effort to trace the course taken by the concept of totalitarianism in Eastern Europe. It is possible to speak of two major phases which correspond to two attitudes towards the concept of totalitarianism: the first, corresponding roughly to the period of de-Stalinization (1956–68), could be called the East European contribution to efforts to demolish the concept; the second, sparked off by the Soviet-led invasion of Czechoslovakia in August 1968 and 'consolidated' by the establishment, in December 1981, of martial law in Poland, has taken the form of an original effort to redefine the concept of totalitarianism, its sources, its means of social control and its present crisis. It remains to be seen whether the Gorbachev era will inspire a reappraisal of the totalitarian phenomenon.

Totalitarianism Redefined

The events of 1968 represent the zenith of both Communist 'reformism' and the challenge to the concept of totalitarianism. But the crushing of reform and, more generally, the ensuing period of conservative restoration throughout the Soviet bloc were perceived as the defeat of the very idea of a fundamental reform of the system from within, and the ultimate proof of the impossibility of 'detotalizing totalitarianism' (Svitak). It also meant, according to Kolakowski, the 'clinical death' of Marxist revisionism in Eastern Europe. From that moment, Communism 'ceased to be an intellectual problem and became merely a question of power'. One is tempted to add: Communist ideology ceased to be an intellectual problem, whereas power became one.

The second, related aspect of this evolution is the progressive jettisoning of the concept of 'Stalinism', the jettisoning so dear to the 'revisionist' Marxists of the 1960s in the East and the 'Euro-communists' of the 1970s in the West. Solzhenitsyn is categorical on the subject: 'there never was any such thing as Stalinism (either as a doctrine, or as a path of national life, or as a state system). . . . Stalin was a very consistent and faithful – if also very untalented – heir to the spirit of Lenin's teaching.' The touchstone of Solzhenitsyn's argument is the gulag, the concentration-camp system whose origins go back to Lenin's time, and, most importantly, whose extent and central role in the system are what makes Communism akin to Nazism. Indeed, the bulk of writings by the survivors of the gulag, such as Solzhenitsyn, Evgenia Ginzburg, Varlam Shalamov and Anatoly Marchenko, makes the concentration-camp system and its links with Marxist–Leninist ideology the pivot of Communist totalitarianism.

It was within this new intellectual framework that the concept of totalitarianism surfaced once more, and subsequently became a common denominator in independent political thinking in Eastern Europe. This rediscovery of the concept (and realities) of totalitarianism was by no means a return to the American political science of the 1950s. It was a completely new attempt to redefine the concept in the light of the system's evolution and the new methods of Communist rule. One can distinguish two basic approaches, corresponding to two definitions of the concept of totalitarianism. The first of them – more literary and philosophical – attempts to discern the 'essence' of totalitarian rule. The second approach relies on political analysis in seeking to lay bare the new workings of totalitarian or 'post-totalitarian' rule; both approaches nevertheless converge in exploring the origins of the totalitarian phenomenon.

The Orwellian Heritage: The 'Institutionalized Lie'

Tell me what is your reading of *Nineteen Eighty-Four* and I will tell you who you are. The Orwellian year of 1984 has brought from East and West a new spate of very contrasting interpretations of the famous novel.

One example among many. In 1984 an *Orwell Kalender* was published in West Germany with contributions from leading writers depicting the slow slide of Western societies into something supposedly resembling an Orwellian world of television screens, nuclear weapons and environmental destruction. Cases of people being sacked from their jobs for political reasons were mentioned as further evidence. In order to illustrate Orwell's insight into the superpowers

(Oceania and Eurasia) waging wars by proxy, *Der Orwell Kalender* gave a detailed chronology of conflicts since 1945, including a long list of US involvement in Central and Latin America and even, curiously, the 1969 'football war' between El Salvador and Honduras. No mention, however, was made of the Warsaw Pact invasion of Czechoslovakia or of 'martial law' in Poland.

The same year another Orwell calendar was published in Warsaw by the NOWA independent publishers. Under each month it lists appropriate anniversaries which leave no doubt whatsoever of the real identity of Big Brother (and its totalitarian alter ego Little Brother): '2 April 1948. The Big Brother starts blockade of a city soon to be surrounded by a Wall'; '3–6 August 1940. The Big Brother swallows up his three little neighbours' (the Baltic Republics): '1 September 1939. Little Brother marches eastwards.' '17 September 1939. Big Brother marches westwards and together they swallow up their common neighbour' (Poland).

The two calendars (and one could give many other similar examples) point to the contrasting interpretations of Orwell and more generally to the totalitarian phenomenon in the two halves of Europe. In the West *Nineteen Eighty-Four* now tends to be read as a prophecy or a warning about the threat to open government stemming from the emergence of new technologies of communication and social control. In the lands of so-called 'real socialism' Orwell is read as an allegory, as a lucid and often incredibly accurate analysis of the nature of Communist rule. This duality might well be inherent in the ambiguities of Orwell's novel, which would also account for its universal success. But the contrasting ways in which the novel is read in the two Europes reveal different perceptions and assumptions about the totalitarian phenomenon. They also point to some of the difficulties of East–West intellectual communication.

> Many have read Koestler's *Darkness at Noon*, but few have a knowledge of Orwell's *Nineteen Eighty-Four*. Because of the difficulties in obtaining the book and the risk faced by anyone possessing it, it is only known to a handful of members of the 'Inner Party'. These privileged individuals are fascinated by Orwell's Swiftian manner of observing details so familiar to them. It is impossible to employ such a style in the countries of the New Faith because allegory, being by nature capable of several interpretations, would run counter to the precepts of socialist realism and the requirements of the censor.

This observation by Czeslaw Milosz in 1952 deserves to be 'updated'. First, it is difficult these days to overestimate the profound impact that Orwell's novel has had on the intellectuals of East-Central Europe. It is one of the great post-war literary works that have marked a whole generation. The book escaped from the sanctum of the 'Inner Party', to which Milosz refers, and has been widely distributed in *samizdat* form. Orwell's readers have recognized themselves in this book, which, in the countries of 'existing socialism', is regarded not solely as a work of science fiction but as a description – a precise and pertinent one at that – of their reality. Intellectuals of the Other Europe read *Nineteen Eighty-Four* with the same feelings as Winston Smith on discovering the key to the system in Goldstein's book: they discover 'what they knew already'.

The Czech philosopher Milan Simecka describes movingly his identification with Orwell's hero: 'Like Winston, I had grown up in a totalitarian system, had never been elsewhere, lacked all knowledge of the past, the present, not to speak of the future. In a way too I was an employee of the Ministry of Truth and lived in the thrall of its ideology. Just like Winston, I knew only too well how lies were manufactured....' Simecka says he felt 'invariably stunned when, again and again, I would come across situations in *Nineteen Eighty-Four* resembling my own, events and experiences which were so like those I had seen only the day before'. Those who, like Simecka, 'have lived through the "victories" and defeats of real socialism, are struck when reading *Nineteen Eighty-Four*, by the many astounding similarities, until the London of *Nineteen Eighty-Four* becomes willynilly synonymous with home'. When he finished Orwell's novel, Simecka says, 'the book lay in front of me, I looked at its last page, and I think my hands shook a little. I had an incommunicable feeling of identification, and the feeling would not be chased away even outside in the sun. I was alone with my comrade Winston Smith, and we both knew what it was all about.'

Not surprisingly, an Orwellian or Swiftian literary genre, well suited to describing and interpreting the Communist system, has evolved over the past decade, the masterpieces of the genre being Tadeusz Konwicki's *Minor Apocalypse* and Alexander Zinoviev's *Yawning Heights*.

'Mendacity is the immortal soul of Communism,' said Leszek Kolakowski. This sums up what it is that constitutes the essence of the totalitarian system in the view of Central European intellectuals: the primacy of ideology as the institutionalized lie. The Orwellian theme of 'the lie' and resistance to it (or 'living in truth' as Havel put it) is the point of departure for the reconstitution of independent political thinking in the Soviet bloc countries.

Kolakowski provides the most lucid explanation of the lie's function in the totalitarian system. By systematically destroying historical memory and manipulating all information, the totalitarian regime destroys the basic criterion of truth. Since truth changes in accordance with the needs of the rulers, a lie can become the truth, or rather the notion of truth disappears: 'This is the great cognitive triumph of totalitarianism. By managing to abrogate the very idea of truth, it can no longer be accused of lying.'

In other words, we are not talking about the 'white lies' or half-truths in which politicians in all possible political systems indulge. We are talking about the Lie with a capital L, which constitutes the foundation of a political system, what Kolakowski calls a 'new civilization'.

Defined in this way, the totalitarian lie rests on double pillars: the destruction of memory, and totalitarian language. Consciousness is impossible without memory. And the destruction of the past and of historical memory is precisely at the heart of the totalitarian endeavour: 'A people whose memory – either individual or collective – has been nationalized and passed into state hands, and is therefore perfectly malleable and manipulable, are entirely at the mercy of their rulers; they have been robbed of their identity' (Kolakowski). Under the 'regime of oblivion', any attempt, however limited, to preserve one's memory and hence one's freedom to think represents, according to Simecka, 'an act of self-preservation, and self-defence in the face of total disintegration, as well as an assertion of human dignity. Nowhere in the world does history have such importance as in Eastern Europe.' In Milan Kundera's words: 'The struggle of man against power is the struggle of memory against forgetting.'

Needless to say, the totalitarian power's manipulation of history is enforced in the name of history, since the regimes claim to be the embodiment of historical necessity. In Vaclav Havel's words: 'It began with an interpretation of history from a single aspect of it; then it made that aspect absolute and finally it reduced all history to it. The existing multiplicity of history was replaced with an easily understood interaction of "historical laws", "social formations" and "relations of production", so pleasing to the order-loving eye of the scientist.'

The destruction of history as memory goes hand in hand with the replacement of actual events, 'stories' that constitute history, by a timeless succession of preordained rituals. In a 1987 essay Havel describes the 'normalization' period in Czechoslovakia as a 'cessation of history':

History was replaced by pseudo-history, by a calendar of rhythmically recurring anniversaries, congresses, celebrations and mass gymnastic events; in other words by precisely the kind of artificial activity that is not an open-ended play of agents confronting one another but a one-dimensional, transparent and utterly predictable self-manifestation (and self-celebration) of a single, central agent of truth and power.

Czeslaw Milosz subtitled his *Captive Mind* an 'Essay on the People's Logocracies'. While the conquest of power could be achieved through 'the barrel of a gun', the maintenance of power is achieved through the 'muzzle of language'. This key idea of Orwell's *Nineteen Eighty-Four* – that totalitarian power cannot be maintained without a totalitarian language which is not solely the vehicle of the state ideology but is above all intended to prevent the emergence of 'heretical' ideas – has been taken up again by dissident intellectuals in Russia and East-Central Europe alike. And rightly so. Indeed, the historian Michel Heller has convincingly shown this Orwellian heritage through official Soviet reference books, which exemplify the concept of discourse and language current in the Soviet system.

The aim, according to Heller, is to 'confer a political nuance on all words', in line with the regime's goal of 'politicizing all areas of life'. Looked at in this way, Soviet Communism would appear to be a 'linguistic dictatorship' by the MacLuhan method (the 'medium is the message'): 'the state has rationalized language and the means of information; it has become both the medium and the message; its subject of discourse is itself. It declares that the state is the most important thing of all, of which the citizens are no more than minuscule parts. Hence power must be maintained. Earlier ideologies admitted discussion. In contrast, this magnificent technology of power – the rationalization of the vocabulary – prevents any response.' This is not solely a theoretical model but, as Milan Simecka points out, 'a process which is already so far advanced in Eastern Europe that it truly threatens to destroy the capacity of a defenceless population freely to articulate a non-official evaluation of political, social and economic realities'.

How can this vision of a totalitarian 'logocracy' be reconciled with what has been said about the bankruptcy of the official ideology? The answer is to be found in the notion of the 'existential lie', which is quite distinct from conscious (or even enthusiastic) support for the ruling ideology. Indeed, in the present situation, according to Vaclav Havel, 'one need not believe all these mystifications, but one must behave as if one did, or at least put up with them tacitly, or get along with those who use them. But this means living within a lie. One is not required to believe the lie; it is enough to accept life with it and within it. In so doing one confirms the system, gives it meaning, creates it . . . and merges with it.' Looked at this way, it is irrelevant whether, in terms of 'effectiveness', the official propaganda receives conscious support or merely arouses more or less cynical indifference. Most importantly, the institutionalized lie is an impersonal one. One can live in the lie without being taken for a 'liar'. 'The impersonal lie and the impersonal murder are two forms of the political art that the totalitarian states have brought to perfection' (Fidelius).

From Social Control to 'Social Contract'

Western political science in the 1950s (especially the classic work of Friedrich and Brzezinski) defined totalitarianism by a set of criteria which included the presence of a charismatic leader, mass terror, the 'permanent purge' and ideological mobilization. These criteria were superseded not only by Khrushchevian (or now Gorbachevian) reformism, but also by the conservatism of the Brezhnev era. Instead of rejecting out of hand the concept of totalitarianism in favour of others, borrowed either from the study of Western political systems (such as interest groups, political participation), or from theories of 'modernization', independent political thinkers in East-Central Europe have redefined it in the light of their experience of the past twenty-five years. These analyses tend to stress the new machinery of social control: an evolution of the means of power, rather than of its nature. Among these studies one should also distinguish between the more theoretical approaches, such as those of Zinoviev and Mlynar, which seek to supply a coherent explanation of the relative non-violence of social control, and the analytical approaches which try, by observing closely the realities of the 'normalization' process, to discern how a model of 'totalitarian normality' functions in practice, so as to bring out both the factors of its stability and its current changes.

The theoretical trajectory of Zdenek Mlynar (an 'official' Czech politologist turned Politburo member in 1968, turned 'dissident' and forced into exile in the 1970s) provides a good illustration of the time-lag between Eastern and Western thinking on totalitarianism. At the very moment in the 1970s when Western Sovietology was coming to accept Mlynar's ideas from the 1960s about how a 'limited pluralism' and the existence of interest groups could be institutionalized, the Czech author himself – by then a signatory of Charter 77 – was discovering the merits of the concept of totalitarianism, which he considers to be the most 'adequate' interpretation of the Communist system. And irony of ironies, in order to (re)discover and reformulate the concept, and rid it of certain outdated parameters, Mlynar invokes cybernetics and the concepts of power elaborated by another political scientist, Prague-born Karl Deutsch. The latter, at a celebrated symposium organized in 1953 by the American Academy of Sciences, asserted the inevitability of the centrifugal dynamics which would eventually strike at the very heart of the Communist system. Now Mlynar has redefined totalitarianism precisely by taking as a starting point Deutsch's definition of power:

> By power we mean the ability of an individual or an organization to impose extrapolations or projections of their inner structure upon their environment. In simple language, to have power means not to have to give in, and to force the environment or the other person to do so. Power in this narrow sense is the priority of output over intake, the ability to talk instead of listen. In a sense, it is the ability to afford not to learn.

In terms of this definition, says Mlynar, totalitarian power is able, in all spheres of activity and in relation to all 'subjects' (social groups, economic agents, citizens), 'to impose the extrapolation or projection of its internal structure'. The chief characteristic of totalitarianism is its continuing capacity to limit all scope for independent action in every possible sphere of social activity. In other words, it has nothing to do with the degree of violence or terror employed. Power remains 'totalitarian' even when the forms of repression are less visible (albeit still virtually present). One could go so far as to say that a system becomes truly totalitarian only when the 'terrorist' phase is completed, i.e. when all the subjects have lost their autonomy and capacity for self-government (the opportunity to change objectives, behaviour, etc.). Consequently, it is not a matter of interpreting the limitation of autonomy solely in terms of legal or penal constraints; it must always be interpreted also in the 'cybernetic' sense with which Deutsch invests it:

> A society or community that is to steer itself must continue to receive a full flow of three kinds of information: first, information about the world outside; second, information from the past, with a wide range of recall and recombination; and third, information about itself and its own parts. Let any one of these streams be

long interrupted, such as by oppression or secrecy, and the society becomes an automaton, a walking corpse.

Autonomy is thus limited by the fact that those in power tend to control all these sources and circuits of information. In Mlynar's view, it is possible to talk of totalitarianism in those cases where the only contact that the overwhelming majority of the population is able to have with other subjects or the outside world is through those circuits controlled by the regime (which is consequently able to determine the nature and extent of that information).

Through his reflections on the relationship between memory and autonomy, Mlynar renews the theme dear to Orwell (and now Kundera) of the erosion of memory as the permanent goal of total itarian power. In this respect, ideology continues to be the mainstay of the 'real socialist' countries by creating a system based on the 'jamming' of information and memory. Hence all the talk of the revolutionary break with the past, the 'New Age', the 'new community of socialist nations', the 'new social forces' and, last but not least, the 'New Man'. The ultimate logic of totalitarianism would be the instrumentalization of all components of society as a consequence of its lost autonomy. What Mlynar proposed was no more than a model, and he is the first to admit that in reality there is a whole range of situations as well as of possibilities for future developments. The main thing is to discover the 'threshold ' at which autonomy is lost in order to provide a definition of a totalitarian situation. Thus, as soon as one moves from the theoretical model to the analysis of reality, the concept of totalitarianism gives way to notions such as 'totalitarian situations' or an 'underlying trend towards totalitarianism'.

Alexander Zinoviev has gone furthest towards constructing a theoretical model explaining the mechanisms of non-violent social control and the stability of the Soviet system. In fact, he rejects the very concept of totalitarianism because, in his view, it overemphasizes the similarities between the terrorist methods of wielding power employed by Nazism and Stalinism. Such apparent similarities apply solely to the installation phases of those regimes; consequently, the concept of totalitarianism ignores the specific features of the Communist phenomenon. Zinoviev regards Nazism as essentially violence 'from above', whereas Communism, in its mature phase, is 'totalitarianism from below'. In contrast to Solzhenitsyn, who regards the concentration-camp system as the incarnation of Communism's true nature – a yoke foisted on people from outside – Zinoviev sees the camps at most as an epiphenomenon and regards

Communist society as the culmination of 'mankind's natural, inherent' activity. Communism as a form of social organization corresponds, according to this interpretation, to a natural phenomenon in the history of mankind, which he calls the communal spirit; it is a system in which the usual counterbalances or safeguards of community life (law, morality, religion, etc.), that is, 'civilization', are suppressed.

Taking up a position somewhere between Hobbes and Henri Laborit, Zinoviev sums up the essence of communalism in the phrase: 'Man is wolfish towards Man.' The key component of the system is the 'cell', by means of which the individual is slotted into society. This cell (the factory, the state farm, the institute, etc.) constitutes the microstructure whose salient features are reproduced at the level of the state macrostructure. In other words, in contrast with the dominant theories in Central Europe which present totalitarianism as a conflict between the Party-state and a fragmenting society, Zinoviev regards the Communist state as a reflection of a communalist society whose cell is the key reproductive link and the chosen place for the formation of the 'New Man', *homo sovieticus*. This view ultimately leads to the conclusion that every action, whether individual or collective, must necessarily be 'manipulated', even when it is directed against the regime. From such a standpoint, resistance becomes meaningless, since everything is programmed or manipulated. Thus, however original Zinoviev's idea of regarding Communism as a social rather than a political system, and however much he puts his finger, even hyperbolically, on one of the major sources of the system's stability, his *homo sovieticus* nevertheless borders on caricature, and is in sharp contrast to the analyses of 'Communism as reality' coming out of Central Europe.

The Contours of Totalitarian Power

What, then, are the contours of totalitarian power in its post-ideological and post-terrorist phase? The 'polymorphous Party' is the sole autonomous organization in a system in which all other institutions of state and society are subordinated to it. The Party ensures the monopoly of use of the state apparat and thereby all organized forms of social life. This subordination of state to Party operates by means of the nomenklatura, which ensures the Party's control over key posts in the state's administration. This unified and unifying Party can, occasionally, diverge from the political line formulated in Moscow but may never abdicate its monopoly of power. Any failure on this point (as in Czechoslovakia in 1968) calls for a massive purge. There is always a new 'vanguard' waiting in the wings.

For the benefit of Western observers, unimpressed by the quiet, boring façade of everyday life, Vaclav Havel attempted to explain why Czechoslovakia is not a poorer and duller version of Switzerland:

> Almost every day I am struck by the ambiguity of this social quiescence, which is essentially only the visible expression of an invisible war between the totalitarian system and life itself. It is not true therefore to say that our country is free of warfare and murder. The war and the killing merely assume a different form: they have been shifted from the sphere of observable social events to the twilight of an unobservable inner destruction . . .; the slow, secretive, bloodless, never quite absolute yet horrifying ever-present death of 'non action', 'non-story', 'non-life' and 'non-time'; the strange collective deadening – or more precisely anaesthetizing – of social and historical nihilization.

'Civilized violence', as Simecka calls it, has replaced the arbitrary terrorist violence of the Stalin era. It is harassment rather than physical terror, selective non-bloody repression. The police and judiciary make a show of respecting the regulations in force and prefer interrogations during office hours to those at three o'clock in the morning. This change is perfectly illustrated by the role of the 'confession' in the functioning of the Communist system, as analysed by historian Karel Bartosek. Defining the confession as the 'total submission of the individual to the lie and the agents of the lie', Bartosek traces the development from the 'big confessions' of the 1950s show-trials to the 'petty confessions' of 'normalization' in the 1970s. The 'big confessions' of the show-trials had a deterrent function *vis-à-vis* the population, who had to take part in institutionalizing the lie in the course of campaigns in which the media whipped up a climate of hysteria. By contrast, the 'petty confession' method exacts submission to the lie from the population by means of purges, screening and 'loyalty oaths', as in Poland during martial law. The goal is to create 'complicity' with the system, and to smash the individual as the 'last step in the subjugation of civil society'.

Although violent methods and the use of tanks prove necessary in times of open crisis, the Communist regime possesses other, no less effective means of atomizing society. The system of 'petty confessions' is able to function only because the state is the sole employer. Simecka provides a remarkable definition of this system:

The totalitarian state has far more powerful weapons at its disposal [than violence]: all citizens are its employees and it is no problem to shift them up or down a scale of incentives – rewarding the good and punishing the bad. This capacity is a thoroughly modern weapon. It has worked well, because it was brought into play only when existing socialism, in its infra- structures, most resembled a consumer society, i.e. when it had something to reward or punish with.

Not only did this recipe prove particularly effective in the period of 'normalization', but it in fact represents the very basis of the Communist system in its post-terrorist phase. Since employment of labour is the pre-eminent instrument of social control, the workplace, as Peter Kende points out, is 'the prime location for the regimentation of Sovietized societies'. Within this system, police repression is replaced by the personnel office, the police officer by the personnel officer. Hungary, which enjoys the reputation of being 'different' from other Communist countries, is a past master in the use of more sophisticated methods of repression and social control.

From social control it is a short step to an implicit 'social contract' between the state and the citizen: the citizens 'adapt themselves' by giving up their individual rights (civil liberties) and collective rights (freedom of association), and receive in exchange job security and a slowly – though fairly steadily – rising standard of living. The advent of the consumer society has reinforced this 'contract' which has been in gestation since the 1960s. According to Simecka, the contract 'is a far more reliable guarantee of order in the state than all those expensive and ever-expanding organs of surveillance. The essential condition for the functioning of this contract is the level of enjoyment the state permits its citizens in their private lives.' This system has been perfected since 1968 with the creation of a (small) 'army of unemployed', i.e. dissident intellectuals. The 'new social contract' in fact requires the intellectuals to submit to censorship, in other words to renounce their function as intellectuals. But, even here, things have greatly changed since the 1950s. 'Under Stalin,' says György Konrad, 'censorship was both positive and aggressive, now- adays it is negative and defensive. Before, it used to tell you what to say. Now it advises you what not to say. . . . In a totalitarian situation, censorship cannot be formalized.' In the same way that the transition has been made from mass terror to 'civilized violence', totali- tarianism now prefers internalized self-censorship to insti- tutionalized censorship. The relative isolation of dissident intellectuals (except in periods of open crisis) would seem, in a way, to confirm the effectiveness of these new techniques of totalitarian social control.

Totalitarianism or Authoritarianism?

Might not these new non-violent mechanisms of social control and the very emergence of dissidence since the 1970s in fact prove that it would be obsolete to speak in terms of totalitarianism?

Ideology which was once – with terror – the pillar of the system, has been reduced to a ritual, and over the past fifteen years Communist regimes have tended to seek legitimacy either through nationalism (Romania) or through economic measures (Hungary). This inevitably recalls the sort of values that, Juan Linz tells us, are espoused by right-wing 'authoritarian' regimes: nationalism, economic development, order. If one also takes into account the growing role of the military – particularly in Poland – one is tempted to see there the signs of an evolution from totalitarian to authoritarian/bureaucratic regimes. The latter display a 'very limited pluralism', do not have any precise ideology but instead exhibit a typical 'mentality' in which, according to Linz, 'a leader or a small group exercises power within formally ill-defined but perfectly predictable limits'. Interestingly, the two political scientists who seem closest to this position turn out to be Polish (one close to the regime, the other to the opposition). The first is Jerzy Wiatr: he formulated his idea of Polish-style 'authoritarianism' (or Bonapartism) on the eve of the military *coup d'état* in 1981; he was calling for 'a new political system' in which the army and the Church (as institutions enjoying legitimacy, representing the state and society respectively) would take the place of the Party and Solidarity, which were engaged in a suicidal confrontation. After the coup, Wiatr was appointed by General Jaruzelski to head the Institute of Marxism–Leninism, but was relieved of this post after the Soviets publicly denounced his views.

The other theory of the slide from 'totalitarianism' into 'authoritarianism' came from quite a different standpoint. In her book entitled *Poland's Self-Limiting Revolution*, Jadwiga Staniszkis analysed the dynamic of relations within a Communist regime, seeking 'a reduction from above of totalitarian domination' to prevent its happening 'from below'. It is in order to be better able to absorb this pressure from society that 'post-totalitarianism' resorts to a 'bandy-legged pluralism' or to the 'fragmentation' (horizontal and vertical) of state structures and a sort of 'corporatism' whose appar-

ent aim is that of 'borrowing from the Catholic Church its legitimacy'. The aftermath of the 13 December coup would seem to
have put paid to the hypothesis of a slide towards an 'enlightened
authoritarianism' having more in common with Pilsudski than Marx
and Lenin, and practising a corporatism legitimized by the *modus
vivendi* with the Church. With the 'restoration of order', one also
saw the re-emergence of the Party and its (admittedly moribund)
ideology. Poland perhaps illustrates a double failure: a 'failed totalitarianism', given that the Party can no longer claim to control all
spheres of social life, and a 'failed authoritarianism' as well.

In the end, all these debates over whether or not the Communist
systems deserve the authoritarian label hinge on the status of ideology. Is the Soviet system still 'utopia in power', as Heller and
Nekritch maintain, or is it being transformed, as Castoriadis
suggested, into a 'stratocracy' with nationalism taking the place of
Marxism? Writers from East-Central Europe have made some very
apposite contributions to this debate. Whereas none of them seems
to discern an incipient 'stratocracy' in East-Central Europe, and
although the plausibility of the phenomenon with respect to the
Soviet Union is sometimes recognized (by Vajda, for example),
most writers concur in the view that the ideology is in a state of
decomposition. The 'radiant future' has given way to the 'cold
utopia' (Simecka).

In the 'post-totalitarian' phase, ideology nonetheless remains not
only the sole means of communication between the state and the
citizen, but also, and perhaps above all, the chief means of homogenizing and integrating the ruling apparat. The upshot of this is a
dichotomy in the system, which is 'totalitarian' inside the Party
(clinging to an ideological legitimacy) and 'post-totalitarian' outside
(with a mere ideological ritual).

No so-called 'totalitarian' system can achieve total control over
society. It would be better, therefore, to talk of the system's totalitarian tendencies (anchored in the ideology, with its own inherent
self-perpetuating logic, according to Havel). What differentiates
Communist totalitarianism from other so-called 'authoritarian' dictatorships is not the degree of violence but its intention.

The Origins of Totalitarianism

Authors from the Other Europe have breathed new life into the
debate about totalitarianism; they are equally thought-provoking
about totalitarianism's sources. For the East-Central Europeans, the

chief source is, understandably, external – that is, in Jacek Kuron's words, Soviet:

> The totalitarian system was imposed on Poland thirty years ago by the armed forces of the Soviet Union with the approval of the Western powers, in particular the United States and Great Britain. The system's stability is assured by the Soviet Union's propensity – demonstrated on three occasions already – to reimpose itself by force on any nation which might attempt to liberate itself.

Apart from this fact, which is as essential as it is elementary, one notes in the course of the past decade a new approach to the internal factors. This approach might help reveal the more deep-seated social and cultural supports of the totalitarian system's hold over societies.

The Czech philosopher Jan Patočka takes up Husserl's view on the crisis of the European conscience, a crisis whose origins he sees in the triumph of an impersonal rationality which he contrasts with the subjective universality of *das Lebenswelt*. Thus, in the same way that, in Patočka's view, Galileo based the science of nature on a mathematization of the universe, so also according to one of Patočka's most talented disciples, Vaclav Beloradsky, does Machiavelli reduce politics to a technology of power. Looked at in this way, modern political theory from Machiavelli to Max Weber converges towards an autonomization of the state, whose functions obey a rationality divorced from conscience. From the moment that legitimacy is founded on (or confused with) rational–bureaucratic legality, there is the risk that legitimacy and conscience will be absorbed by the institution or the apparat. This theme of 'law' devoid of 'human meaning' and therefore, in the extreme, absurd runs through the whole of early-twentieth-century Central European literature, and it is no accident that it is in Kafka, Musil, Broch or Ruth (i.e. somewhere between Prague and Vienna) that one discovers the most enlightening premonitions of the totalitarian potential within impersonal rationality. And, for certain writers, there is a great temptation to see in socialism – first imaginary and then 'real' socialism – the culmination of modern state power's long march towards 'transparency' and 'innocence'.

From this point of view, the factor which transformed these potentialities into realities was Marxism and (for Kolakowski or Shafarevich) socialism as such. The Machiavellian state may well be 'impersonal', but it remains circumscribed within the field of politics: it has no ambition to change 'human nature'. The Marxists, and even Gramsci (precisely in his study of Machiavelli) maintain that mankind is no more than a 'fixed ensemble of historically determined social relations'; consequently, by changing these conditions, regimes can transform human nature. When interpreted in this way, Karel Kosík argued, the theory of the 'New Man' risks drifting towards an 'insane utopia' legitimizing unlimited and irresponsible power.

Kolakowski and Shafarevich share the view that all socialist doctrines involving the central control of production and distribution inevitably engender the temptation to control minds. Starting with Plato's Republic, Shafarevich draws up the family tree of what he considers to be the 'kernel' of the 'socialist doctrines of the medieval heresies' (Cathari, Hussites, etc.) and the various types of utopia, not forgetting the eighteenth-century Enlightenment. These all bear in his rendering an uncanny resemblance to twentieth-century 'existing socialism', with its 'destruction of private property, religion and the family' and its corresponding 'demand for equality'. In short, when the socialist utopia is made into a science, the result is fairly predictable. Kolakowski, on the other hand, believes that the socialist utopia only becomes totalitarian when it is combined with a revolutionary will: it is in this sense that Bolshevism and fascism for him are closely related, incarnating the internationalist and nationalist variants of socialist totalitarianism respectively.

Intellectuals, the State and the Regime

Although, as we have seen, bureaucratic étatism and Marxism are often perceived as the sources of totalitarianism, one should not forget the factor that links them, i.e. 'the intellectuals' march to power' (Konrad and Szelenyi). Milosz and Kundera explored the individual reasons for the fascination of intellectuals with the 'magic circle of power' and its ideology. The contribution of the Hungarian school has been to investigate the motives of the intelligentsia as a social group.

The 'Hungarian thesis' can be summed up in the following way. In the absence of a real bourgeoisie, it is the state in Eastern Europe which becomes the actual driving force of economic modernization; the intelligentsia naturally identifies with the state and, more than elsewhere, its nationalist and socialist ideologies acquire a clearly étatist complexion. Looked at in this light, the Marxist phase (the triumph of Communism) was no more than the culmination of a lengthy process in which the intelligentsia, as the repositories of teleological and technological knowledge, gradually merged with the modernizing state: 'whether bureaucrats or revolutionaries, the East European intellectuals had long since taken on board a teleology of either the nationalist or the socialist variety. Thus they forged themselves a redoubtable weapon in the battle to establish their own class power. As victors they married the two brands of teleology to produce the ethos of state-run socialist redistribution.' Marxism, Haraszti says, is the perfect ideology for an intelligentsia which, by identifying with the state, becomes the sole repository of the keys to 'rational distribution' and 'social engineering'.

This is the genealogy of what the Polish sociologist Paulina Preiss called 'total bureaucracy'. A basic trait of this phenomenon is the elimination of the autonomy of subsystems. Budapest Professor Mihaly Bihari analysed this 'descent' of politics into the economic sphere and its consequent 'incorporation into the political system'; 'the result of the total politicization of the economic system and the economization of the political system was the fusion of these two subsystems and the total disappearance of their relative autonomy'. According to another Hungarian author, Béla Polok, Communism, particularly in its Stalinist phase, by homogenizing the agents of the different spheres of social action has represented a regression: the suppression of the achievements of several centuries of modernization.

At this point, discussion of the totalitarian phenomenon merges with a critique of the étatism which made the East-Central European societies vulnerable to Communist takeover. Notwithstanding the specific nature of the Communist system, and the break it represented with the cultural and political tradition of those countries, the discussion does not omit an analysis of the endogenous factors which may have played a role.

This accounts for the current appeal of neo-liberalism and the rediscovery of the theories of Hayek and von Mises, who based their critique of modern étatism on its Austrian incarnation, of which several countries now incorporated in the Soviet bloc were the legatees. The other aspect of this approach, which one finds in the writings of historians, philosophers and writers alike, is the idea that the twin phenomena of war and revolution brought about the totalitarian systems of the twentieth century. These phenomena not only provoked enormous political changes, but also rocked the values which were the very foundation of civilization. Hence Solzhenitsyn's fixation in *The Red Wheel* upon the way in which the interaction of war and civil war paved the way for the first Communist state. One finds a similar preoccupation among several Central European historians, for whom the establishment of the Communist system after the Second World War was not just the unfortunate outcome of the Cold War, but rather the continuation of the destruction or reshaping of social, political and cultural structures which started with the war and Nazi occupation.

Jan Patočka examined the issue from a philosophical perspective in his celebrated essay, 'The Wars of the Twentieth Century and the Twentieth Century as War'. He views the problem of totalitarianism as symptomatic of the crisis of European cultural identity and the triumph of a metaphysics of history, which identifies being with force, which in turn paves the way for the 'totalitarian night', in which an external 'state of war' goes hand in hand with an internal 'state of war':

> in the twentieth century war has become a revolution against existing everyday values.... War is a universal declaration that 'everything is permitted'; as savage freedom, war invades states and becomes 'total'. Everyday life and the orgy are organized by one and the same hand. The author of five-year plans is also the director of show-trials, which form part of the witch-hunt of modern times. War represents at one and the same time the greatest project of industrial civilization; the product and the instrument of total mobilization (as Ernst Junger saw so well) and the release of an orgiastic potential which nowhere else could cause destruction to such an extreme limit of intoxication.

Beyond Totalitarianism

When a social order survives for more than seventy years, it is relevant to raise the question of its legitimacy. The Hungarian philosopher Agnes Heller regards the Soviet Union as possessing a 'negative legitimacy' derived from the absence from society's consciousness of a recognized alternative to the existing social order; here too is a fundamental difference between the Soviet Union and Central Europe as to the way totalitarianism is experienced and perceived. Indeed, Poland, Czechoslovakia and Hungary differ from the Soviet Union, in Heller's view, in that they find themselves in a 'state of permanent crisis of legitimacy', which in periods of open crisis (1956, 1968, 1980) not only affects society but also provokes the decomposition of the Communist Party itself. It is a crisis of legitimacy fuelled both by the 'demise of ideology' and by the economic crisis. According to Vajda, the chief contradiction of the system is the 'fact that it can maintain its totalitarian power structure only by channelling all human activity into the private sphere; to this end, however, it is forced to introduce a mechanism which threatens the system as much as the socially orientated initiatives.' In the face of what Djilas calls the 'disintegration of Leninist totalitarianism', the gulf is widening between the centre of the empire and its peripheries. This gulf is also reflected in dissident writings on totalitarianism.

Tolstoy's novel *Anna Karenina* begins with the famous sentence: 'Happy families are all alike; each unhappy family is unhappy in its own way.' One is tempted to say that in the view of dissident writers all regimes of the 'radiant future' are alike in terms of their political systems, while each of the societies concerned has its own particular experience of the 'unhappy' realities of totalitarianism. Whereas most of the unofficial writings refer to the concept of totalitarianism, each of them defines it differently, and the approaches of the different authors naturally reflect the situation of their own country and the characteristics of their political culture.

The notion of civil society is clearly at the centre of the divide between images of totalitarianism and alternatives to it in the Soviet Union and East-Central Europe.

In Polish oppositional thinking of the 1970s and 1980s, Communist power, invariably defined as totalitarian, is to be 'rolled back' by the revival or reconstitution of civil society. Adam Michnik's famous 'new evolutionism' was the key turning point when the opposition ceased addressing the Party-state and turned directly to society. The Party was to be driven back, so to speak, into the state by the steady emancipation of civil society through a continuing process of self-organization. The corollary of this idea is that one can try to 'undo' totalitarianism at the peripheries of the empire so long as one keeps the Party-state as a necessary umbrella and intermediary with the 'centre'. General Jaruzelski's military coup cut short the Solidarity debate over the limits of 'new evolutionism', but without being able to restore the *ancien régime*. To the extent that Solidarity represented a 'self-limiting' revolution, what followed was a 'self-limiting counter-revolution'. Thus the present situation is no longer shaped by a powerful social movement like Solidarity, but there are a variety of old and new ways in which the societies of Poland, Hungary and Czechoslovakia try with mixed results to sustain their aspirations for autonomy. The economic decay of the system created space for market and privatization; the collapse of Marxist ideology enhanced the search for autonomy in the sphere of culture.

This leads Kuron to reformulate the idea of the autonomy of civil society: 'Today Polish society is outside the totalitarian system. Now we have to bring ourselves to inject our independence into dependent state structures. Now is the time for what I call the "interdependent economy". It is the time to form self-management workers' councils in factories, to make state enterprises autonomous, to replace administrative control with the market.'

This is very much in line with Hungarian poli .cal thinking of the last decade in which references to the totalitarian features of the system are a by-product of discussions concerning the political obstacles to a genuine evolution in the direction of a market economy. Hungarian economic thinking (by no means confined to the democratic opposition) identifies the economy with society and calls for its independence from the Party-state. Whether belonging to the liberal variant (e.g. Tibor Liska as a 'Friedmanite' proponent of the integral market) or to the more socially aware libertarian self-managing one (e.g. T. Bauer and Forintos), the Hungarians tend to agree that a Polish-style solution is to be avoided, and that in Hungary the economy (the local equivalent of society) should become an autonomous sphere while keeping the Party-state involved in a self-limiting process or retreat.

In Czechoslovakia, too, the thinking about totalitarianism and civil society reflects a specific situation. In the face of the apparently unending 'normalization' process, considerations tend to focus on the 'metaphysics' of totalitarian language and modes of thinking relentlessly imposed on society by the system. Hence the importance of the emergence of a 'parallel' or 'underground' culture which helped to bring about the Charter 77 movement as a community of citizens, a 'parallel polis', as Catholic philosopher Vaclav Benda called it. As in the 'Age of Darkness', the period of the Counter-Reformation in the Czech lands in the seventeenth century, culture becomes the substitute for politics. From this point of view, totalitarianism's victory over society can never be lasting so long as the nation's culture has not been quelled, so long as there survives the 'resistance of the typewriter'.

There are, however, two mutually reinforcing theses concerning totalitarianism in East-Central Europe which downplay the notion of civil society. The first, put forward by several Hungarian historians and sociologists, stresses that the weakness of civil society in the region actually predates Communism (and sometimes even contributed to its introduction). The second is a reminder that totalitarian systems have systematically attempted to destroy whatever civil society was left at the end of the Second World War. The first thesis tends to lump Russia and Central Europe together, the idea being to seek in social history the rationale for post-1945 Eastern Europe under Soviet rule (the boundaries of the so-called 'second serfdom' roughly coincide with those of the Warsaw Pact). Stimulating responses to this view can be found in Jeno Szucz's essay showing that there were 'three Europes' (if one wishes to go back to historical regions in Europe). The history of the Hungarians, the Poles or the Czechs might not fit the Western model but it certainly had even less to do with the Eastern, or Russian, model. Kundera's article on the 'tragedy of Central Europe' torn between its cultural allegiance to the West and its political 'kidnapping' by the East takes the argument one step further: the 'Caesaro-Papist' tradition of subservience to the state and its ideology, and the very absence in Russia of the notion of civil society, are seen as primary historical–cultural features separating Russia and Europe.

The second, less loaded argument is that, as Raymond Aron pointed out, 'fortunately or unfortunately, political systems rarely entirely fulfil their essence'. This was all the more so in Central Europe where a political culture radically different from that of Soviet Russia helped to sustain the idea of society as something distinct from the state and thus created the conditions for the emergence of new society-centre dissent after 1968.

Georges Nivat, a leading French expert on Russian culture, once observed that the key word for understanding Russia was *narod*, the people. In contrast, the key word for understanding contemporary Poland is society. It could also be argued that most of the countries in East-Central Europe represent an intermediate stage between the atomized Soviet-style people and Polish-type civil society. Vaclav Benda's 'parallel polis' or Elemer Hankiss' 'second society' are the nearest Czech and Hungarian approximations to the Polish model of the emancipation of civil society in the post-totalitarian era.

There is no better illustration of the gulf that separates Central European and Russian ideas about totalitarianism than the thinking of Solzhenitsyn or that of Alexander Zinoviev. The latter sees a totalitarianism from below, *homo sovieticus* belonging to a 'community' but certainly not a 'society'. Solzhenitsyn believes that Communism came from without, and that it has 'stifled Russia'. At the root of the catastrophe is the fact that people have 'forgotten God'. Communism is the fruit of unbelief, the result of a process of secularization of the state which can be traced back to the Renaissance. Whereas Communism has suppressed the spirituality of the Russian people, it is the West, the origin of the 'disease' of atheism and secularization, which is now in a state of internal decay, warns Solzhenitsyn.

In contrast, the Central Europeans insist on their Western cultural ties even in the field of political or economic thought. Significantly, the Poles centre their thinking on the notion of 'civil society'; the Hungarians on the market economy and the liberal tradition; and the Czechs on their attachment to European culture. In other words, here are three components of their European and Western heritage which are all obstacles to the ambitions of totalitarian power. As far as the Russian participants in the debate are concerned, these are mostly writers of genius who, when it comes to political thinking, turn into prophets of doom who blame their 'misfortune' either on the hated West or on a Sovietized people who, when all is said and done, have got what they deserve.

However, above and beyond their different analyses of the 'essence' of totalitarianism, its mechanisms or its strengths and weaknesses, all the *samizdat* authors mentioned here, who represent the emergence of independent political thinking in Russia and Central Europe, are united in contradicting Orwell's vision of *Nineteen Eighty-Four* on one point. In contrast to the pessimistic message conveyed by the case of Winston Smith, who ends up 'loving' Big Brother, running through the writings of independent intellectuals is the implication that the resistance to totalitarianism, even in the gulag as Solzhenitsyn shows, is possible and necessary. This stance is echoed in the break with the 'enslavement to everydayness' and the 'solidarity of the shaken' that Patočka speaks of, in Adam Michnik's 'living in dignity' or Havel's 'living in truth'. But at this point we have already gone beyond political analysis of the totalitarian phenomenon to enter the field of ethics and 'spiritual resistance'. It is symptomatic that this should happen, because it suggests that it is precisely this ethical unity of resistance which in the end is the common denominator, among dissident thinkers, of reflections on totalitarianism. If this is so, we can justifiably conclude that we are not dealing with a 'scientific' concept, but a 'subjective' notion which, like 'democracy' or 'liberty', rests on a value judgement and inevitably implicates those who employ it.

Part 4
THE LAST EMPIRE

10 Reform and Revolution

'The peoples of Europe enjoy only the degree of freedom that their audacity conquers from fear.

(Stendhal)

When Moscow sneezes Central Europe catches a cold. Change at the centre of the Empire is bound to have repercussions at the periphery. However, because Communist rule is weaker there and because these societies have a stronger democratic tradition, the risks of change are much greater there than in the Soviet Union itself.

Gorbachev has little experience with the countries of Central Europe, but he must have on his mind the unrest and revolt in Poland and Hungary prompted by Khrushchev's de-Stalinization. He might also ponder that the Red Army's suppression of the Czechoslovak reform movement in 1968 was followed by two decades of conservative stagnation not just in Prague but in Moscow as well. Are reform of the system and reform of the Empire compatible? Is Gorbachev the great white hope of disillusioned Central Europeans? Or might, as many in the West already worry, the unruly Central Europeans jeopardize the prospects of *perestroika* and provoke a setback for East–West relations? Perhaps the best way to understand the Central European response is to recall that, if anything, it is the nature of Soviet domination which has been the prime cause of instability in the area. The crises of Budapest in 1956, Prague in 1968 or Warsaw in 1980 were all separate attempts to reform or shake off a Soviet-imposed system in countries with a radically different political and cultural tradition.

Budapest 1956 was the first anti-totalitarian revolution to shake the foundations of a Communist state. The subsequent practice of calling it a 'revolt' or an 'uprising' is essentially an attempt to present it merely as a violent outburst, at the expense of its political significance. It is also a way to gloss over the fact that the violence (as well as the decision to leave the Warsaw Pact) was provoked by a first Soviet intervention on 24 October, which in turn brought about a second one on 4 November. The year 1956 also brought the first war between Communist countries.

In 1968 the Czechs and Slovaks were anxious to avoid the Hungarian syndrome: they wanted not the collapse of the Party but its rejuvenation. The fact that it was the Party itself which initiated a reform carried out in the name of socialism, combined with the absence of anti-Russian feeling in the population, had convinced the Dubček leadership that their comrades in Moscow would show understanding for a reform not directed against them or against the system, but designed to improve it and make it more attractive. In retrospect, of course, there was some naivety in Dubček's attempt to persuade Brezhnev that the abolition of censorship and the curbing of police control were good for the popularity of the Party and for socialism in Europe. Brezhnev, as we know from Zdenek Mlynar's account of the post-invasion talks in Moscow, replied that he could not care less about the image of socialism in the West, that security for him meant control, and that, as they had been since the end of the war, Czech borders were also Soviet borders. Twenty years later, only Dubček still believes that it was all a terrible misunderstanding.

Twelve years after the Warsaw Pact troops rolled into Prague, Solidarity was born in Gdansk. It was the first genuine workers' revolution since the Paris Commune of 1871. But instead of pictures of Marx they carried pictures of the Polish Pope; instead of the 'Internationale' they sang 'Poland is Not Yet Lost'.

The lesson from Budapest and Prague had not been forgotten: neither a violent revolution against the Party nor a reform from within, Solidarity emerged as a powerful social movement from the roots. Solidarity was also the first revolution which aimed not to seize state power but to gain autonomy for society. It was a self-limiting, non-violent revolution – not quite the stereotype of Polish revolutionary Romanticism. Its violent suppression had far-reaching consequences for the whole Soviet bloc. After a revolution in Budapest and a Party-led reform in Prague, the defeat of Solidarity seemed to bar all prospects for fundamental change; it left a feeling of hopelessness, a feeling that everything had been tried and everything had failed.

Moscow too showed that it had learned a great deal about crisis management in Central Europe (if not actually about its causes and significance): a bloodbath by the Red Army in Budapest in 1956, a collective Warsaw Pact invasion in 1968, then a domestic military coup by proxy in Poland in December 1981. In each case the methods used to suppress a reform movement were more sophisticated – repression was quicker, casualties were fewer – than in the previous one. And each time, Soviet involvement in repression was less direct. The effectiveness of the 'restoration of order', Moscow found out, was related to the degree of its delegation. But there are drawbacks as well: the delegation of repression makes Soviet control over the ensuing process of 'normalization' more difficult. General Jaruzelski liquidated Solidarity with considerable aplomb, but his policy of seeking a compromise with the Catholic Church, instead of root-ing out the heresy as Gustav Husak had done in neighbouring Czechoslovakia, has proved to be a considerable constraint on 'normalization'.

'Normalization, in Communist language means the restoration of Soviet control over the country, and of the Party's self-confidence and control over society. It rests not just on repression, but above all on society's acceptance of defeat. Indeed 'normalization' has succeeded when overt violence becomes no longer necessary. Kadar's Hungary provided the model: the Party had experienced its first great scare and had seen how quickly its rule could crumble. It realized that after 1956 things could never be the same. Hungarian society also knew that it stood little chance against the might of Soviet tanks; evolutionary change would have to take place within the system. According to one argument, something good could come out of the tragedy: severe punishment (the execution in cold blood of Imre Nagy in June 1958, and the continuing executions of hun-dreds of participants in the years up to 1960) in a way prepared the ground for Kadar's offer of compromise – 'Who is not against us is with us.' This, of course, is a cynical argument. Kadar had never read Machiavelli and his 'discovery' was purely a pragmatic one: to avoid a repetition of 1956 repression is not enough; the Party should keep its exasperation with society to a minimum while remaining within the limits of what is acceptable to Moscow.

Kadar was helped by the favourable context created by Khrush-chev's second wave of de-Stalinization in the early 1960s. Kadar also obtained the co-operation of the intellectuals, by allowing them to publish without humiliating recantations. Finally, he was able, for some twenty years, to offer the workers a slow but steady increase in living standards. This does not mean that Kadar *had* to follow a flexible policy. Ceausescu's Romania or Husak's Czechoslovakia are reminders that there is no such thing as an imperative for reform, nor set limits to the suffering inflicted on a society by the local satraps.

When Gustav Husak took over from Alexander Dubček in April 1969, many thought he would be a Czechoslovakian Kadar. After all, like Kadar, he was a former victim of Stalinist purges and a prominent reformer during the Prague Spring. Who remembers that on the eve of the invasion of 21 August 1968, Husak declared: 'I am firmly convinced that the new course represented by Comrade Dubček is so powerful among the Czech and Slovak people that there is no force capable of turning us back'? Except, of course, a Soviet invasion, which gave Husak the opportunity to offer his services to the Russians. Only a week after the invasion Husak concluded his speech at the Conference of Slovak Communists with the words: 'For my part, I support Dubček's concept, I took part in its elaboration and will support it fully: either I'll stay with him or I'll leave.' Within months Husak had signed a new 'treaty of friendship' with the Soviet Union, accepting the Brezhnev doctrine of limited sovereignty, and embarked on an extensive and ruthless eradication of reform. In contrast to Kadar, who never allowed Rakosi's old guard to return after 1956 (Rakosi's rule had preceded the reforms of Imre Nagy), Husak allied himself with the ultra-Stalinist faction led by Vasil Bilak. What followed were twenty years of repression and stagnation. Compared to the Hungarian model, the Czechoslovak 'normalization' was only a semi-success, or a semi-failure. True, it brought Moscow twenty years of quiet. The economic carrot helped to buy the passivity of the population; the skilful use of the Slovak card, as part of a 'divide and rule' strategy, did help find a constituency for a 'normalized' status quo. But the intellectuals have not been co-opted, and rigid control rather than the search for consensus is still official policy. After two decades of complete immobility and paranoia about the spectre of 1968, Husak has been unceremoniously ousted. 'What did you do in 1968?' was the question asked by Husak's inquisition in all the purges and 'verifications' which led to the expulsion of half a million people from the Party. Husak assuredly deserves Kundera's nickname as the 'President of forgetting'. By clinging to power he tried to impose amnesia on a whole nation.

In Poland martial law and the repression of Solidarity were effective, but certain ingredients of 'normalization' in the Hungarian or even the Czechoslovak style were lacking. The leaders of Solidarity were neither physically liquidated as Nagy was in Hungary nor forced to capitulate as Dubček was in Czechoslovakia. Walesa and

Solidarity remain as a symbol of continuity and resistance. The co-optation of intellectuals is impossible. The Church can be used as a moderating, stabilizing influence, but in exchange it has obtained the recognition of its ideological dominance in society. Over the last decade the Polish Church has incorporated the notion of human rights into its doctrine. The Pope's homilies on this subject during his successive visits to his homeland suggest that, whatever practical arrangements Primate Glemp may have conceded, the Polish Church stands for spiritual resistance to 'normalization' – another major difference with post-1956 Hungary or post-1968 Czecho-slovakia. Finally, the economic disaster of the 1980s meant that Jaruzelski had nothing to offer the workers after the crackdown on Solidarity. The result is sporadic strikes in the factories and, as Jacek Kuron points out, the new official trade unions are often closer to the legacy of Solidarity than to the old-style 'transmission belt' of the Party.

Bronislaw Geremek, the well-known historian and an adviser to Solidarity, says that society is tired of confrontation, but that the experience of martial law has deepened the 'them and us' divide.

After Budapest in 1956 resistance was destroyed within weeks. After 1968 in Prague resistance was destroyed in one year. In Poland, more than six years after the coup, you still have the same movement, weaker than before, but still in existence. You have hundreds of underground publications. For the first time in the Eastern bloc we are a country in which the opposition is a political fact. When I say the opposition, I mean a civil society with its own means of communication and expression, with an independent public opinion. How could one call this real normalization?

Looking back at the three major crises it is clear that the techniques of repression have proved each time to be more effective. But 'normalization', what Simecka called the 'restoration of order', each time proved more difficult: fairly good in Hungary, mediocre in Czechoslovakia, very dubious in Poland.

At the end of the 1980s the legacy of the three interrupted revolutions is being reclaimed, though nobody believes they will be repeated. In Hungary, the end of the Kadar era also ended what Janos Kis called the 'contract of silence' concerning 1956 which a traumatized society had tacitly accepted. Today the legacy of 1956 is reclaimed not just by the opposition but especially by the young generation, which does not remember the repression of the 1950s and sees the promise of consumerism rapidly fading away. There is a symbolic and a political legacy at stake. 'Our problem,' says György Konrad, 'is that of Antigone. We have to bury our dead; those who fell during the revolution or were afterwards executed in so cowardly a manner.' On 16 June 1988 a demonstration to commemorate the assassination of Imre Nagy was dispersed by police, whereas only two weeks later a much larger demonstration, in support of the Hungarian minority in Transylvania, received official blessing. Ironically, thirty years after 1956, nationalism is more acceptable to the Hungarian Party leadership than rehabilitating one of its sons, perhaps the only one whose name is really popular in the country. A year later they were forced to grant a national funeral to Nagy without being able to claim credit for it. The reason for their lagging behind the public mood was their inability to accept the substance of the 1956 legacy. For a nation that had suffered two humiliating defeats in this century, a nation divided along cultural and political lines, 1956 provided a liberating experience of unity around the defence of democratic ideas. Nobody wishes a replay of 1956, but the reclaiming of its values by the democratic opposition is of importance for the future of Hungarian politics.

In contrast to Kadar's post-1956 'contract of forgetting', the Prague regime's relentless settling of accounts with the ideas and the protagonists of 1968 means that, even twenty years later, the question still touches a raw nerve in Czechoslovakia. There are essentially three responses to its legacy. That of Dubček and the Communist dignitaries expelled from the Party: after a long period of silence (and criticism from non-Communists) they, at last, feel vindicated by Gorbachev. Their only mistake was to be right twenty years too early. 'The basic ideological directions are the same,' says Dubček.

> The needs and the aims in both cases are the same: economic reform and the democratization of the Party and the whole society. . . . In our official propaganda to this day the idea prevails that there is no similarity between the two programmes. But you need only look at our Action Programme of 1968 and their programme and you'll find that they are very alike. . . . But Gorbachev has one advantage: for him there is no danger of the tanks which rolled over us in 1968.

Zdenek Mlynar, who was a member of the Party Politburo in 1968, is critical of Dubček's illusions:

> There was the illusion of the Party leadership about its own

possibilities within the Soviet bloc. You had the idea of reform, but under no conditions was a rift envisaged with the Soviet Union, as had happened in Yugoslavia. And with such assumptions one could only do what the majority of the leadership would agree to at the time; that is, roughly what Kadar was doing in Hungary. In that case there was hardly any point in starting at all. Illusion number two was that, because twenty years of totalitarian diktat had freed the way to democratization, the Czechoslovak Party leadership enjoyed enormous support and that this was likely to continue and to guarantee that people would always be satisfied with what the leadership granted. Finally, there was the population's illusion about the leadership: that it can transgress certain limits provided there is sufficient push from below.

The more plausible, Realpolitik approach favoured by Mlynar would have been a slower and more controlled process of reform. To abolish censorship while keeping the hardliners in the Party apparatus, even at the highest level, was a recipe for disaster. Meanwhile Prague intellectuals seemed to follow the slogan of their Parisian counterparts: 'Be realists, demand the impossible!'

The non-Communists, in their assessment of 1968, are less concerned with the merits of Party tactics in the clash of reformers and conservatives. Vaclav Havel sees in the Prague Spring the culmination of a long process of 'self-awareness and self-liberation of society'. If anything, the lesson of 1968 was that a Communist monopoly of power cannot be dismantled by the Party itself. In a *samizdat* study entitled *Prague Spring 1968: Hopes and Disillusionment*, published twenty years later, Miroslav Synek writes:

> Just as the nations of our continent are unlikely to forget the Napoleonic Wars, the slaughter at Verdun or Hitler's European campaign, so the year 1968 will be forever etched in the historical memory of the Czechs and Slovaks. That sudden and spontaneous outburst of popular activity and its cynical suppression provided unmistakable proof that a ruling Communist Party is incapable of restoring democratic liberties to a closed society. 1968 is a permanent warning to all nations and peoples that grand talk about peace and friendship, sovereignty and territorial inviolability count for far less than the interests of naked power.

As an attempt to reconcile a ruling Communist Party with the democratic political culture of its people, the Prague Spring came too late for Khrushchev and too early for Gorbachev. It is not an experience that will be repeated. Yet it is a reminder of how quickly things can change, of 'all the potentialities that slumber within the soul of the populace'. 'Who', says Vaclav Havel, 'at the time of Novotny's decaying regime, could have anticipated that in the space of half a year genuine civil awareness would stir within that self-same society, or that a year later a society so recently apathetic, sceptical and virtually demoralized would resist foreign invasion with such audacity and resourcefulness!'

In Poland, Solidarity and General Jaruzelski's military coup showed the success and the limits of the strategy of 'new evolutionism'. But even the crushing of the independent trade union did not mean a return to the situation that existed before 1980. There is a cumulative effect in the emancipation of Polish society from the state through a series of crises. In 1956 the Church and the peasantry (allowed to return to private agriculture) gained autonomy from the state. In 1968 intellectuals made their break with the ideology of the regime. Through a series of strikes in 1970, 1976 and 1980 the workers made their bid for self-organization. In the periods between crises the regime has, of course, tried to regain control and withdraw its concessions but with only partial success. Thus the whole period since 1956 can be seen as a gradual process of the emancipation of civil society.

For Jacek Kuron the crises are essentially periods when the social movement expands:

It goes back to 1956. We had not yet abandoned Communism but we were already of the opinion that social movements should be independent of the Party and the government. 1968 and 1970 were crucial times for the relationship between the intellectuals and the workers. In 1968 the intellectuals realized that they must ally themselves with the workers. After 1970 the workers reached a similar conclusion about the need for an alliance with the intellectuals. KOR [the Workers' Defence Committee] was born from this experience, and its attempts to foster the self-organization of social movements eventually bore splendid fruits in 1980. True, Solidarity has been crushed and driven underground, but this cannot change the fact that the foundations of the totalitarian system have been broken. We have created and sustained freedom of expression so that the authorities have had to open up the official media. Because of the pressure of the Solidarity underground, even all those dummy social movements which they created now cease to be dummies.

There is only one road: from totalitarianism to democracy, and we have covered a great length of it. If you compare the way in which we live today – this very conversation, here – with the times when for a word, for a joke, one went to prison, you will see that we live in a different country, in a different social order.

Poland, as always, magnifies a trend. A would-be totalitarian state coexists with a society which it can no longer control with the old methods. As Adam Michnik put it, this is not 'socialism with a human face, but totalitarianism with broken teeth'. Its relative tolerance is proof not of enlightened liberalism, but of weakness and disintegration. Between abortive reforms and abortive 'normalizations' society tries to assert its autonomy.

On three occasions attempts at democratic change have been suppressed by Moscow all the more easily because the countries which made them were isolated from the other countries of the Soviet bloc. But today there is change in Moscow and a crisis brewing simultaneously in several countries. There is a growing awareness – at least among the opposition – of the interdependence of the fate of the nations of Central Europe. The optimistic view is that, for the first time, conditions might be ripe. The greater breathing space conquered by society, the argument goes, combines with change and adaptation within the political system. Thanks to Gorbachev there is a chance for the long-awaited synthesis of change from above and from below, from within and from outside the system.

There is also the dramatic, catastrophist reading of the new situation: historically, the combination of economic crisis and political liberalism is a known recipe for disaster. Some, like Zbigniew Brzezinski, at one time America's National Security Adviser, believe that Central Europe is in a pre-revolutionary situation. In 1988 a new Spring of Nations is in the offing, parallel to that of 1848. This, of course, would mean the end of Gorbachev's *perestroika*, with unpleasant repercussions for East–West relations.

The problem with the revolutionary scenario is that it rests on a concept of 'crisis' which is used as a common denominator for situations which are completely different. To say that Poland is in crisis is hardly new; 'crisis' has been on and off the 'normal' state of the country since 1956. Crisis, used to describe Ceausescu's Romania, is a polite understatement. For Hungary it is a slight exaggeration: crisis there means a sharp deterioration in comparison to the apparent prosperity of recent years. In Czechoslovakia 1988 has been launched with Husak's departure from office and Dubček's interview in *L'Unità* claiming that the difference between him and

Gorbachev is no more than twenty years. Exciting, but hardly evidence of 'crisis'.

The 'optimo-pessimistic' view of the situation is that few people in Central Europe expect anything from hypothetical upheavals because there is little reason to believe that, with or without Gorbachev, the Soviet Union would behave any differently from how it has in the past. Gradual change of far-reaching significance is taking place, but in a context of decay, even disintegration: the steady erosion of imperial Soviet control over Central Europe combines with the erosion of state control over society. Ideology has collapsed under the combined forces of the use of tanks against 'socialism with a human face' in Prague and against workers in Gdansk. Ideocracies without an ideology, the Communist regimes have been looking for substitutes, of which nationalism is the favourite. Ceausescu has followed the Balkan pattern of authoritarian nationalism. After his military coup General Jaruzelski abandoned the language of Communism for that of nationalism. The Hungarian Party, so reluctant to express any national feeling under Kadar, is now endorsing the cause of the Hungarians in Transylvania. Even the East German Party, for whom the very word 'nation' used to be taboo, is now reclaiming the Prussian past; Clausewitz and Bismarck are rehabilitated, Martin Luther and Frederick the Great are presented as forerunners of socialism. The immediate advantages of attempting to tap the nationalist feelings of the population are obvious. But it might also prove to be a dangerous game. The dynamics of popular nationalism might outrun those who wish to manipulate it; Moscow too might find it useful to play 'divide and rule'. Yet, in the long run nationalism is bound to foster centrifugal tendencies within the Soviet Empire.

Economic decline has become the prime cause of change. In the 1970s it was fashionable to predict that economic modernization and more trade with the West would eventually also bring greater freedom in the East. Statesmen such as Chancellor Schmidt and President Giscard d'Estaing were convinced that economic interdependence would make the systems of the Other Europe more stable and thus more relaxed. These hopes have failed to materialize. In the 1980s the Soviet bloc economies have been sliding into decay and demodernization. At the end of the war, as one observer put it, the Communist Parties of Central Europe claimed to follow 'national roads to socialism'; today, they seem to follow national roads from socialism. The degree to which the Party retreats from the economy reflects the scale of the disaster: this, as much as political circumstances, explains why Poland and Hungary are the forerunners of reform, while the conservative economies of East Germany and Czechoslovakia are doing relatively better. The combination of decay and retreat opens more space for independent private initiative. But this is not a zero-sum game in which the crisis of the Party-state system of control automatically means greater freedom for society. The economic collapse, especially in Poland, affects social services, the fabric of everyday life. The Party's partial withdrawal from the economic sphere gives society the opportunity and the challenge to provide alternative answers to the crisis. The question for the future is, as Janos Kis suggested, whether after decades under anaesthesia the pace of self-organization in civil society can match the pace of disintegration in the Communist system.

As the Soviet bloc regimes fall into decay, it has dawned on some of the more enlightened Party leaders that the crisis might have something to do with the Party's obstinate insistence on controlling things. Besides, if you control everything, you also get blamed for everything. Hence the idea that the Party should retreat from the sphere of culture and the economy and relax political control as well. But this is easier said than done. Can you shake off your Stalinist legacy and yet retain power? And once you start retreating, where do you stop? Each Party has to find its own answers to these questions, answers which depend not so much on Gorbachev as on the strength and the resistance of each society.

11 Dismantling Communism

The most dangerous time for a bad regime occurs when
it tries to improve itself.

(Alexis de Tocqueville)

The Gorbachev Factor

Is Gorbachev really a reformer? Adam Michnik, the Polish historian
and political writer, calls him a 'counter-reformer'. A counter-reformation, he argues, is not a restoration of the old order, but rather
an attempt to restructure institutions from within, to absorb critical
thinking and defuse radical change. 'If one accepts that Solidarity
was a great reformist movement in the orbit of Communist civilization, then Gorbachev deserves the title of the "Great Counter-
Reformer". This is the meaning of "reform from above" – this is
the counter-reformation which is to save the Communist system.'

Is Gorbachev good for Poland? Michnik sees the prospects of
Polish freedom today as dependent on the success of Gorbachev's
reform in the Soviet Union. Neither cause would survive an
explosion at the periphery of the Empire. There is a historical
precedent for this: the 1863 Polish uprising which blocked the
reforms of Tsar Alexander II. Thus the author of a seminal essay on
'new evolutionism', which suggests that dissidents should care less
about what the Party thinks and more about how a society can act,
now shows concern for Gorbachev's imperial dilemma.

The contradiction is only apparent: even the staunchest advocates
of the autonomy of civil society know that, since the destruction of
Solidarity, lasting change will depend not just on pressure from
below, but also on the process of 'counter-reformist' retreat and
adaptation from above. Moreover, there is an understandable hope,
after 1956, 1968 and 1981, that Gorbachev's *perestroika* will lead

Moscow to rethink the imperial predicament.

This is where hopes might lead to illusions. Gorbachev's dilemma in East-Central Europe can be summarized as follows: given the centralized nature of the Communist system, reform at the centre cannot but have repercussions on the periphery. But the risks there are much greater and could jeopardize reform in the USSR itself. Still, even assuming that change in Moscow without change at the periphery was possible, it would not be without dangers: after all, as François Fejtö observed, the first signs of independence from Moscow in the 1950s came not from reformers, but from conservatives eager to insulate their country and their Party from the effects of de-Stalinization. Those countries happen to be the same as those who now resist *perestroika*: East Germany, Romania, Czechoslovakia. And if both the spill-over effects of reform and resistance to it are difficult to manage, can one really believe that Gorbachev would wish anything but the perpetuation of the status quo?

The reactions in East-Central Europe to changes under way in the Soviet Union reflect the variety of local situations. Two paradoxes illustrate this. General Jaruzelski's enthusiasm has no equal: he called Gorbachev's reforms 'breathtaking' for the Poles, and gave the Polish Party's 'full support to the new strategy against the lazy, the stiff-necked dignitaries, the political sclerosis'. His close associate and Politburo member Mieczyslaw Rakowski added: 'For the first time since the war, what takes place in the Soviet Union has acquired, thanks to Gorbachev, a positive connotation in Polish society. This is a new situation, which also has relevance for the credibility of our Party among the population.' In other words, and this is no small irony, the Polish Party now relies on its identification with Moscow in order to legitimize itself at home.

The Prague paradox is no less amusing. After twenty years of all-out 'normalization' in the name of unconditional allegiance to the Soviet model, the Czechoslovak leadership found itself out of step with the reform policies advocated by the Kremlin. At first Gorbachev's speeches were censored when they mentioned the need for multiple candidacies, the rule of law or restrictions on the role of the police and the judiciary. Then came a relentless campaign against parallels between Dubček and Gorbachev, with Vasil Bilak, the most orthodox of 'internationalists', arguing the case for an inverted version of the theory of 'national paths to socialism' which he repeatedly used against advocates of *glasnost* in Prague. This prompted Prime Minister Strougal, the leading moderate, to refer ironically to:

those who wish to limit to the U S S R alone the relevance of the CPSU experience. . . . While they used to consider the pool of common characteristics as paramount, now for a change they try to make particularity an absolute principle. One may be forgiven for wondering if this attitude is not just an attempt to hide their reluctance to change anything at all of the basis of our Czecho-slovak experience.

One may indeed.

The East German reluctance is a mixture of conservatism and self-satisfaction. It rests on three points. Since the Gorbachevian enthusiasts in Moscow do not tire of repeating that there is no longer a model to be imitated, East Germany should not be afraid to assert with its chief ideologue Kurt Hager that 'there is no need to change your wallpaper just because your neighbour has done so'. To which the editor of the Communist youth journal *Junge Welt* added: 'the Soviet Union has won great historical merit for having defeated Hitler and won the war, but as far as technology and progress is concerned it is no model for us.' *Perestroika* is certainly necessary to improve the failing Soviet economy, but it would be superfluous in East Germany since the necessary changes have already been intro-duced and since its economy is already the most successful in the socialist camp: 'you don't change a winning team.' As for *glasnost*, the line in East Berlin is that it remains to be proved that political liberal-ization and economic performance are complementary. The East German experience even suggests that the opposite could be the case.

In Romania there is not reluctance but outright opposition. Not, as one might expect, in the name of a nationalism that would find it demeaning to seek inspiration abroad, but rather in the name of the purity of the Marxist–Leninist doctrine. Referring to Gorbachev's reforms, Ceausescu has stated: 'It is unthinkable that a revolutionary Party could say "we are going to let enterprises and the economy manage themselves".'

The distinction between reformers and conservatives is, however, of only limited use. Reactions to Gorbachev are rather like a menu *à la carte*: each Party chooses to support or ignore what it deems fit. In Warsaw and Budapest there is vocal support for the policy that there can be no *perestroika* without *glasnost*, no reform without political openness. In East Berlin and Bucharest neither is really accepted, though Soviet foreign policy is warmly endorsed. In Prague and Sofia there are purely verbal commitments to *perestroika*, preferably without *glasnost*. In other words: to each a Gorbachev according to his needs.

The reactions of the peoples are inversely proportional to those of the regimes. In Hungary and Poland, where Gorbachev's policies are officially endorsed, there is widespread scepticism and indifference to developments in Moscow. In East Germany and Czechoslovakia people are much more attentive and often hopeful. Gorbachev's welcome in Prague in April 1987 was astonishing for the representative of an occupying power that had imposed 'normalization' on the country. In East Berlin young people wishing to listen to a rock concert on the other side of the Wall demonstrated with shouts not just of 'Down with the Wall!' but also of 'Gorbachev! Gorbachev!' Again the leader of the power that has imposed the Wall is perceived as a symbol of hope. This reflects not just naivety, mirroring the image of Gorbachev as a 'liberator' promoted in East Germany by the West German media, but the pragmatic realization that in a petrified system, after decades of internal immobility, any movement seems good to latch on to, even if it comes from outside, even if it comes from the East. Besides, this is playing it safe: using the supreme authority of the Communist system to point to discrepancies in local policies.

Whatever the tactical uses of Gorbachevism, the realities of Central Europe are very different from Soviet Russia. And this applies especially to those who pride themselves on being, at last, in tune with the Moscow line. Gorbachev's main obstacle is a conservative, entrenched Party bureaucracy. Jaruzelski's problem is to establish a degree of credibility in Polish society. Similarly, Jaruzelski now finds in *glasnost* an *ex post facto* justification for the concessions he has been forced to make not because of Moscow but because of the formidable pressure from his society. The relative freedom of expression enjoyed by the Poles has little to do with the *glasnost* graciously bestowed by Moscow, but is on the contrary the result of twenty years of unofficial *samizdat* counter-culture and the Solidarity experience.

The problem for Hungary today is not to decide whether a reform of the economy is desirable and if so in what form (which is still the debate in Moscow), but what to do with a reform that has failed. The order of the day is not, as it is in Moscow, to give a larger role to private initiative in agriculture and the service sector, but whether the industrial core of the command economy can be dismantled through privatization. Most importantly, the debate among Hungarian reformers is not, as it is in Moscow, about economic and social pluralism, but about political pluralism. The Hungarian economic failure makes it much more difficult for Gorbachev's supporters in Moscow to use Hungary as a reference point, if not as a 'model'. But the reverse is even more true: there is nothing in Soviet *perestroika* that can help reformist Hungary to solve its deadlock.

Put simply: for Central Europeans there is absolutely nothing new about *perestroika*. They were the first to introduce it and have practised it, in one form or another, for at least two decades. There is not a single new idea in Gorbachev's programme. All this has been said – and better – in the reform programme of the Prague Spring of 1968; all this has been experimented with in Poland and especially in Hungary. There is a feeling of *déjà vu* in Central Europe about the latest discoveries in mother Russia. Of course, it is satisfying for the reformist old hands in Prague to see some of their ideas of yesterday now rehabilitated by those who sent in the tanks to crush them. But in the meantime twenty years have been lost and the landscape has changed: mere reform, a 'humanization', of socialism has lost its appeal. The current trend is liberalism and the rebirth of a civil society.

In his superb collection entitled *A Cup of Coffee with My Interrogator*, the Czech writer Ludvik Vaculik, one of the *enfants terribles* of 1968, writes:

> So they again think they are better than us. And again on the basis that might is right. True, the country has for a long time needed someone to come and shake it up, and yet it's all rather sad: by the time an idea has been grasped by the Russian bureaucracy, it is hardly new where the rest of the world is concerned. . . . To manufacture quality goods: what a revolutionary and daring idea! More than one candidate to stand for election: now there's a discovery for you! . . . Independent thought, too – for how long, this time? Conscience to be your highest guide: even if it goes against the grain? . . . There are still more amazing discoveries to be made: for instance the separation of legislative, executive and judicial power. But whatever you may discover, just leave us alone.

Can Moscow leave Central Europe alone? Does the presence of Gorbachev mean acceptance of greater autonomy and diversity? In his speech for the seventieth anniversary of the Bolshevik revolution Gorbachev said that 'unity does not mean uniformity', adding that 'there is no model of socialism to be imitated by all'. The principles that should guide the relations between socialist countries are: 'complete and full equality, the responsibility of each party in power for its own country, the commitment to the common cause of socialism, mutual respect and strict adherence to the principles of peaceful coexistence.' The last time these lofty principles were enunciated with such clarity was by Khrushchev in the famous declaration of 30 October 1956, the *magna carta* of new relations between Moscow and its allies. The next day the Russian tanks were in Budapest. And there is little reason to expect that in the case of a crisis at the periphery of the Empire Gorbachev would behave differently.

Still, there is in Gorbachev's formulation a clear departure from the Brezhnev doctrine of limited sovereignty which made the socialist community as a whole ultimately responsble for the fate of socialism in each country. 'Peaceful coexistence' was used only for relations with the capitalist West. Now Soviet allies will benefit from the same 'peaceful' treatment as its alleged enemies have enjoyed, which is progress of sorts. Academician Smirnov, director of the Institute of Marxism–Leninism, even hinted in April 1987 that there was a case for 're-thinking the events of 1968', but nobody has since dared publicly to follow that suggestion. The Prague leadership had protested with great vehemence and anxiety.

This highlights the main feature of Gorbachev's policy with the allies: leave each leadership to choose the methods it considers best to ensure internal stability. Even Ligachev, Gorbachev's main rival and not exactly an adept at *glasnost*, said in Budapest in April 1987 that 'each country can act independently. In the past one said that the orchestra was conducted by Moscow and that all the others just listened. This is no longer the case.' This means that Gorbachev can accommodate at the same time Jaruzelski and Honecker, Grosz and Ceausescu, reformists, pragmatists and authoritarian hardliners. He has refrained from changing the Brezhnevite old guard in charge, but many expected that he would install his own men when vacancies became available. The results so far are disappointing. After twenty years of 'normalization' Husák is at long last gone. Yet he has been replaced not by a pro-reformer supporter of Gorbachev such as Lubomir Strougal, but by one Milos Jakes, a pure product of the apparat and, according to Zdenek Mlynar, a Soviet security man. More importantly, as head of the Control Commission Jakes personally presided over the great purge of half a million Dubčekite Communists that followed 1968. Promoted by Brezhnev to the Secretariat in 1981, he has been in charge of economic policies and as such managed to block even the most modest attempts at reform. If anything, Jakes, even more than Husák, is the symbol of 'normalization'. If he is now supposed to represent *perestroika*, the word really has no meaning whatsoever.

The next candidate for succession is probably Ceausescu. There, whomever he chooses, Gorbachev will earn universal praise: from

an exhausted population, and from neighbouring socialist countries
worried about their own minorities in Romania, and from the West,
which in the recent past has contributed so much to the creation of
the Ceausescu myth of independence. This has a precedent: the
sense of relief after the Vietnamese invasion which delivered
Cambodia from the murderous Pol Pot regime, though not from
Communism.

Moscow is not going to force reform on its allies, as Leonid
Yagodovsky, Deputy Head of the Institute of the World Socialist
System in Moscow, explains:

> Should the reform process in any East European country stop,
> or perhaps regress – this has been known to happen – we shall,
> naturally, not be pleased with this change. But that is not to say
> that the Soviet Union would enforce or carry out reforms in
> those countries with the use of tanks or what have you. Tanks
> can be used to stop reform, but reform cannot be introduced by
> tanks.

What the Communist regimes in the Soviet Union and in East-
Central Europe have in common is a process of decay. At the periphery this decay is more advanced; most importantly, a civil society
is badly lacking in Soviet Russia. After a long war of attrition with
the state society has gained more freedom, but it also shows signs
of exhaustion: the wear and tear of forty years of Communism.
Democratic change in the future will depend not just on Gorbachev's
reformist disciples but on the capacity of the peoples of Central
Europe to invent new forms of democratic life in an undemocratic
environment.

Under Gorbachev the limits of Soviet tolerance have become
blurred. But, to paraphrase Churchill, can a Soviet leader, especially
if he is serious about reforming Russia, afford to preside over the
liquidation of the last empire in the heart of Europe?

A Transition to What?

We know that an aquarium can be turned into fish soup. But can
fish soup be turned into an aquarium? This is the question – or
rather the somewhat hyperbolic version of the question – now facing
Eastern Europe. The near-universal acknowledgement of the bankruptcy of Communism permits us for the first time to think seriously
about the de-Sovietization of the area and a transition to democracy
and a market economy. Yet the bankruptcy itself – the toll taken by

forty-five years of Communism – could prove to be an overwhelming impediment to the Eastern bloc countries' return to Europe. This paradox is evident all across the region. In the course of a single day in mid-February 1989, the chairman of the Hungarian Parliament, Matyás Szuros, suggested in Strasbourg that Hungary might want to join the Common Market, even as the leader of the reformist wing of Hungary's Communist Party, Imre Pozsgay, declared Eastern Europe 'the greatest crisis zone in the world'.

How compatible are the two statements? Both highlight the contradictory nature of the present situation in East-Central Europe. We are witnessing a formidable acceleration of history in the area, but one which entails risks that are proportional to the opportunities offered to overcome the Yalta legacy and the partition of Europe. For more than forty years Soviet domination of Eastern Europe has been identified with a potential threat to Western Europe. Today, the Soviet hold on the area is being undermined, offering unprecedented possibilities for Western influence. But is Western Europe, preoccupied with the prospects of a single market in 1992, prepared to meet this challenge? The Yalta system was morally unacceptable, but it was predictable. Can it be dismantled without unleashing an extended period of turmoil and instability? Current developments in Poland and Hungary clearly suggest a redefinition of Moscow's attitudes towards internal change in the Eastern bloc; but can we conclude that the Brezhnev doctrine of limited sovereignty is dead? After the traumas of failure in 1956, 1968 and 1981, what are the prospects for peaceful change?

The word 'crisis' is actually a bit misleading. In Poland, crisis has been on and off the 'normal' state of affairs since 1956. For Romania the word crisis is a polite understatement; for Hungary a slight exaggeration. The uneven pace of decay and the greater degree of tolerance in Moscow has encouraged diversity and a variety of responses to the new situation. After the war Communists in Eastern Europe claimed to be following different roads to socialism. Today they are searching for different paths *from* socialism.

These differences notwithstanding, all the Warsaw Pact states are now being unsettled from within by growing popular pressure for change, and from without by the Gorbachev factor. The economies in Eastern Europe continue to decline while the populace grows restless, but the regimes now find themselves unable to count on Moscow for support, whether in the form of money or – should push come to shove – in the form of tanks.

The most common reaction to this problem has been withdrawal into the past. The majority of the Warsaw Pact regimes (East

Germany, Czechoslovakia, Bulgaria and Romania) have embarked on a policy of conservative resistance. They understandably find the immediately destabilizing effects of *glasnost* more alarming than the prospects of missing out on the alleged long-term benefits of *perestroika*. The idea of the 'rejection front' is to wait for Gorbachev either to fall from power or be brought to abandon his reformist ambitions. So, for the foreseeable future, the out-and-out dismantling of Party rule will be an issue only in Hungary, Poland and Slovenia (the most prosperous and most liberal Yugoslav republic). They are by far the most creative laboratories for reform in the Soviet bloc.

It is important not to confuse the current changes in Hungary and Poland with Gorbachev's reforms. Gorbachev offers these countries no intellectual inspiration, merely a greater margin of manoeuvre. After all, Hungary and Poland have been practising *perestroika* and *glasnost* for some twenty years. The result is what might be called 'catastroika'. The lesson both countries have drawn from this failure is one that still may not have been driven home to Gorbachev: nothing short of a thorough unraveling of centralized economic control and a genuine introduction of market mechanisms will work. And, no less importantly, you cannot have an economic market without some form of political market. The regimes in Poland and Hungary have thus come to accept the idea of a gradual Party retreat from the sphere of ideology as well as the economy. But the retreat is now turning into a rout, as the Party's monopoly of political power crumbles.

Dissent has been a fact of life in East-Central Europe since the 1970s. Now it is turning into an organized and legalized political opposition that will have a chance to shape the transition to the post-Communist era. But that implies that a number of hurdles must be jumped before the basic hallmarks of democracy are introduced in Poland and Hungary. The first is the transition from symbolic politics to real politics. Until now the spokesmen for change have been intellectuals and writers, and the enemy has been an easy target: the coercion of a totalitarian state. Once that enemy leaves the stage, politics becomes an expression of competing interests: of differing opinions about the conditions of freedom, about the allocation of resources, about how the pie gets cut up. How easily can dissident intellectuals who were expert practitioners of moral indignation turn into professional politicians who can orchestrate the compromises of everyday political life? The transition to democracy presupposes the emergence of a new political elite, and the revival of a democratic political culture badly damaged by four decades of Sovietization.

What are the basic features of the current dismantling of the Old Régime? First, the restoration of capitalism. The 1960s' ideas of a 'socialist market' or a 'socialist democracy' have been abandoned. In Eastern Europe, the adjective 'socialist' now tends to be seen as a weasel word, emptying words such as 'market' or 'democracy' of their content. By the early 1990s half of the Hungarian economy should be in private hands. Socialism is the longest – and most arduous – road from capitalism to capitalism.

Secondly, freedom of the press is being *de facto* restored. In Budapest you can now read Koestler, Orwell or the writings of Imre Nagy, the prime minister executed after the 1956 revolution. The Hungarian Democratic Forum publishes *Hitel*, the first independent weekly in Eastern Europe, while in Warsaw Adam Michnik launched *Gazeta* in May 1989, the first opposition daily newspaper in the history of Communism. There is only one remaining taboo: the nature of Soviet responsibility for the past and of Soviet constraint on the future.

Third, the rule of law is being restored. New constitutions centered on the rights of the citizen (rather than on his absolute subordination to the state) are being prepared. Instead of constitutional monarchy, this is constitutional communism.

Fourth, a separation of Party and state seems to be in the works in both Poland and Hungary, as the Communists grudgingly relinquish their claim to a 'leading role'. In Budapest, the Party's share in the state budget has been revealed for the first time, and promptly cut in half. This may remind you of 1789 France (*'Combien coûte la cour?'*), but it is not merely a Hungarian contribution to the bicentennial celebrations.

Fifth, power-sharing will be the crucial political test of the Communists' readiness to abandon their monopoly, known as the 'leading role' of the party. The opposition parties are already gearing up for the occasion. In Poland Solidarity has been legalized, and a new law on political parties has been drafted in Hungary, where the transition towards a multiparty system is already well under way. Two of the main protagonists of the 1945–47 democratic interlude (the Smallholders party and the Social Democrats) have been restored, while two new parties are in the offing: the Free Democrats (liberals), led by Janos Kis, and the Democratic Forum, representing a populist tradition. In the June 1989 election in Poland a third of the seats in the Sejm were reserved for the opposition, while genuine elections were held for an upper chamber (with admittedly limited powers). Out of 100 seats in the Senate, the Party won only one.

In both Poland and Hungary the democratic transition is made possible by the combination of Communist Party disarray and Moscow *laisser faire*. Prospects for success seem better in Hungary than in Poland. The economic collapse is less dramatic there, and the country seems less threatened by the fear of a social explosion. In Poland, there was a sharp polarization between state and society, between the Jaruzelski regime and Solidarity. This accounts for the success of Polish resistance to the post-martial law regime, but might prove an obstacle to a peaceful transition to democracy. In Hungary there is no coherent social movement opposed to the Party state. Economists and lawyers are the Hungarian equivalents to the Polish bishops and Solidarity militants. Reformist ideas were never eradicated in the Hungarian Party under Kadar, and a continuum has developed over the last decade ranging from Communist reformers (such as Poszgay and Nyers) to the democratic opposition. This is a network of people who have been arguing the finer points of reformist policy for years – in short, a political elite. In Poland Solidarity has been an umbrella organization for the whole opposition, and its goals have been broad, basic ones. Once specific and drastic economic choices have to be made, it will have trouble serving both as a trade union and a surrogate political party; the latent factionalism within Solidarity will be brought into the open.

The difference between the two nations was captured in March 1989, when one conference on the transition to democracy was held in Warsaw, and another in Budapest. The Warsaw conference was somewhat Polono-centric in outlook and concluded that complete, unabashed economic liberalism was the only way forward. In Budapest, people toyed with various models of a mixed economy and compared the future of their country variously with Spain, Austria and Finland (rather than Poland).

Hungary also has the luxury of occupying territory that is of less strategic importance to the Soviet Union than Poland (which is a vital link between Soviet Russia and East Germany and therefore an important element in the East-West equation). The Hungarians can therefore experiment with less fear that Gorbachev will go back on his pledge of non-interference. All this helps to explain the starkly different moods in the two countries. Hungary is full of optimism and aggressive pragmatism, while Poland remains gloomy even after a triumph – the agreement to legalize Solidarity – that few people could have predicted a year ago.

For the first time since the war the unthinkable has become not only thinkable, but in some cases even feasible. Yet there are limits, or at least serious constraints, too. Aside from sheer political obstacles to democracy, there are economic ones. Can you introduce a free market and private enterprise in a collapsing economy? The existence of a market economy is, as we know, a necessary though not the only condition for a transition to democracy. Typically, in cases of successful democratization – in Spain, Latin America or South Korea – the displaced dictatorships had not destroyed the very foundations of a market economy. The same cannot be said for the Soviet bloc. This is the heart of the question about turning fish soup into fish: can the disastrous effects of forty-five years of Communist rule be effectively reversed? Freeing a nationalized economy is much harder than nationalizing a free one.

This is not to say that things are hopeless in Eastern Europe. In both Poland and Hungary, free enterprise has for some time been spreading in agriculture and in the service sector, where small-scale entrepreneurship is practical. But in the large-scale industries, shifting into reverse is not so easy. Leaders in Poland and Hungary are now pondering the question of how to privatize large state-owned enterprises. Selling stock in them – to workers, or to others – is one possibility. But who has the money to buy it? And even if buyers materialize, how will the workers be cushioned from the resulting blow? If Polish industries were suddenly exposed to market forces, about half of them would go bankrupt and millions of workers would lose their jobs. Already during the last decade of *perestroika*, the real incomes of labourers in Hungary have declined by 40 per cent, largely because of inflation accompanying the abolition of price control. And the resistance of workers in highly subsidized industries is matched, at the opposite end of the spectrum, among the *nomenklatura* who fear for their power and their privileges. The problem, when the market has been destroyed, is how to restore its legitimacy in societies where it must mean at least in the short term hardship and insecurity. The positive results of a free market might take twenty years to materialize whereas the social costs are immediate. So collectively Poles and Hungarians favour market reform, but individually everybody resents it.

It has long been assumed that economic change under Communism is easier, less threatening, than political change. Now we may discover that ideological and political changes might prove easier than economic ones.

On the brighter side, a new entrepreneurial class is emerging out of what used to be known as the second economy or the parallel (black) market, which has now been legalized. And the new bourgeoisie, says Hungarian writer György Konrad, will also demand 'bourgeois' rights. At the same time we are seeing the 'embourgeoisement' of some sections of the Communist ruling class. They are now trying to convert their privileges into rights. Not just the children of Solidarity, but also the children of the *nomenklatura* are now going into business and setting up shop on Main Street: Daddy is a Party apparatchik, the son manages in an import-export firm, the daughter runs a fashion boutique on Vaci street in downtown Budapest, and Granny owns a hotel on Lake Balaton. While East German and Czechoslovak state socialists are living off their bourgeois past, some of their Polish and Hungarian counterparts prepare for a bourgeois future. So much for the East European contribution to Barrington Moore's famous thesis on the *Social Origins of Democracy and Dictatorship*.

The development of both private economic activity and new rights contributes to the revival of 'citizenship' and of a civil society which remains an essential precondition for the democratic transition. This also brings with it the return of politics: no longer the symbolic politics of dissent about the freedom from *coercion*, but 'real' politics about freedom from *constraints*. Politics as an expression of competing interests, but also of competing arguments about the conditions of freedom in the City.

Can you introduce a semi-democracy based on an economic disaster? The transition in Spain was preceded by more than a decade of economic prosperity. In Poland and Hungary it has been preceded by a decade of economic decline. True, it is the latter that has made political change possible, but the downward slide into democracy and decay entails a number of large risks.

One is that the Party retreat remains only half-hearted or too constrained, and that the Communists will try simply to hide behind or to 'borrow' the legitimacy of the opposition (just as they have already done with the Polish Church) and make it share the responsibility for the state of the country. When Prime Minister Rakowski told representatives of Solidarity, 'The nation is watching us and judging us,' he meant, 'You are already co-responsible for the state of the country', or 'We might be powerless in the face of the economic disaster, but so are you.' The opposition takes the risk of being discredited or cut off from society before it has had a chance to push through its new policies of radical reform. Already (as the May Day demonstrations have shown) grass-roots radicals in Wroclaw, Lodz and on the Baltic coast protest against the 'betrayal' by the Solidarity leadership. There is a danger, expecially in Poland, that the population will see the opposition elites as having been 'coopted'. Yet it is hard for the opposition to shy away from a challenge like this; you cannot for years demand democratic institutions and power-sharing, yet chicken out when the chance arrives.

The second risk faced by the opposition is that the collapse of the Communist regime is too rapid for alternative institutions and new channels of communication between rulers and ruled to emerge. Such a power vacuum combined with economic disarray could be a recipe for chaos and social explosion – not for peaceful democratic change.

And then there is the third, more familiar risk – that change will exceed the limits of Soviet tolerance even in the Gorbachev era. A most dangerous combination, from Gorbachev's point of view, would be an interaction of crises at the inner (Baltic, Ukrainian) and outer (Polish) peripheries of the Empire. Could Gorbachev behave differently from his predecessors if faced with such a threat – or even with the collapse of a single Communist regime in Eastern Europe? He has been sending conflicting signals. While Oleg Bogomolov, Head of the Institute of Economics of the World Socialist System, claimed in Budapest that a multi-party system in Hungary would be acceptable, Gorbachev himself described the idea as 'rubbish'. In Belgrade, in March 1988, he pledged his commitment to non-interference. Bogomolov even said that a 'neutral' Hungary would not be seen as a security threat by Moscow. Still, there has been no formal repudiation of the Brezhnev doctrine of limited sovereignty. To the extent that the word 'socialism' has lost all meaning, the Brezhnevite idea of a collective responsibility for the safeguard of socialism might be considered obsolete. But even if the Brezhnev doctrine were dead, it does not mean you could not have – if need be – a 'Gorbachev doctrine' for the preservation of the Empire. However, Gorbachev, more than any other Soviet leader, seems to have doubt as to what a hypothetical invasion could achieve. True, the technology of repression is nowadays more sophisticated and it seems preferable, from Moscow's point of view, to rely on the local Warsaw Pact armies. But here too the doubts must have set in: how many times can you impose martial law in Poland? Jaruzelski did postpone the emergence of Solidarity by a decade, but he did not manage to roll back the emerging civil society. No wonder Moscow is in two minds.

The result of this 'confusion of sentiments' (as Stefan Zweig would put it) is raising expectations among the East European populations and divisions in the ruling elites. All this amidst announcements of – admittedly limited – Soviet troop withdrawals from Hungary (to be followed in due course by East Germany and Czechoslovakia). Militarily speaking, this is of little consequence:

the Soviet troops will simply be moved a couple of hundred miles eastwards, without substantially altering the East-West strategic balance. And Gorbachev seems to understand that no amount of military presence in East-Central Europe can ensure stability in the area. Yet the psychological and political effect of such troop withdrawals is considerable in East-Central Europe. The Hungarian opposition is already calling for a withdrawal from the Warsaw Pact. And once the genie of national sovereignty is out of the bottle, *perestroika* – or indeed the imperial idea – might well be living on borrowed time. If the process of emancipation of the nations of the Other Europe gets out of control, the use of force — or, for that matter, the failure to use force – could trigger a conservative backlash against Gorbachev.

A final threat to the democratic transition is nationalism. The return of democracy starts with the return of history. In most of Eastern Europe the pre-war experience with democracy foundered on the shoals of unbridled nationalism. As Communism collapses, what is coming to the surface is not just liberal democracy, but also populist nationalism, which in the past has combined more readily with authoritarian rather than democratic rule. So far (just as in the 1848 'Spring of Nations', or in 1918) democratic and national aspirations have combined in opposing the Communist dictatorship. But it is far from clear that the future of Polish politics will be shaped by the likes of Michnik and Geremek. And one can only hope that Janos Kis and his liberal friends do not suffer the fate of Oskar Jaszi, their democratic predecessor of 1918, swept aside by a nationalist tide.

What East Europeans are asking now is how much of the future lies in the past. Their history offers at least three likely models for the course that reform is likely to take. The most obvious (and perhaps the most likely) is the return to a self-limiting coalition resembling the 1945–47 pattern: the Communists would remain in charge of the army, the police and foreign affairs, but would let the other parties get on with restoring a market economy and the rule of law. The second (and least desirable) scenario would be a return to the inter-war pattern of nationalist and semi-authoritarian autarchies exporting their *Gastarbeiters* and their tribal feuds to the rest of Europe. The third (and most desirable) model would be a 'Habsbur-gization' of the Soviet Empire, along the lines of the 1867 Austro-Hungarian compromise. Such a compromise between the Soviets and the genuine representatives of the nations of East-Central Europe is the only way they might willingly accept limitations on their sovereignty.

A century ago Marx thought the key to the workers' paradise lay in the combination of German philosophy, English political economy and French socialism. Today, after forty-five years of Communist rule, East Europeans dream of a European future that would combine English-style parliamentary democracy, the Swedish welfare state and German living standards.

The economic realities, however, leave little hope for such a dreamlike future. Instead there is the unattractive possibility of 'Latin Americanization' – after a period of chaos, an authoritarian regime emerges with generals at the helm or lurking in the background. Nationalism, rather than Marxism, would then be the dominant ideology. Market reforms would be imposed on a reluctant Communist *nomenklatura* and a disgruntled populace. The transition from totalitarianism to authoritarianism could, some might argue, turn out to be a transitory phase toward democracy. But East Europeans have reasons to be wary of such rationalizations for the postponement of liberty. (Such a militarized post-Communist state cannot be excluded from the future of the Soviet Union itself. The more important the role of the Red Army plays in preserving the imperial order, the greater will be its say in the internal political set-up.)

There is, finally, the optimistic scenario that is being widely discussed in both East and West: 'Finlandization'. The assumption here is that the Soviet Union could be turned into a classical empire, willing to divest itself of liabilities if the costs became too high. (Gorbachev does show signs that he is amenable to the logic of cost-benefit calculus.) Eastern Europe would then be transformed from a sphere of dominance into a sphere of influence. It would have security links to the Soviet Union but growing economic ties with Western Europe.

Beyond the Central Europe of nostalgia (identified with the Habsburg monarchy) and utopia, a middle Europe emerges which does not match up with either of the two competing visions of Europe: that of the unified West European market after 1992 (with its *de facto* economic barriers between East and West) or that of Gorbachev's notion of a 'Common European House' stretching from the Ural mountains to the Atlantic. Rather, this is a third Europe, straddling the two Cold War alliances as their internal cohesion, and perhaps their *raison d'être*, deteriorates.

This naturally brings up the German question. Germany is the European nation with the deepest long-term interest in altering the post-war status quo. It is also the nation best equipped to fill the Central European power vacuum, thus recovering in the area its traditional sphere of economic and cultural influence. This would, of course, ultimately depend on Soviet consent, which means keeping German political ambitions toned down. (The prospect of Germany as the dominant power in the heart of Europe would be as frightening to the Russians as it would be, for that matter, to the French.)

An East-Central Europe stabilized with German assistance would be a double-edged weapon. On the one hand it would challenge West European cohesion and America's solidarity with Western Europe. Gorbachev is the ultimate master at using the internal weaknesses of his Empire as foreign policy assets. The process of de-Sovietization would thus be compensated by German neutralism and American isolationism. Gorbachev's 'Common European House' would be a more fragmented one and, perhaps, one more open to change. But it would also be a Europe which would have room for Russia but not for America.

On the other hand, a neutralized Central Europe, by reducing the external threat to the Soviet Union, could also facilitate democratic change and the long-term dismantling of Soviet influence in Eastern Europe. The result could be to hasten the symmetrical decay of the two alliances. Thus overcoming the partition of Europe raises hopes for the return of democracy but also the question: Who is Finlandizing whom?

Bibliography

This is merely a selected bibliography designed more as a guide for further reading than as an exhaustive indication of my own sources. To these one should add more than a hundred interviews with leading political and cultural figures (official and unofficial) conducted in East–Central Europe in 1987 and 1988.

Part I

Berdiaev, Nicolas, *Les Sources et le Sens du Communisme Russe*, Paris, 1951
Berend, Ivan T., *The Crisis Zone of Europe*, Cambridge, 1986
Berlin, Isaiah, *Russian Thinkers*, London, 1988
Bibó, Istvan, *Misère des Petits Etats de l'Europe de l'Est*, Paris, 1986
Borsody, Stephen, *The Tragedy of Central Europe*, New Haven, 1980
Busek, Erhard and Willfinger, Gerhard (eds.), *Aufbruch nach Mitteleuropa*, Vienna, 1986
Canetti, Elias, *The Tongue Set Free: Remembrances of a European Childhood*, London, 1980
Cioran, E. M., *Histoire et Utopie*, Paris, 1960
Cohen, Gary B., *The Politics of Ethnic Survival: Germans in Prague 1861–1914*, Princeton, 1981
Davies, Norman, *God's Playground: A History of Poland*, Oxford, 1981
Fejtö, François, *Requiem pour un Empire Défunt*, Paris, 1988
Gombrowicz, Witold, *Souvenirs de Pologne*, Paris, 1984
Halecki, Oscar, *The Limits and Divisions of European History*, New York, 1950
Hammel, Claus, *Die Preussen Kommen*, East Berlin, 1981
Janos, Andrew, *The Politics of Backwardness 1855–1945*, Princeton, 1982
Jaszi, Oscar, *The Dissolution of the Habsburg Monarchy*, Chicago, 1929
Johnston, William M., *The Austrian Mind*, Berkeley, 1972
Kann, Robert A., *A History of the Habsburg Empire*, Berkeley, 1980
Kundera, Milan, 'The Tragedy of Central Europe', *New York Review of Books*, 26 April 1984
Lukacs, John, *Budapest 1900*, New York, 1988

Magris, Claudio, *Danubio*, Rome, 1986
Masaryk, Tomas, *The Spirit of Russia*, 3 vols., London, 1968
Milosz, Czeslaw, *Une Autre Europe*, Paris, 1964
Polonsky, Antony, *The Little Dictators*, London, 1975
Ripellino, A. M., *Praga Magica*, Rome, 1973
Rothschild, Joseph, *East-Central Europe Between the Two World Wars*, Seattle, 1974
Schlögel, Karl, *Die Mitte Liegt Ostwarts*, Berlin, 1986
Schorske, Carl E., *Fin-de-Siècle Vienna*, New York, 1979
Seton Watson, Hugh, *Eastern Europe Between the Wars 1918–1941*, Cambridge, 1945
Spengler, Oswald, *Prussianité et Socialisme*, Paris, 1986
Stern, Fritz, *Dreams and Delusions: The Drama of German History*, New York, 1987
Stone, Norman, *Europe Transformed 1878–1919*, London, 1983
Szücs, Jenö, *Les Trois Europes*, Paris, 1985
Taylor, A. J. P., *The Course of German History*, London, 1945
Thaden, Rudolf von, *Fragen an Preussen*, Munich, 1981
Walicki, Andrzej, *A History of Russian Thought*, Stanford, 1981

Part II

Banac, Ivo, *The National Question in Yugoslavia*, Ithaca, 1984
Bruegel, J. W., *Czechoslovakia Before Munich*, Cambridge, 1973
Brzezinski, Zbigniew, *The Soviet Bloc: Unity and Conflict*, Cambridge, Mass., 1981
Buber Neumann, Margarete, *Under Two Dictators*, New York, 1949
Charlton, Michael, *The Eagle and the Small Birds*, London, 1984
Djilas, Milovan, *Conversations with Stalin*, London, 1962
Fejtö, François, *History of the People's Democracies*, New York, 1970
Gati, Charles, *Hungary and the Soviet Bloc*, Durham, 1986
Gross, Jan T., *Polish Society Under German Occupation*, Princeton, 1979
Gross, Jan T., *Revolution from Abroad*, Princeton, 1988
Herling, Gustav, *A World Apart*, Oxford, 1987
Hodos, George H., *Show Trials*, New York, 1987
Kaplan, Karel, *The Short March*, London, 1987
Koštunica, V. and Čavoski, K., *Party Pluralism or Monism*, Boulder, 1985
Kovaly, Heda, *The Victors and the Vanquished*, New York, 1973
Leonhard, Wolfgang, *Child of the Revolution*, Chicago, 1950
Loebl, Eugen, *My Mind on Trial*, New York, 1976
London, Artur, *The Confession*, New York, 1970
McCauley, Martin (ed.), *Communist Power in Europe 1944–1949*, London, 1977
Mastny, Vojtech, *Russia's Road to the Cold War*, New York, 1979
Meyer, Peter (ed.), *The Jews in the Soviet Satellites*, Syracuse, 1953
Milosz, Czeslaw, *The Captive Mind*, London, 1953

Pelikan, Jiři (ed.), *Czechoslovak Political Trials, 1950–53*, Stanford, 1971
Polonski, A. and Drukier, B. (eds.), *The Beginnings of Communist Rule in Poland*, London, 1980
Rupnik, Jacques, *Histoire du Parti Communiste Tchécoslovaque*, Paris, 1981
Seton Watson, Hugh, *The East European Revolution*, New York, 1951
Thomas, Hugh, *Armed Truth: The Beginnings of the Cold War 1945–46*, London, 1986
Toranska, Teresa, *Oni*, London, 1987
Ulam, Adam, *Expansion and Coexistence: The History of Soviet Foreign Policy, 1917–67*, New York, 1968

Part III

Beloff, Nora, *Tito's Flawed Legacy*, London, 1985
Bethell, Nicholas, *Gomulka: His Poland and his Communism*, London, 1972
Borsody, Stephen (ed.), *The Hungarians: A Divided Nation*, New Haven, 1988
Bown, A. and Gray, J. (eds.), *Political Culture and Political Change in Communist States*, London, 1977
Brandys, Kazimierz, *A Question of Reality*, London, 1981
Brandys, Kazimierz, *A Warsaw Diary 1978–81*, London, 1983
Brus, Wlodzimierz, *Institutional Change Within a Planned Economy*, Oxford, 1986
Davies, Norman, *Heart of Europe*, Oxford, 1986
Haraszti, Miklos, *The Velvet Prison*, New York, 1987
Havel, Vaclav (ed.), *The Power of the Powerless*, London, 1980
Howe, Irving (ed.), *1984 Revisited*, New York, 1984
Ionescu, Ghita, *Communism in Romania 1944–62*, Oxford, 1964
Jowitt, Kenneth, *Revolutionary Breakthrough: The Case of Romania*, Berkeley, 1971
Kaplan, Karel, *The Communist Party in Power*, Boulder, 1987
Keane, John (ed.), *Civil Society and the State*, London, 1988
Kolakowski, Leszek, *Main Currents of Marxism*, 3 vols., Oxford, 1978
Konrad, G. and Szelenyi, I., *Intellectuals on the Road to Class Power*, London, 1979
Labedz, Leopold (ed.), *Revisionism: Essays on the History of Marxist Ideas*, London, 1962
Liehm, Antonin, *The Politics of Culture*, New York, 1973
Liehm, Antonin and Mira, *The Most Important Art*, Berkeley, 1977
Michnik, Adam, *L'Eglise et la Gauche: Le Dialogue Polonais*, Paris, 1979
Molnar, Miklos, *De Bela Kun à Janos Kadar*, Paris, 1987
Patočka, Jan, *Essais Heretiques*, Paris, 1981
Pavlowitch, Stevan, *The Improbable Survivor: Yugoslavia 1918–1988*, London, 1988
Schopflin, George (ed.), *Censorship and Political Communication*, London, 1983

Shafir, Michael, *Romania*, London, 1985
Skilling, Gordon, *Samizdat and Independent Society in Central and Eastern Europe*, London, 1989
Škvorecký, Josef, *The Engineer of Human Souls*, Toronto, 1984
Tismeanu, Vladimir, *The Crisis of Marxist Ideology in Eastern Europe*, London, 1988
Tökes, Rudolf (ed.), *Opposition in Eastern Europe*, London, 1979
Vaculík, Ludvík, *A Cup of Coffee with My Interrogator*, London, 1988
Volgyes, Ivan, *Politics in Eastern Europe*, Chicago, 1986

Part IV

Brumberg, Abraham (ed.), *Poland: Genesis of a Revolution*, New York, 1983
Brzezinski, Zbigniew, *The Grand Failure*, New York, 1989
Garton Ash, Timothy, *The Polish Revolution*, London, 1984
Gordon, L., Brown, J., Hassner, P. and Moreton, E., *Eroding Empire*, Washington, 1987
Havel, Vaclav, *Letters to Olga*, New York, 1988
Kende, P. and Pomian, K. (eds.), *Varsovie-Budapest 1956*, Paris, 1978
Konrad, György, *Antipolitics*, New York, 1984
Lomax, Bill, *Eyewitness in Hungary*, Nottingham, 1980
Lomax, Bill, *Hungary 1956*, London, 1976
Michnik, Adam, *Letters from Prison*, Berkeley, 1985
Mlynář, Zdeněk, *Nightforst in Prague*, London, 1980
Pfaff, William, *Barbarian Sentiments*, New York, 1989
Šimečka, Milan, *The Restoration of Order*, London, 1987
Skilling, Gordon, *Czechoslovakia's Interrupted Revolution*, Princeton, 1976
Terry, Sarah Meiklejohn (ed.), *Soviet Policy in Eastern Europe*, New Haven, 1984

Index

JACQUES RUPNIK was born in Prague in 1950, and was educated at the University of Paris and at Harvard. He has worked as a specialist on East-Central Europe for the BBC World Service, and at present is a Senior Fellow at the Fondation Nationale des Sciences Politiques in Paris. He is the writer and narrator of the documentary television series *The Other Europe*.